Applied Edge AI

Applied Edge AI

Concepts, Platforms, and Industry Use Cases

Edited by
Pethuru Raj Chelliah
G. Nagarajan
R.I. Minu

CRC Press
Taylor & Francis Group
Boca Raton London New York

CRC Press is an imprint of the
Taylor & Francis Group, an **informa** business

AN AUERBACH BOOK

First Edition published 2022
by CRC Press
6000 Broken Sound Parkway NW, Suite 300, Boca Raton, FL 33487-2742

and by CRC Press
2 Park Square, Milton Park, Abingdon, Oxon, OX14 4RN

CRC Press is an imprint of Taylor & Francis Group, LLC

Library of Congress Cataloguing-in-Publication Data
A catalog record has been requested for this book

ISBN: 978-0-367-70236-6 (hbk)
ISBN: 978-1-032-21728-4 (pbk)
ISBN: 978-1-003-14515-8 (ebk)

DOI: 10.1201/9781003145158

Typeset in AGaramond
by MPS Limited, Dehradun

Contents

Contributors

N. Raakin Ahamed
Department of Aerospace Engineering
B. S Abdur Rahman Crescent Institute
    of Science and Technology
Chennai, India

D. Aishwarya
Department of Computing Technology
SRM Institute of Science and
    Technology
Chennai, India

G. Bharath Ajay
Department of Aerospace Engineering
B. S Abdur Rahman Crescent Institute
    of Science and Technology
Chennai, India

Peter Augustine
CHRIST University
Bangalore, India

Anastasios-Stavros Charismiadis
Department of Informatics &
    Telecommunications National and
    Kapodistrian
University of Athens, Panepistimiopolis
Ilisia, Greece

A. Dulvi
Department of Aerospace Engineering
B. S Abdur Rahman Crescent
    Institute of Science and Technology
Chennai, India

Andreas Foteas
Department of Informatics &
    Telecommunications National and
    Kapodistrian
University of Athens, Panepistimiopolis
Ilisia, Greece

Murali G
Department of Mechatronics
SRM Institute of Science and
    Technology
Chennai, India

Parthiban Jovin
CHRIST University
Bangalore, India

S. Karthikeyan
Department of Aerospace Engineering
B. S Abdur Rahman Crescent
    Institute of Science and
    Technology
Chennai, India

Harilaos Koumaras
NCSR "Demokritos"
Institute of Informatics and
  Telecommunications
Paraskevi, Greece

Vijayalakshmi M.
Department of Computing
  Technology
SRM Institute of Science and
  Technology
Chennai, India

R.I. Minu
Department of Computing
  Technology
SRM Institute of Science and
  Technology
Chennai, India

G. Murali
Department of Mechatronics
SRM Institute of Science and
  Technology
Chennai, India

G. Nagarajan
Department of CSE
Sathyabama Institute of Science and
  Technology
Chennai, India

R. Raghavi
Department of Aerospace Engineering
B. S Abdur Rahman Crescent Institute
  of Science and Technology
Chennai, India

Ashwini S.
Department of Computing Technology
SRM Institute of Science and
  Technology
Chennai, India

Sony Priya S.
Department of Computing Technology
SRM Institute of Science and
  Technology
Chennai, India

T. Sasikala
Thejus Engineering College
Kerala, India

S. Sharanya
Department of Computer Science and
  Engineering
SRM Institute of Science and
  Technology
Chennai, India

A. Sharun
Department of Aerospace Engineering
B. S Abdur Rahman Crescent Institute
  of Science and Technology
Chennai, India

Serin V. Simpson
Sathyabama Institute of Science and
  Technology
Chennai, India

S. Sivabalan
Department of Computing Technology
SRM Institute of Science and
  Technology
Chennai, India

R. Sivarethinamohan
CHRIST University
Bangalore, India

V.J.K. Kishor Sonti
Department of ECE
Sathyabama Institute of Science and
  Technology
Chennai, India

P. Beaulah Soundarabai
CHRIST University
Bangalore, India

S. Sujatha
K. Ramakrishnan College of
   Technology
Tamil Nadu, India

G. Sundari
Department of ECE
Sathyabama Institute of Science and
   Technology
Chennai, India

S. Sai Suresh
Department of Aerospace Engineering
B. S Abdur Rahman Crescent
   Institute of Science and
   Technology
Chennai, India

Dimitris Tsolkas
Department of Informatics &
   Telecommunications National and
   Kapodistrian
University of Athens, Panepistimiopolis
Ilisia, Greece

Revathi Venkataraman
School of Computing
SRM Institute of Science and
   Technology
Chennai, India

Smitha Vinod
CHRIST University
Bangalore, India

Chapter 1

Edge Computing: Opportunities and Challenges

S. Ashwini and R.I. Minu

SRM Institute of Science and Technology, Chennai, India

G. Nagarajan

Sathyabama Institute of Science and Technology, Chennai, India

Contents

DOI: 10.1201/9781003145158-1

1

Introduction

Recently, the artificial intelligence applications have seen a significant growth across the world. Cloud computing has been formed as an important component of artificial intelligence's advancement as a result of corporate action. As the rate of consumers who use their devices are increasing, there have been drastic changes in businesses that has brought technology into the devices that serve the consumers' needs in a better way. Edge AI is a considerable field of artificial intelligence that would protect the user from privacy issues and slowdowns that occur due to the transmission of data. Edge AI enhances people's access to artificial intelligence in a better way by providing wider areas of AI in which it leads the devices to get outputs for the inputs in an easier and quicker manner without letting it go to cloud. Let's learn about the features of Edge AI in a deeper sense.

The increasing human knowledge and advancements in hardware technology have resulted in a market for AI on edge devices. The cloud-based ecosystem has proven to be a viable forum for a variety of AI applications. However, the cloud-based approach has a number of drawbacks that preclude it from being used in all AI applications.

Edge AI is a type of data computing in which data is distributed among decentralized data centers and certain information is saved locally at the edge. In fact, edge computing is similar to the cloud by its key purpose. The major difference is that cloud computing prefers to store data in remote data centers, while edge computing makes partial use of local drives. In the following circumstances, edge computing is an excellent backup solution:

- There is sufficient bandwidth on the network to send files to the cloud.
- Businesspeople are hesitant to store sensitive data on remote servers.

■ Edge computing provides smooth access to files, even in offline mode, when the network is always reliable.

Cloud computing on the other hand has its own unique advantages:

■ In securing local networks, investment is not needed.
■ Large amounts of data are allowed to be stored without limits.
■ Multiple devices and software can be deployed easily.

The key aspect of an edge device is that it connects to a network that can be called a connected device. It gets information from sensors and could do some computations as well. It could also send to the data center and it should travel through an edge computer device.

From the IoT devices and microprocessors' point of view, the edge is the network edge where all the sensors come into these edge servers. So, there's a lot of different ways but it's all about where the sensors are capturing data. If we're doing the computations at that point, then we do edge computing through the data center. For example, many of us would use Alexa at home. We would talk to the data center and then the data centers would send it back after the computing works and it would seem like a fairly low latency but actually it's a very long latency. There's a lot of power being consumed. So, when we do compute at the edge, we get immediate results and we could have very low latency, low power, and privacy. There are lots of benefits in doing edge computing. Thus, lower cost and power are the whole goals.

We have billions of zettabytes of data that will be generated by the year 2025. A hundred zettabytes is quite a lot of data and the problem faced by industries is, if they don't take advantage of checking out the data and processing that data then they're missing out on opportunities to make their businesses more efficient. It's really transforming the way we live and work.

According to Gartner, more than 50% of all data produced by businesses will be created and analyzed outside of data centers and clouds by 2022. Organizations would need a new plan to keep up with the explosion of new devices and apps that demand real-time decisions. Therefore, this problem can be solved by edge computing. Edge computing enhances the action of bringing processing power closer to the data source to decrease network congestion and latency.

The following section is organized as follows: Section 2 highlights the fact of artificial intelligence, Edge AI with a list of benefits, and how Edge AI integrates with other technologies. We present advancements in the edge computing-based smart applications and detailed analysis on edge chip innovation in Sections 3–4. A discussion on future opportunities and challenges is presented in Section 5 and, finally, we conclude the paper.

Background

Artificial Intelligence

Artificial intelligence is defined as a program able to perform tasks normally associated with human intelligence. AI technology in general is growing very fast. If we look at Figure 1.1, we have estimated the growth of AI technology and we're talking about $50 billion and growing in terms of hundreds of billions of dollars over the next few years. We believe that it will create about $13 trillion of additional economic activity in the next 10 or 11 years, so there's actually a lot of activity in many different industries going on with AI. AI is actually the mimicking of a human brain, a very general kind of topic, but if we dig down into various aspects of AI there's something called machine learning, a subset of AI where a machine is actually iterating, learning, training, and reducing errors. In a machine algorithm, the machine is learning, but more specifically when we get to something called deep learning, that's where we hit the ability to do machine learning, but in a very regimented way with kinds of model neurons and layers of these neurons. We are basically passing through information from layer to layer and it's called a deep neural network. So deep learning is all about implementing a deep neural network and these actually have been tuned so that many people have been doing research on deep neural networks for decades and they're a very efficient way on a microprocessor in multiply in editions to be able to implement an algorithm that does machine learning.

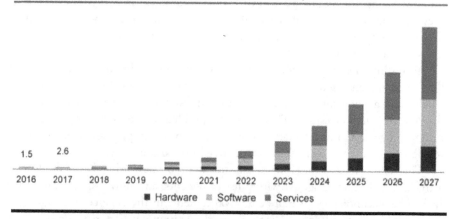

Figure 1.1 Asia Pacific Artificial Intelligence Market Estimate.

Source: www.Grandviewresearch.com

Edge AI

At the local level, the data from a hardware device will be processed by Edge AI systems using machine learning algorithms. To process such data and make decisions in real time, in milliseconds, the computer does not need to be connected to the Internet. The cloud model's connectivity costs are significantly reduced as a result of this. Edge AI, in other words, brings data and its processing to the user's closest point of contact, whether it's a phone, an IoT system, or an edge server.

To fully comprehend Edge AI, we must first learn edge computing, and the easiest way to understand edge computing is to compare it to cloud computing. The delivery of computing services over the Internet is known as cloud computing. Edge computing systems, on the other hand, are not connected to the cloud and instead run on local devices. A dedicated edge computing server, a local computer, or an Internet of Things (IoT) device may all be used as local computers. The use of edge computing has a variety of benefits. For example, Internet/cloud-based computation is constrained by latency and bandwidth, while edge computing is unconstrained. Now that we understand edge computing, we can take a look at Edge AI.

Artificial intelligence and edge computing are combined in Edge AI. The AI algorithms are run on computers with edge computing capabilities. The benefit is that the data can be processed in real time without the need for a cloud connection.

Since they need a lot of computing resources, most cutting-edge AI processes are done in the cloud. As a consequence, these AI processes are resistant to downtime. Since Edge AI systems run on an edge computing system, the requisite data operations can be performed locally before being sent over the Internet, saving time. Deep learning algorithms will work on the computer itself, which is where the data starts.

Edge AI is becoming more relevant as more devices are required to use AI in cases where they do not have access to the cloud. Consider how many manufacturing robots and automobiles now have computer vision algorithms. In these circumstances, a pause in data transmission may be disastrous. When detecting objects on the road, self-driving cars cannot experience latency. Since a fast response time is critical, the device must have an Edge AI system that can analyze and identify images without requiring a cloud link.

As edge computers are tasked with data processing tasks that would normally be performed in the cloud, the result is real-time, low-latency processing. Furthermore, by limiting data transmission to only the most critical data, the data volume itself can be reduced, and communication interruptions can be reduced.

Advantages of Edge AI

- Edge AI has a number of key benefits, including latency times and lower costs for a better user experience. This makes it easier to integrate wearable devices that are based on the user experience, such as bracelets that monitor your exercise and sleep habits in real time.

■ Through local processing, it raises the level of protection in terms of data privacy. In a centralized cloud, data is no longer transmitted.

■ Technically, the decrease in needed bandwidth could result in a decrease in the contracted Internet service prices.

■ Edge technology devices don't need data scientists or AI developers to maintain them. It is an autonomous technology since the graphic data flows are delivered automatically for monitoring.

How Edge AI Helps

Edge AI facilitates decision making, secures data processing, enhances user experiences, reduces costs, and makes devices more energy efficient. Figure 1.2 shows the key benefits of Edge AI.

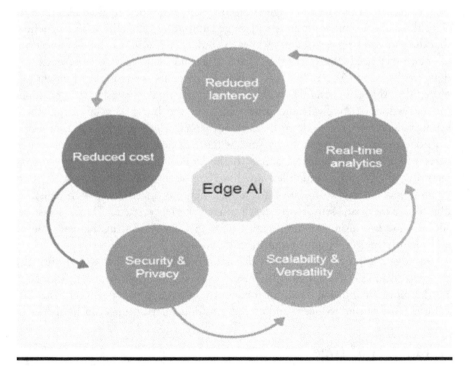

Figure 1.2   Edge AI Benefits.

Reduced Latency

Edge computing operates with a distributed network that eliminates the round-trip journey to the cloud and provides local authority and real-time responsiveness, whereas cloud computing relies on a single data center. It maintains the traffic and processing close to the end-user applications and the devices that generate and consume data, such as home security systems, tablets, and smartphones. This reduces latency significantly and allows for real-time, automated decision making. It provides a faster user experience to end users.

Scalability

Storage of large amounts of data in edge networks and remote centers are allowed by edge computing. According to IDC, there will be 41 billion connected IoT devices in use by 2025, generating 79 zettabytes of data. New innovative methods for efficient data analysis and processing are needed as data volumes grow.

A centralized service or data transmission does not become a bottleneck when the majority of data processing happens locally, on the edge. In most Edge AI use cases, large amounts of data are involved.

Real-Time Analytics

Edge AI's most important benefit is that it brings high-performance computing capacity to the edge, where sensors and IoT devices are found. AI edge computing allows AI applications to perform directly on field devices. For autonomous applications, such as semi-autonomous vehicles, the systems can process data and perform machine learning in the field using deep learning (DL) algorithms. Consider what would happen if it took the autonomous vehicle a few seconds to process data in the cloud versus a few milliseconds to process it at the edge. Mistakes would happen even more often, putting lives at risk.

Reduced Cost

We save energy costs because we won't need to stay connected to the cloud to move data back and forth between the edge system and the cloud, because we process data locally. Furthermore, edge computing systems are built with energy efficiency and power consumption in mind. Edge computers must balance power and efficiency since many edge applications are deployed in remote and uncontrolled environments.

Edge AI, of course, necessitates local computing power and hardware investment, but it is frequently the most cost-effective solution.

Privacy and Security

Safety is also major advantage. Edge computing allows control over data to companies through storing of information at the local level when data processing takes place locally. As a result, gaining access to data without authorization becomes increasingly difficult and a network of many devices is often more difficult to bring down.

Edge computing is far more secure than cloud computing in a technical way because it doesn't give sensitive information to third-party providers. In reality, this is only possible if we invest in securing local networks despite all these challenges. This technology can be very useful in a variety of industries.

Including security for IoT devices that link to the devices of the edge and for themselves is very important. If the network elements are over-extracted, it could compensate other devices that consist of valuable properties. It is also a requirement that edge computing does not act as a single point-network failure as edge computing is becoming more essential. So, there is a need to bring architects that would build redundancy and would serve fail over occurrence to prevent crippling downtime in case a primary node went down. The industry has already gone a long way toward addressing the demands of edge computing and it is becoming mainstream. As the usage of real-time apps is emerging more prevalently, its importance grows.

Edge AI and the Internet of Things

Edge AI integrates with other emerging technologies such as 5G and IoT. Edge AI systems can use data generated by IoT, and 5G technology is needed for both Edge AI and IoT to continue to progress.

IoT is a term that links a collection of smart devices that are connected to one another through the Internet. All of these devices produce data that can be fed into the Edge AI system, which can also serve as a temporary storage unit before the data is synced with the cloud. The data processing approach allows for more flexibility.

Edge AI and the IoT will also benefit from the fifth generation of mobile networks, or 5G. 5G is capable of transmitting data at much faster rates, up to 20 Gbps, while 4G can only transmit data at 1 Gbps. 5G also has much more simultaneous connections (1,000,000 per square kilometer vs. 100,000) and a faster latency speed than 4G (1 ms vs. 10 ms). These advantages over 4G are critical because as the Internet of Things expands, so does data volume, and transmission speed suffers as a result. 5G allows for more communication between a broader ranges of devices, many of which can be fit with AI at the edge.

Edge AI networks feature software platforms and hardware connected with IoT technologies. Recently, companies have offered a set of edge computers, IoT edge servers, and multi-service IoT edge gateways that are capable of supporting advanced machine learning and deep learning applications.

The idea of connecting embedded systems to the Internet isn't exactly new. The IoT is proving to be very useful in areas such as industrial automation where things like robots and sensors can remotely report potential issues before they arise, possibly saving companies losing millions in cost repairs but, once again, we run into the problem of collecting, transporting, and analyzing all the data.

For example, we have Internet-connected sensors in the warehouse. These are sending massive amounts of data to servers across the Internet where we're running some ML algorithms to try and predict throughput maintenance needs. All of these statistics are sent to a dashboard on our computer systems where we can decide what actions to do next from the comfort of our office or home. However, as you begin to scale up operations in our warehouse, we might start to run into physical limitations in our network bandwidth. The Wi-Fi might get too crowded with all those sensors or we might start having to pay way more than we intended to our Internet service provider for extra bandwidth and that's where we get to this idea of edge computing where we run our own local computers or servers to help manage all that data. These servers don't exist out in the cloud. We likely own or have control of them. So, they're said to be on the edge of the cloud. They may not be as powerful as the remote servers, but they can help alleviate some of the bandwidth requirements. These servers can collect, arrange, and perform a basic analysis of our data before shipping it off to the remote servers, and here's where the interesting things begins. If we start running machine learning algorithms on that local server, we've entered into the realm of Edge AI. Even if the algorithms aren't as accurate or as fast as they would be on a remote server, they still might be more useful closer to the collection devices rather than having to rely on the Internet and all of its latency and it gets even more exciting when we start running ML algorithms on the collection devices themselves; assuming the processing power is present, we could perform basic analysis and accuracy before sending it off to our servers. A detailed comparison is shown in Figure 1.3.

Smart Applications

Smart glasses, remote control devices, medical devices, smartphones, smart TVs, and IoT devices may all benefit from Edge AI.

Edge AI is particularly useful in manufacturing and traffic, including transportation sectors autonomous vehicles and machinery. Electricity and retail are two of the other fast-growing industries in Edge AI.

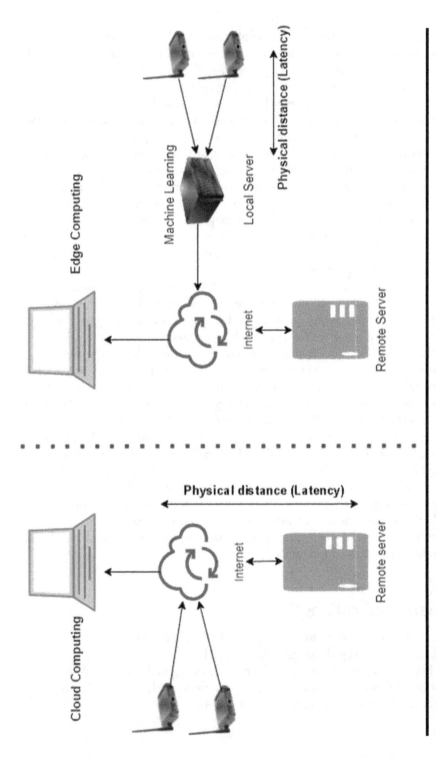

Figure 1.3 Cloud Computing vs Edge Computing.

Manufacturing

Manufacturing quality management is one of the promising Edge AI applications. Edge computing allows industrial equipment to make decisions without the need for human intervention. The decentralized design aids in time and cost reductions. Mobile equipment may be set up on-site with minimal data infrastructure footprints since the data is collected and processed locally. The supply chain will be shortened, and markets will be more available.

Video analytics is a form of Edge AI that can continuously, accurately, and precisely track product quality. Even the tiniest quality anomalies, which are almost impossible to spot with the naked eye, can be detected using video analytics.

Additionally, the "always on" connectivity of edge computing would reduce the occurrence of device downtime, allowing for greater organizational versatility.

Transportation and Traffic

For a long time, passenger aircrafts have been highly automated. Real-time analysis of sensor data will help to increase flight safety even further. Although fully autonomous and automated ships might not be possible for several years, modern ships already have a lot of sophisticated data analytics.

Edge computing can help cities handle traffic management more efficiently. Controlling the opening and closing of extra lanes and, in the future, managing automated car flows are all examples of this. Edge computing eliminates the need to transport vast amounts of traffic data to a centralized cloud, lowering bandwidth and latency costs.

Health Care

Distributive analytics allows healthcare professionals to gain information from data obtained by IoT devices, allowing them to move beyond physical patient visits to hospitals. By establishing a continuous real-time patient management system, edge computing broadens the field of vision and facilitates a transition from reactive to proactive treatment. In health care, edge computing aids in the acceleration of machine-to-machine and machine-to-human communication. By bringing computing processing closer to the data sources, this brings localized processing to the sensor. By spreading workloads across branch data center locations, this computing mechanism will also aid in the delivery of medical applications and services to remote rural areas. The use of virtualization technology like hyper-convergence will help patients and healthcare providers communicate more effectively. When connected to edge data centers, IoT healthcare devices will expand medical personnel's scope to even the most remote patients.

Other edge computing applications in health care include, but are not limited to, assisting health centers with inventory management, manual ordering, eliminating time-consuming paperwork, and speeding up the shipping of essential medication and equipment.

Energy and Retail

The amount of data generated by a smart grid is enormous. Demand elasticity, usage tracking and forecasting, renewable energy use, and decentralized energy production are all possible with a truly smart grid. A smart grid, on the other hand, necessitates communication between devices; as a result, using a conventional cloud service to transmit data might not be the best choice.

To understand the customer behavior, retailers gather a lot of data about their consumers both internally and externally. Customer analytics has been used by large retail stores for a long time. Currently, the analytics are mainly based on the analysis of completed, receipt data. While this approach yields good results, the receipt data does not contain all of the necessary details. It doesn't say much about how people walk around the store, how satisfied they are, what they're viewing, or anything else. Video analytics examines entirely anonymized data derived from a video picture to gain a better understanding of people's buying habits, which can help enhance the overall shopping experience and customer service, as shown in Figure 1.4.

Edge Chip

The opportunity in computing chip technologies in edge computing chips is actually growing. There's going to be a growth in the endpoint device and edge computing. By the year of 2019, there was a number of new deep learning chips being announced by companies such as the deep learning chip "Goya" by Habana, Intel's deep learning inference chip "NNP-I", full self-driving computer with two chips by Tesla, Huawei's deep learning IP core "Da Vinci", and deep learning inference accelerator multi-chip module by Nvidia.

What Do Edge AI Chip Functions Do?

The demand for Edge AI chips will continue to expand at a much faster rate than the overall chip market. Edge AI chip revenues are expected to reach 1.5 billion by 2024, probably by a large margin [1–5]. These cutting-edge AI chips are expected to make their way through an increasing number of consumer devices, such as

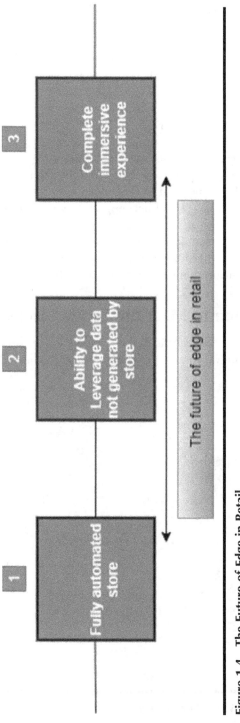

Figure 1.4   The Future of Edge in Retail.

high-end smartphones, laptops, and wearables. Robots, cameras, sensors, and other IoT devices would all benefit from them.

What they don't do, maybe, is a better query. Machine learning underpins a wide range of capabilities today, including biometrics, facial detection and recognition, fun image filters, speech recognition, voice assistance, and language translation.

These tasks can be carried out on processors without an Edge AI chip, as well as in the cloud, but when done by an Edge AI chip, they perform much better, run far faster, and use much less energy. Personal data that never leaves a phone cannot be intercepted or misused. As a result, keeping the processing on a computer is more convenient in terms of privacy and security. Even if the phone is not connected to the Internet, the Edge AI chip mounted on the handset will perform all of these functions.

Edge AI can open up a slew of new opportunities for businesses, especially in IoT applications. Companies will increase their ability to analyze rather than just collect data from connected devices, and transform the analysis into action using Edge AI chips, all while avoiding the cost, complexity, and security risks associated with sending large quantity of data onto the cloud (Figure 1.5).

Chip Innovation to Meet the Edge's Needs

Edge requirements for doing this heavy computation in low latency with low power is actually causing companies to build chips that are efficient for moving

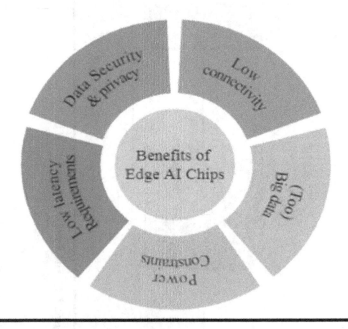

Figure 1.5   Issues Where Edge AI Can Help.

data around and having very efficient data flow on the chip. The company also have to build better algorithm processing and need to be using memory more efficiently because memory isn't free even if they're very small chips and the silicon process technology is still an issue. Gordon Moore's law of trying to improve the size of the transistor in order to get more speed from a chip is still there, and there's tons of investment in that kind of problem. So, there's still a lot of challenges in the chip industry in order to meet this insatiable desire to deploy AI algorithms everywhere because of course the cost to being able to deploy such complex algorithms to get high accuracy.

Discussion on Edge AI

Artificial intelligence is exceptional for how quickly this has slipped into the main field of modern society. Televisions, tablets, automobiles, robots, wearables, buildings, and industrial systems have all acquired capabilities and their facilities that were considered a futuristic thing once. They now have the ability to see, hear, and sense. They have the ability to make decisions that closely resemble and, in some cases, exceed human thinking, conduct, and acts.

Despite these impressive advances, one pesky fact remains: smart systems should still be a lot smarter and handle even more challenging tasks. Furthermore, as the IoT takes shape, ultra-low energy sensors and reduced latency with onboard processing are becoming increasingly important. Systems should depend on data centers and clouds to process data. The complete value of artificial intelligence can't be realized [6–19].

Edge AI is aimed at these problems. To genuinely and pervasively engage AI in the processes within our lives, AI computation must be pushed away from the data center and toward the edge [20–50]. This method reduces latency by reducing the need for a distant data center and, in some cases, bypassing it entirely. Computation occurs on the system in many situations. Edge AI will allow new types of systems to work all around us at the speed of life, with data that is intimate and essential to us [20].

This framework's strength lies in its ability to process data precisely when and where it is needed. Between the user devices and the cloud, Edge AI adds new computational layers. Between these layers, it distributes app computations [51,52].

Apart from the Data Center

A basic yet profound challenge lies at the important part of Edge AI: Computing systems that can make decisions at the speed of a human mind and in real time.

For AI to reach its full potential, any device implementing AI must run at a high level of speed and accuracy. This usually necessitates a delay of less than 10 ms. Nowadays, clouds, on the other hand, react in the range of 70 ms or more; connections that include networking without wires are even slower in speed [6].

The present method of funnelling data via a few massive data centers limits the strengths of increasing digital technologies. Edge AI grabs a unique approach: Instead of running algorithms in distant clouds and data centers, it runs them locally on chips and specialized hardware. This means that a machine can function without maintaining a constant link to a network or the Internet, and it can connect to remote networks and transmit data on an "as-needed" basis. Since chips aren't optimized for AI and networks aren't explicitly built for Edge AI, current implementations, such as edge computing and fog networks, only have marginal benefits.

However, a low-latency framework necessitates the creation of new processors, storage devices, and algorithms. It has a huge impact in changing traditional computing models. Today's mainstream data-driven AI methods, especially in decision-making and machine learning (ML), are designed to be run in a cloud environment, with all data items always available for learning or inference on abundant and homogeneous computing resources observed [51]. The cloud-native model is ill-suited to the opportunistic, distributed, and heterogeneous edge computing world, where devices appear and vanish, links fail, and system batteries die and where user and edge devices have widely disparate computational resources.

Smart Devices

The article [20] states that decision making and other roles to the network's edge results in drastic changes. An autonomous vehicle, for example, may use on-board machine learning to dynamically respond to various environments and drivers. A network of sensors installed in a house or in a hospital could help monitor patients, including the older age people, and identify issues such as ability to not get out of bed or failure to take medicines. Edge AI could also track the state of underground pipes for decades without the need to replace a sensor battery. Right now, what we do at the edge is pretty simple, says Kurt Busch, co-founder and CEO of SYN-TIANT Corp., a company that develops Edge AI chips. But within a few years, we will possibly see robust functionality, says Busch.

While all of these items can be done without the help of Edge AI today, removing the circle trip to the cloud will drastically change the functions. It's safe to say a language translating application would work well in Barcelona today, but things get harder in places like Mongolia's Gobi Desert, where cellular service is unavailable. Even when there is a good signal, the process of jumping phrases to the cloud and back takes a long time, resulting in inconvenient and sometimes inappropriate lags. Edge AI can fix this by keeping all necessary data on the computer and only connecting to the Internet when absolutely necessary.

Wake-on-command functions are another attractive aspect of Edge AI. When a computer isn't in operation, these devices will reduce power consumption to near zero. This gives permission to certain devices to run for years without needing to be recharged or replaced. This function will be useful for embedded sensors, medical implants, and remote video cameras. Furthermore, several appliances, such as coffee makers and microwave ovens, don't need a lot of computing power or a Siri to operate; a few thousand hard-wired terms will suffice. Since we don't have to deal with the roundtrip of the cloud, the system becomes more responsive and has better privacy [20].

Smart glasses, smartphones, medical devices, watches, smart TVs, smart speakers, remote control devices, and other IoT machines may all benefit from Edge AI. Edge AI, according to Amit Lal, an electrical engineering professor at Cornell University [20], may have far-reaching implications apart from microwave ovens that enable humans to say cooking commands or hearing aids that voluntarily respond to the user and their surroundings. As component of a team that was in charge of the NZERO program for the United States between 2017 and 2019, Lal and others at the Defense Advanced Research Projects Agency (DARPA) investigated ultra-low-power or zero-power nanomechanical learning chips that could harness acoustic signals or other types of ambient energy and wake as required. The research can eventually lead to automobiles and other devices that can be identified by a distinct acoustic signature. Before the car or other device gets near enough to pose a threat, you can check its identity.

Rethinking and Reconnecting AI

Edge AI's full potential necessitates emphasis on both practical and technological issues. Network models and new devices are needed that do not rely on on-screen assistants, speakers, or the cloud. Microprocessors built particularly for the depth learning process and on-chip artificial intelligence functions, such as wake-on-demand functionality and speech processing, are a good place to start when tackling this issue. According to article [20], Edge AI needs an entirely different system for data collection, modeling, validation, and the development of a deep learning model.

SYNTIANT Company is working on chips designed particularly for Edge AI. Flex Logix, Ambient, Mythic, Coral, BrainChip, and GreenWaves are among the others. Machine learning algorithms are usually run as 8- or 16-bit computations on such chips, which not only improves local efficiency but also decreases energy consumption by orders of magnitude. Edge AI chips, unlike standard Von Neumann or stored-program chips including central processing units and digital signal processors (DSPs), do not require data to be swapped between the memory and processor. Instead, they use in-memory or near-memory data flow designs, which bring the logic and memory data closer together. According to article [20], a neural decision processor outperforms stored program architectures including CPUs and DSPs by a factor of 100.

However, the latest generation of Edge AI chips is just the beginning. Future edge chips, according to Busch, would likely have different structures and features depending on the use case. Developing memory technologies such as magnetoresistive random-access memory (MRAM) and resistive random-access memory (ReRAM) could promote power and performance efficiency for particular use cases, such as a ultra-low-power app that operates outside of a data center. Nonvolatile flash memory (NOR) is being investigated by other chipmakers as a method to save code on systems for more ultra-machine learning features.

To bring Edge AI into the main field, however, more than new and better chips will be needed. According to [6], cloud computing must be deployed in completely new ways [6]. Pioneered the concept of cloudlets, which are basically data centers in a box that can be installed in aircraft, cars, vehicles, homes, and offices. "To suit the area, the same Xeon hardware that occupies a football-sized building will be tailored to a small box or shelf. Hyperconverged clouds carry compute to the customer. You end up with a lot of bandwidth and very little latency" declares with the implementation of 5G, which supports Internet of things (IoT) architectures, such systems and edge AI could be further improved [6].

The concept of cloudlets and Edge AI has been gaining momentum recently. Wavelength, from Amazon Web Services, and Edge TPU, from Google, are hardware and software solutions that support edge functionality. Despite the fact that Edge AI technology raises concerns about how to best handle physical security and cybersecurity, the model is gaining traction. Widely distributed cloudlets will radically change how data flows, processes occur, and machines make decisions [6].

On the Top Ledge

A few more items will be needed to get cutting-edge AI off the board and into daily life. Distribution learning processes and inference algorithms that work in a fragmented, heterogeneous, and opportunistic edge setting with non-IID data are one of the most critical requirements, according to [51]. The effectiveness of these systems and the value they provide will be determined by how well they complete the mission, especially in highly connected IoT ecosystems.

Additionally, libraries and structures that make new and more effective algorithms are needed. Developers of Edge AI applications and machine learning tasks on-chip or on-device would need ready-made tools and resources. Furthermore, these libraries must work in a variety of edge settings, such as ad-hoc clouds or cloudlets from various Compatibility, data quality, and manufacturer issues will arise if this system is not in place, and Edge AI will fall away. Existing frameworks like Tensorflow, Ray, and Spark are basically cloud-native, and their computational models are an unrated fit for the edge setting, according to [51].

Edge AI will earn popularity over the succeeding years, despite technological problems and new security issues. Edge chips and other parts will not only emerge in appliances, sensors, and smartphones, but they will also open up completely new methods to use AI, neural networks, and ML, possibly reclaiming a factor of privacy that has been largely immersed in the digital age. According to reference [20], "Edge AI has a staggering number of applications and possibilities. You will open up a world of possibilities by making devices and sensors smarter and lowering their power requirements".

Conclusion

Companies and developers have recognized the need of using edge technology to deliver immediate and efficient service while increasing profit margins as users spend more time on their mobile devices. As a result, enterprise-level artificial intelligence–based technological services have started to emerge.

The Edge AI system has grabbed a huge investment in the millions by big companies like Google and Amazon. So, there is heavy competition in this field. As there was heavy demand for the IoT devices, it has led to the adoption of edge computing and 5G network.

However, there is a common misconception that edge technology would replace the cloud; this is not the case. Edge technology will complement cloud computing. Although data will continue to be handled in the cloud, user-generated data that belongs solely to them can be operated and processed on the edge.

References

[1] C. Hao, J. Dotzel, J. Xiong, L. Benini, Z. Zhang, and D. Chen. "Enabling Design Methodologies and Future Trends for Edge AI: Specialization and Co-design." *IEEE Design & Test* (2021).
[2] F. Foukalas and A. Tziouvaras. "Applications." *IEEE Industrial Electronics Magazine* (2021).
[3] R. Marculescu, D. Marculescu, and U. Ogras. "Edge AI: Systems Design and ML for IoT Data Analytics," In *Proceedings of the 26th ACM SIGKDD International Conference on Knowledge Discovery & Data Mining* (2020): 3565–3566.
[4] A. Libri, A. Bartolini, and L. Benini. "pAElla: Edge AI-Based Real-Time Malware Detection in Data Centers." *IEEE Internet of Things Journal* 7, no. 10 (2020): 9589–9599.

[5] H. A. Imran, U. Mujahid, S. Wazir, U. Latif, and K. Mehmood. "Embedded Development Boards for Edge-AI: A Comprehensive Report." *arXiv preprint arXiv:2009.00803* (2020).

[6] M. Satyanarayanan and N. Davies. "Augmenting Cognition Through Edge Computing." *Computer* 52, no. 7 (2019): 37–46.

[7] T. Rausch and S. Dustdar. "Edge Intelligence: The Convergence of Humans, Things, and ai," In *2019 IEEE International Conference on Cloud Engineering (IC2E)* (2019): 86–96. IEEE.

[8] Arm Blueprint, "Edge AI: From the Art of the Possible to the Art of the Tangible." June 3, 2019. View in article

[9] T. Bai, C. Pan, Y. Deng, M. Elkashlan, A. Nallanathan, and L. Hanzo. "Latency Minimization for Intelligent Reflecting Surface Aided Mobile Edge Computing." *IEEE Journal on Selected Areas in Communications* 38, no. 11 (2020): 2666–2682.

[10] Arm, "From Cloud to The Edge: On-Device Artificial Intelligence Boosts Performance," *MIT Technology Review*, May 16, 2019. View in article

[11] Research and Markets. "Global Artificial Intelligence (AI) Chip Market Set to Record a CAGR of 45.2% Between 2019 & 2025 - ASIC Segment Anticipated to Overtake the GPU Type in the Near Future, in Terms of Revenue." press release, August 28, 2019. View in article

[12] S. Deng, H. Zhao, W. Fang, J. Yin, S. Dustdar, and A. Y. Zomaya. "Edge Intelligence: the Confluence of Edge Computing and Artificial Intelligence." *IEEE Internet of Things Journal* 7, no. 8 (2020): 7457–7469.

[13] K. Cao, Y. Liu, G. Meng, and Q. Sun. "An Overview on Edge Computing Research." *IEEE Access* 8 (2020): 85714–85728.

[14] T. Wang, L. Qiu, A. K. Sangaiah, A. Liu, M. Z. A. Bhuiyan, and Y. Ma. "Edge-Computing-Based Trustworthy Data Collection Model in the Internet of Things." *IEEE Internet of Things Journal* 7, no. 5 (2020): 4218–4227.

[15] L. U. Khan, I. Yaqoob, N. H. Tran, S. Ahsan Kazmi, T. Nguyen Dang, and C. S. Hong. "Edge-Computing-Enabled Smart Cities: A Comprehensive Survey." *IEEE Internet of Things Journal* 7, no. 10 (2020): 10200–10232.

[16] C. Jiang, T. Fan, H. Gao, W. Shi, L. Liu, C. Cerin, and J. Wan. "Energy Aware Edge Computing: A Survey." *Computer Communications* 151 (2020): 556–580.

[17] R. I. Minu and G. Nagarajan. "Bridging the IoT Gap Through Edge Computing." In *Edge Computing and Computational Intelligence Paradigms for the IoT*, pp. 1–9. IGI Global, 2019.

[18] G. Nagarajan, R. I. Minu, and A. Jayanthiladevi. "Cognitive Internet of Things (C-IOT)." In *Sensing Techniques for Next Generation Cognitive Radio Networks*, pp. 299–311. IGI Global, 2019.

[19] S. V. Simpson and G. Nagarajan. "An Edge Based Trustworthy Environment Establishment for Internet of Things: an Approach for Smart Cities." *Wireless Networks* (2021): 1–17.

[20] S. Greengard. "AI on Edge." *Communications of the ACM* 63, no. 9 (2020): 18–20.

[21] W. Shi, J. Cao, Q. Zhang, Y. Li, and L. Xu. "Edge Computing: Vision and Challenges." *IEEE Internet of Things Journal* 3, no. 5 (2016): 637–646.

[22] W. Shi, and S. Dustdar. "The Promise of Edge Computing." *Computer* 49, no. 5 (2016): 78–81.

[23] M. Satyanarayanan. "The Emergence of Edge Computing." *Computer* 50, no. 1 (2017): 30–39.

[24] Y. Mao, C. You, J. Zhang, K. Huang, and K. B. Letaief. "A Survey on Mobile Edge Computing: The Communication Perspective." *IEEE Communications Surveys & Tutorials* 19, no. 4 (2017): 2322–2358.

[25] B. Varghese, N. Wang, S. Barbhuiya, P. Kilpatrick, and D. S. Nikolopoulos. "Challenges and Opportunities in Edge Computing," In *2016 IEEE International Conference on Smart Cloud (SmartCloud)* (2016): 20–26. IEEE.

[26] W. Yu, F. Liang, X. He, W. G. Hatcher, C. Lu, J. Lin, and X. Yang. "A Survey on the Edge Computing for the Internet of Things." *IEEE access* 6 (2017): 6900–6919.

[27] H. Li, K. Ota, and M. Dong. "Learning IoT in Edge: Deep Learning for the Internet of Things with Edge Computing." *IEEE network* 32, no. 1 (2018): 96–101.

[28] G. Premsankar, M. D. Francesco, and T. Taleb. "Edge Computing for the Internet of Things: A Case Study." *IEEE Internet of Things Journal* 5, no. 2 (2018): 1275–1284.

[29] C. Sonmez, A. Ozgovde, and C. Ersoy. "Edgecloudsim: An Environment for Performance Evaluation of Edge Computing Systems." *Transactions on Emerging Telecommunications Technologies* 29, no. 11 (2018): e3493.

[30] Y. Ai, M. Peng, and K. Zhang. "Edge Computing Technologies for Internet of Things: A Primer." *Digital Communications and Networks* 4, no. 2 (2018): 77–86.

[31] F. Liu, G. Tang, Y. Li, Z. Cai, X. Zhang, and T. Zhou. "A Survey on Edge Computing Systems and Tools." *Proceedings of the IEEE* 107, no. 8 (2019): 1537–1562.

[32] Y. Xiao, Y. Jia, C. Liu, X. Cheng, J. Yu, and W. Lv. "Edge Computing Security: State of the Art and Challenges." *Proceedings of the IEEE* 107, no. 8 (2019): 1608–1631.

[33] X. Sun and N. Ansari. "EdgeIoT: Mobile Edge Computing for the Internet of Things." *IEEE Communications Magazine* 54, no. 12 (2016): 22–29.

[34] J. Pan and J. McElhannon. "Future Edge Cloud and Edge Computing for Internet of Things Applications." *IEEE Internet of Things Journal* 5, no. 1 (2017): 439–449.

[35] N. Hassan, S. Gillani, E. Ahmed, I. Yaqoob, and M. Imran. "The Role of Edge Computing in Internet of Things." *IEEE Communications Magazine* 56, no. 11 (2018): 110–115.

[36] X. Wang, Y. Han, V. C. Leung, D. Niyato, X. Yan, and X. Chen. "Convergence of Edge Computing and Deep Learning: A Comprehensive Survey." *IEEE Communications Surveys & Tutorials* 22, no. 2 (2020): 869–904.

[37] P. Porambage, J. Okwuibe, M. Liyanage, M. Ylianttila, and T. Taleb. "Survey on Multi-Access Edge Computing for Internet of Things Realization." *IEEE Communications Surveys & Tutorials* 20, no. 4 (2018): 2961–2991.

[38] S. Liu, L. Liu, J. Tang, B. Yu, Y. Wang, and W. Shi. "Edge Computing for Autonomous Driving: Opportunities and Challenges." *Proceedings of the IEEE* 107, no. 8 (2019): 1697–1716.

[39] N. R. Tadapaneni. "Overview and Opportunities of Edge Computing." *Available at SSRN 3656806* (2016).

[40] A. Yousefpour, C. Fung, T. Nguyen, K. Kadiyala, F. Jalali, A. Niakanlahiji, J. Kong, and J. P. Jue. "All One Needs to Know About Fog Computing and Related Edge Computing Paradigms: A Complete Survey." *Journal of Systems Architecture* 98 (2019): 289–330.

[41] B. Chen, J. Wan, A. Celesti, D. Li, H. Abbas, and Q. Zhang. "Edge Computing in IoT-based Manufacturing." *IEEE Communications Magazine* 56, no. 9 (2018): 103–109.

[42] Y. Huang, X. Ma, X. Fan, J. Liu, and W. Gong. "When Deep Learning Meets Edge Computing," In *2017 IEEE 25th international Conference on Network Protocols (ICNP)* (2017): 1–2. IEEE.

[43] E. Ahmed, A. Ahmed, I. Yaqoob, J. Shuja, A. Gani, M. Imran, and M. Shoaib. "Bringing Computation Closer Toward the User Network: Is Edge Computing the Solution?." *IEEE Communications Magazine* 55, no. 11 (2017): 138–144.

[44] R. Yang, F. Richard Yu, P. Si, Z. Yang, and Y. Zhang. "Integrated Blockchain and Edge Computing Systems: A Survey, Some Research Issues and Challenges." *IEEE Communications Surveys & Tutorials* 21, no. 2 (2019): 1508–1532.

[45] O. Salman, I. Elhajj, A. Kayssi, and A. Chehab. "Edge Computing Enabling the Internet of Things," In *2015 IEEE 2nd World Forum on Internet of Things (WF-IoT)* (2015): 603–608. IEEE.

[46] A. H. Sodhro, S. Pirbhulal, and V. H. C. De Albuquerque. "Artificial Intelligence-Driven Mechanism for Edge Computing-Based Industrial Applications." *IEEE Transactions on Industrial Informatics* 15, no. 7 (2019): 4235–4243.

[47] Q. Pham, F. Fang, V. N. Ha, M. J. Piran, M. Le, L. B. Le, W. Hwang, and Z. Ding. "A Survey of Multi-Access Edge Computing In 5G and Beyond: Fundamentals, Technology Integration, and State-of-the-Art." *IEEE Access* 8 (2020): 116974–117017.

[48] Nvidia, "Autonomous machines: Jetson Nano," accessed October 9, 2019. Although based on a GPU-style architecture, Nvidia's stand-alone AI chip is not a GPU but an AI chip meant for use in devices, not data centers. View in article

[49] M. Satyanarayanan, P. Simoens, Y. Xiao, P. Pillai, Z. Chen, K. Ha, W. Hu, and B. Amos. "Edge Analytics in the Internet of Things." *IEEE Pervasive Computing* 14, no. 2 (2015): 24–31.

[50] M. G. Murshed, C. Murphy, D. Hou, N. Khan, G. Ananthanarayanan, and F. Hussain. "Machine Learning at the Network Edge: A survey." *arXiv preprint arXiv:1908.00080* (2019).

[51] L. Lovén, T. Leppänen, E. Peltonen, J. Partala, E. Harjula, P. Porambage, M. Ylianttila, and J. Riekki. "EdgeAI: A Vision for Distributed, Edgenative Artificial Intelligence in Future 6G Networks." *The 1st 6G Wireless Summit* (2019): 1–2.

[52] A. Nawaz, T. N. Gia, J. P. Queralta, and T. Westerlund. "Edge AI and Blockchain for Privacy-Critical and Data-Sensitive Applications," In *2019 Twelfth International Conference on Mobile Computing and Ubiquitous Network (ICMU)* (2019): 1–2. IEEE.

Chapter 2

Demystifying the Edge AI Paradigm

P. Beaulah Soundarabai, Peter Augustine, and Smitha Vinod

Associate Professor, CHRIST University, Bangalore

Contents

DOI: 10.1201/9781003145158-2

Introduction

Edge computing aspires in the coordination and collaboration of edge devices for processing the data generated in proximity; wherein artificial intelligence aims for creating intelligence on these devices by learning from those data. Edge computing and artificial intelligence are together bringing edge intelligence for creating advantages among them. Individually, each of them has done exceedingly well in contributing to the betterment of society. Now, if they converge, there is a paradigm shift and the impacts will be mesmerizingly profound and phenomenal.

The fusion of these two popular technologies is laying down a spectacular foundation for creating new kinds of experiences and opportunities for people. Newer possibilities can easily come up across business and people domains. There will be premium and people-centric services emerging and evolving for automating and accelerating a number of manual activities in our daily lives. These also smooth the route for the age-old transition from business IT to people IT. This convergence directly impacts people's lives in a distinguishing and deft manner. It not only saves processing time but provides more privacy with an optimum usage of resources, along with low utilization of network bandwidth. The basic concept behind edge computing is fulfilling and flourishing the advantages of distributed computing systems along with enforcing the spread of intelligence all over the network instead of having it only in the centralized cloud structure.

When this intelligence is enforced on the edge devices and servers, it brings lots of benefits together. The first and foremost benefit is reduced network utilization. The live data of audio and video streaming data or any sensed data need not be sent to the distant cloud for processing and decision making. This dramatic data transmission reduction leads to saving network bandwidth and reducing network congestion. There are other advantages, too.

Edge or Fog Devices and Their Roles

According to the leading market watchers and analysts, there is going to be trillions of digitized entities, billions of connected smart devices, and millions of micro-services in the near future for years to come. With the help of faster developments and stability of path-breaking miniaturization technologies, we have state-of-the-art micro- and nano-electronics products flourishing everywhere. Further on, there are competent digitization and edge technologies including LED lights, beacons, stickers, tags, codes, chips, controllers, specks, etc. The other important digitization and edge technologies are disappearing sensors and actuators, which are plentifully and purposefully occupying most of our everyday environments these days. Sensors and actuators are also known as "implantables". By applying these powerful digitization and edge technologies, all kinds of commonly found and cheap things in our living and working spaces are entitled to become smart objects. In other words, ordinary items in our daily places become extraordinary. Any tangible object is bound to become animated and sentient material sent through the smart application of the above-mentioned edge and digitization technologies. Edge devices are being attached or embodied on ordinary and commonly found items. Such a strategically sound transformation is capable of transforming ordinary things into digitized items. What is the result of all this empowerment and enablement? All sorts of physical, mechanical, electrical, and electronics systems in our buildings, manufacturing floors, entertainment plazas, eating joints, railway stations, air- and seaports, auditoriums, sports stadiums, micro-grids, nuclear establishments, shopping malls, etc. are being fruitfully digitized with much care and clarity. These distinct, deeper, and decisive technologies are intrinsically empowering the world to adapt to trillions of digitized smart entities in the approaching future. It is therefore indisputably correct to state that the digitization movement is in full speed. Our shirts become e-shirts; our doors, cots, windows, chairs, tables, wardrobes, kettles, wares, utilities, utensils, etc. will become smart through the attachment of digitization and edge technologies.

Now come to the device world. With the fast-growing device ecosystem, we are being bombarded with a variety of slim and sleek, handy and trendy, resource-constrained and intensive, purpose-specific and agnostic, multimedia, multimodal, and multifaceted devices. There is a growing array of hand-helds, mobiles, portables, wearables, nomadic, and fixed devices. Further on, we have consumer electronics, medical instruments, home appliances, communication gateways, robots, drones, cameras, game consoles, machineries, equipment, medical instruments, single board computers (SBCs), programmable logic controllers (PLCs), SCADAs, etc. yearning to be digitized and connected to attain all the originally expressed benefits. It is forecasted that there will be billions of such higher-end devices soon. With the surging popularity of the Internet of Things (IoT) paradigm, every digitized entity and device is solemnly readied to be Web-enabled. Now, with the overwhelming adoption of the cloud idea, every device in and around us is ordained to be cloud-enabled. In other words, every electronic is slated to be connected. The number of connected entities is expected to be in the billions soon. Device-to-device (D2D) and device-to-cloud (D2C) integration experimentations and scenarios are gaining momentum due to the steady growth of several implementation technologies.

Precisely speaking, digitized entities and connected devices are stuffing and saturating our everyday environments (personal, social, and professional).

About Edge Computing

Edge computing is the computing capability and facility being provided by edge/fog devices. Edge sensors and devices are projected to be in the billions in the years to come; the amount of data getting generated by edge devices is humungous as there is a realization that every type of edge data comprises useful and usable knowledge. Edge data processing is mandated for mining the hidden treasures of meaningful insights from the huge heaps of raw data. Edge computing follows the proven and potential distributed architecture. Cloud computing is quite centralized, whereas edge or fog computing is a distributed model. Multiple heterogeneous devices co-operate with one another to do edge data collection, storage, and processing.

Edge devices are empowered to collect, cleanse, and crunch their data in-stantaneously if they have the requisite data storage and processing power, instead of transmitting those data to nearby or faraway cloud servers. Edge devices form an ad-hoc and dynamic cloud to accomplish bigger and better things. That is, clouds being formed out of edge devices are set to fill the whole earth soon. As there are billions of connected devices, the amount of memory, processing, storage, and IOPS capacities and capabilities are simply phenomenal and hence the future definitely belongs to the pioneering edge computing model. There are edge gateways/servers in order to contribute as a master or control server, whereas other devices in the network help in data storage and processing.

Edge computing, in a way, reduces the storage requirements on the cloud, making the cloud work to its full potential; it also reduces the network bandwidth requirements drastically as there is not many data transactions between these de-vices and the cloud architecture. Edge computing enables the real-time processing instantly by decentralizing the processing power without any latency issues at all. It also makes it possible to visualize and realize a number of next-generation people-centric services and applications. Industries also can convert a lot of manual things by getting them automated and accelerated to enjoy the benefits of smart IoT devices on a variety of value propositions that are available over a vast industrial domain. The prime advantages of edge computing are given below:

- **Low Latency** – With the help of edge analytic tools, the data is analyzed immediately, as and when it is captured, in the local environment and gives the benefit of low latency. This eliminates the unnecessary delays caused by the network and processing queues.

- **Scalability** – The centralized cloud data analytic tools accumulate the received data to do the processing, which hinders the scalability of the analytical model wherein edge analytics have the scalability nature due to decentralized analytical models by processing the data where it is captured.
- **Data Security and Privacy** – When data are stored in the cloud environment, most of that data contains the susceptible information about the business or the users. They are always vulnerable to attacks such as denial of service attack, data loss, and data breach due to malware injection attacks. Since edge computing does not send these sensitive data to remote servers, it gives the advantage of security and privacy;
- **Bandwidth Efficiency** – Edge analytics majorly relies on the local servers and the intelligent applications and thus reduces the need of remote services for analytical purposes. Edge device data gets filtered out and cleansed locally, thereby important data can be transmitted to cloud environments for future references in a secured manner.
- **Robust Connectivity** – Even if there is a network outage, edge technologies and analytics ensure the availability and the accuracy of applications without any disrupt.
- **Real-Time Computing** – Data generation, capture, and processing happen locally and quickly. Edge computing delivers the real meaning and value for real-time applications.

Thus, leveraging one or more edge devices to do real-time implementation of several people-centric applications is gaining momentum with the fast and stable developments of edge devices and the smart computing tools.

Edge Computing Architecture

The key information is that edge computing fully complied with the distributed computing patterns. As articulated above, edge devices are all set to become pervasive and persuasive. Every industry vertical is embracing this new-generation technology in order to hold and serve customers, consumers, and employees in the best way possible. Devices are being increasingly stuffed with more power and capacity that they are penetrating every business domain. In an edge architecture, there are three types of devices contributing immensely. They are edge sensors and actuators, edge devices, and edge gateways.

- **Edge Sensors and Actuators** – As accentuated above, edge sensors are not blessed with high-end memory, processing, and storage power. They are for sensing a variety of things. We know about gas, heat, pressure, presence, movement, gestures, oscillation, and humidity sensors. Hence, they typically collect data about their surroundings and send it to nearby edge devices. Sensors are miniaturized and hence disappearing. On the other hand, extracted information from aggregated sensor data gets supplied to actuators for further actions on time with intelligibility and confidence. Sensors and actuators are not for data processing.

■ **Edge Devices** – These are resource-intensive systems and hence they can run operating systems such as Android, iOS, etc. Further on, they can run data analytics platforms/tools/accelerators in order to do data analytics. They can do streaming analytics of edge sensor/actuator/device data in real time. Further on, artificial intelligence (tools and technologies with machine learning and deep learning (ML/DL) algorithms, computer vision (CV) and natural language processing (NLP)) toolkits and frameworks are being increasingly deployed on edge devices in order to extract predictive, prescriptive, and personalized insights in time. These devices are capable of data processing. These devices can talk directly to faraway cloud servers and services or they can connect edge gateway/broker to talk to cloud applications. These devices form quick clusters (called as edge clouds) to fulfill special needs. Edge clouds are for proximate processing.

■ **Edge Gateways** – They also run on any full-fledged operating system. These gateways serve as an entry point or an intermediary for the edge devices and cloud services, with an uninterrupted power supply and powerful CPUs with data storage capabilities. Edge gateways offer the standardized middleware functionalities.

■ **Cloud Environments** – We have private, public, and hybrid clouds to host business workloads and IT services. These cloud centers involve a huge number of storage architectures, server instances, and networking tools in order to automate cloud operations. Also, all the cloud resources and services are being shared across. Thus, automation and sharing bring down the cloud costs drastically. With the leverage of orchestration tools, most of the simple and complex administration activities get automated and accelerated. With the massive scalability, the leverage of cheaper hardware, deeper automation, and automated orchestration through the containerization movement, the cloud concept is a pithead for affordability, agility, and adaptability. It is projected that more than the 80% of software applications will reside in cloud environments in the years ahead.

We have discussed the prominent building blocks of edge architecture. Besides sensors and actuators, devices and device gateways, we need cloud environments in order to stock all kinds of edge data. Further on, in synchronization with current edge data, a kind of comprehensive and historical data analytics can be accomplished in cloud environments. The increased adoption and adaptation of digital twins is being presented as one of the key drivers for the spread of edge computing across industry verticals.

Edge Cloud Infrastructures

Any computing and analytics activity needs solid infrastructure. For certain scenarios, on-device AI is possible. That is, a single edge device can suffice. For other complicated activities, there is a need for clustering multiple and heterogeneous devices together to form a kind of device cloud dynamically. Clustered or cloud environments are mandatory for doing extremely powerful data analytics. For certain needs, web-scale companies used thousands of compute nodes to do data analytics. For performing edge data analytics, we need edge infrastructures. Thus, edge computing infrastructures include edge devices and their clouds. Some activities are being offloaded to faraway cloud environments. Real-time implementations are predominantly done through edge devices.

As indicated previously, we will have zillions of digitized entities and connected devices on our planet soon. These are subdivided into two major categories: resource constrained and intensive. Resource-constrained digitized entities are focusing on data gathering. Because of the externally or internally embodied communication modules, they can transmit a variety of data to nearby device middleware, which are also called device bus, IoT gateway, and broker, etc. Even devices can send data to the remote cloud environments for real-time processing by crunching the data to extract actionable decisions. However, resource-constrained edge devices are not participating in data processing, whereas resource-intensive edge devices are capable of not only collecting but also involving themselves in data processing, analytics, mining, and learning. Resources-intensive devices can therefore cluster themselves to form ad-hoc, dynamic, and purpose-specific device clouds in time to accomplish real-time data analytics.

The prominent reasons for setting up edge cloud centers are due to the challenges of non-scalability, huge power consumption, excessive network bandwidth utilization, along with a high latency and privacy and data security issues. These critical factors pave the path for the demand of edge cloud services with the micro data centers, cloudlets, or edge clouds/clusters. Edge cloud centers support distributed computing architecture. There are a few important reasons for the surging popularity of edge clouds.

Collection of real-time data, storage, processing, analytics, making the actionable result, and action are being made possible with the realization of edge cloud infrastructures. With the accumulation of sensor devices and actuators, there is a steady stream of sensor and device data. With edge clouds in place, any kind of data can be captured with appropriate sensors, and deeper investigations can be carried out with powerful intelligent tools to uncover hidden patterns in data streams. Real-time customer engagement and fulfillment is being guaranteed through edge centers.

The low-cost Raspberry Pi is the golden standard used for building and powering devices from simple smart devices, tablets, and smart mirrors to robots for single board computing for gaming, and the latest version, Raspberry Pi4, is capable of decoding 4K video from faster storage with a high-speed network connection through gigabit Ethernet. The removable system on module (SoM), used with ML tools for the development board, is from Google Coral, which is highly adapted for building the local AI platform for the benefits of society and the environment for an enriched livelihood. There is a transition here from server-centric cloud environments to device-centric cloud environments. As there are billions of edge devices, the future belongs to device clouds.

Edge Analytics

Analytics are being positioned as the key differentiator for human society. With the number of edge devices going up rapidly in and around us, we can expect more device interactions, collaborations, and correlations and thereby the amount of device data getting generated is also big. That is, the device world is supplying a huge amount of livestream data. The objective is to perform real-time analytics of such device data in order to emit out actionable insights. It is a tough affair to enable the IoT devices to be intelligent in their tasks if they are not proper and prompt in the timely analytics of the captured data.

IoT devices individually or collectively contribute to the building of huge multi-structured data due to which, data analytics acceleration engines and algorithms are gaining prominence. Customers' needs are constantly changing and meeting their demands mandate edge cloud and computing. With a surge in IoT sensors and devices in our work spots, living, and leisure places, real-time monitoring, measurement, and management turn out to be an important factor for the intended success of IoT devices. By doing real-time analytics on IoT device transaction data, the safety, sagacity, and security of IoT sensors and devices are being ensured. Real-time data analytics is essential for creating and delivering real-time applications. Real-time computing is being made possible through edge computing. Newer possibilities and opportunities will emerge with the new normal of edge computing. A host of edge-centric services and applications will see the faster maturity of edge technologies and tools.

Feasibility of edge analytics is even more possible due to the advancements in the internet technology like fifth generation network. 5G is the global standard that emerged after 4G, and this new standard facilitates everyone and every*thing* such as devices, sensors, devices, etc., connect with each other virtually. It delivers high-speed data with significant reduction of latency with a provision for uniform user experiences for a wide range of users. Smart sensors will be ineffective if the data is analyzed somewhere else and the responses come back for actions.

On-site analysis of bulk data is handled by edge analytics in the neighboring switch or router in the connected environment. Real time or closer to real-time insights are possible in this paradigm and due to which analytics can be scalable.

For example, in health care, there is a convincing use case for edge analytics. If we wear a pulse meter and blood sugar monitoring sensor in our body, and there is a sudden spike, then an event is created and communicated to our spouse or family doctor immediately. The smartphone in our pocket acts as the powerful intermediary in capturing and conveying the data to the concerned person to ponder about the counter measures in quick time. This real-time monitoring, measurement, and management of diabetes is being facilitated through edge devices doing fast calculations based on some rules. If there is a break-in in the threshold value, the right information is immediately delivered to the correct person to initiate the proper actions.

For instance, a critical application such as an aircraft passenger safety system, in real time uses a innumerable IoT sensors to monitor and evaluate the turbulence could witness a dangerous change in the internal weather forecast system that could cause damage to the life of its crew and passengers in seconds. If these massive amounts of collected data are required to be sent to a remote server for processing and later comes back to the aircraft for further actions, the aircraft might have crashed.

Edge analytics of IoT is useful in providing an instant and reliable real-time picture of operational sensors and devices to the network controllers. Here, devices transmit the raw sensed data to the centralized location, but the huge data analysis takes place on-site. For example, a fire prevention application, which acts on a fire in a public meeting hall could identify a dangerous event of temperature change that could cause a fire and kill people instantly, should not wait for the data to travel to a remote server for processing and decision making; by then the huge damage would take place. Edge analytics help in preventing such dangerous events instantly by analyzing the data and implementing the decisions that come out of the analysis.

Tending towards Edge AI

Since edge computing has taken enormous growth, it is necessary to optimize the host of services and applications implemented at the edge of the edge computing architecture. The solicitation of artificial intelligence (AI) algorithms can help optimize them, and these algorithms are executed on a hardware device installed locally. Because of this facility to implement the algorithms at the device itself, which does not need any connectivity to the outside world, we can get real-time outputs from the data generated at the edge devices within a few milliseconds.

More complex algorithms are implemented in the hardware to get instant feedback and auto correction in their functionalities in the devices such as phones, laptops, etc. For instance, the face recognition software used in phones and algorithms used in self-driving cars need immediate response based on the inputs they receive from time to time. Every piece of information the sensor gets to be processed, the devices need to adjust and respond immediately. In such a scenario, the processing of these data cannot happen at the cloud to avoid any delay for the intelligence to be enabled.

Nowadays, "smart" is an adjective demanded with any device we use in our day-to-day life. The term "smart" requires intelligence, and it is embedded with devices from the lowest to highest levels. From dawn to dusk, smart devices have become the assistants to human beings to make work more comfortable and elegant. Some of the top-edge devices with artificial intelligence-facilitated comprise smart watches, smartphones, smart speakers, smart gaming devices, head-mounted displays, PCs/tablets, automotive sensors, robots, drones, and security cameras. In the healthcare sector, monitoring vital readings of a patient also includes smart sensors to read, process, and respond to the change in the values such as blood pressure, SO_2 level, sugar level, and heart rate. Major factors such as privacy, security, cost, latency, and bandwidth must be considered when we choose cloud computing centers versus edge processing requirements.

The fields such as computer vision and image processing where deep learning is involved require heavy computing power and storage. The cloud computing environment is the most suitable solution for these applications to run effectively. In deep learning, computing time is relatively less than training the neural network, where latency is more prominent for providing real-time results on a neural network model. The most inference is still achieved in the cloud or on a server, but as AI applications' diversity grows, the centralized training and inference model is coming into question.

It is conceivable and more uncomplicated to run AI and machine learning with analytics at the edge nowadays, based on the edge's capacity and the specific framework being utilized. Whereas computing frameworks used in edge sites are much smaller than those found in cloud centers, they have developed and effectively run numerous workloads due to a colossal development in today's x86 product servers' preparing control. There are many significant preferences of AI-enabled decision making at the edge.

Exceedingly responsive – Edge AI–enabled gadgets handle information quickly compared to IoT models deployed in the cloud.

Greater safety – With a handling time of less than a few milliseconds, the chance of information getting debased and altered amid travel is exceptionally less. These gadgets too incorporate improved security features.

Excellent customer experience – Edge AI gives an arrangement to one of the significant winning issues – idleness. The end user gets an enriched experience due to low latency and real-time experiences.

Incorporating AI on edge will lead to tremendous changes in the real-time processes happening so far. It will increase the demand for smart devices with intelligence, including IoT devices, emerging 5G networks, intelligent gadgets, etc. As the companies progressively make their systems "smart", the market will make substantial advances to persevere with the computing needs of these smart platforms.

Artificial Intelligence (AI) Chips for Edge Devices

Edge-based AI chips and accelerators are being produced and installed in smart mobile handsets, smart speakers, head mounted displays (HMDs), auto-driving machines such as smart cars, vehicles, trucks, etc., and also in laptops, tablets, robots and drones, smart cameras, edge servers, etc.

AI edge processing can be performed in several ways based on the particular application requirement and the hardware device categories. It majorly depends on the choices of central processing units, graphic processing units, field programmable gate arrays (FPGAs), application specific integrated circuits (ASIC), and accelerator of system on a chip (SoC).

Early artificial intelligence (AI) chipsets are general-purpose graphic processing units. They are primarily used in enterprise and cloud servers for creating ML models. They provide high computing capacity and the ability to run state-of-the-art networks at the time. However, the need for AI on the edge devices is inevitable now and so the race to design edge-optimized SoCs has already begun. Edge inference has become an important aspect for achieving intended success of edge computing. Companies are working on major projects such as face identification and recognition, detection of objects, logos of brands, shelf inspection, insights and execution, recognition of text through handwriting and character reading, etc.

The Noteworthy Trends towards Edge AI

A number of technological innovations and disruptions have set the foundation for visualizing and realizing edge AI services and applications. AI-specific chips are being manufactured aplenty these days and this turns out to be a huge differentiator for the huge success and motivation for edge AI. There are several ways being debated for pushing AI to the edge with the aim of taking edge computing to the next level. Edge devices are becoming powerful and can find, bind, and interact with one another in the vicinity and through networks. That is, the formation of dynamic device clusters/clouds has laid down a robust and versatile foundation for Edge AI. There are breakthrough processors emerging to accomplish AI operations within an edge device.

- **Distributed computing** – There is a steady movement from centralized computing to distributed computing in order to gain a number of business, technical, and user advantages. By leveraging the distinct ideals of distributed computing, process and data-intensive AI workloads get divided and distributed across a number of machines to speed up their execution. As we all know, blockchain technology is leaning upon the distributed and decentralized computing models to be efficient and effective for a variety of business verticals.

■ **AI co-processors** – The chipset domain is growing quickly with the spread of the AI domain. As stated previously, there are generic and specific chipsets emerging and evolving in order to simplify and streamline AI processing at the edge.

■ **Advanced algorithms and toolsets** – There are several machine and deep learning (ML/DL) algorithms in the industry now in order to extract predictive and prescriptive insights in time. A number of state-of-the-art algorithms mimicking human brain function are also being unearthed and experimented. With advancements in the domains of deep learning and neural network, computer vision and natural language processing, audio and video processing requirements are being met comfortably. Now AI algorithms are being taken to edge device analysis in order to provide real-time insights. There are enabling frameworks and toolkits to make AI-enabled edge processing simple and swift.

Implementing AI algorithms closer to the environment and location where tasks are happening represents the future. It is all about performing the analytics to make critical decisions that are also critical with respect to immediate action with no delay at the edge by referring to the cloud with historical analysis and intense computing is required.

Organizations continue research to address the challenges of AI data storage and management capabilities by yielding powerful and fault-tolerant edge computing devices; these solutions will in turn reduce the cost payable by customers drastically. The technologies that seem to be very costly will become affordable and valuable over the near future. Massive and expensive cloud data centers were required for the powerful AI smart applications to run; but now, with the ready availability of distributed and decentralized devices in large numbers, AI processing is being done at the edge. With the growing popularity of connected devices, a tremendous amount of data are generated by many manufacturing, retain, power, and energy industries, by networking devices. As indicated previously, edge analytics quickly arrives at a cognitive decision.

Why Edge Site Processing?

The answer is the data security and real-time analytics of edge data. The real-time feature may be lost if we take edge data to cloud servers. That is, proximate processing is mandated for extracting actionable insights in time. Therefore, edge processing is getting the attention.

IoT application environment the data sources are of continuous stream of data with multi variant time series in which analytics strategies are implemented to get meaning insights, aggregations, and hidden inferences. There are many larger-scale data inputs such as forecast systems, alert system using surveillance camera inputs, and audio and video analytics that require very quick but accurate analysis of data for the real-time instant decision making based on the context. For such real-time applications, the cost of performing the data analysis at the cloud would be very costly and time consuming; comparing the data analysis at the edge saves on the cost of network bandwidth and the remote server processing time. Yes, there is a considerable increase of cost on the edge side to replace the regular sensing devices with the powerful AI-based hardware device. But still, the cost of edge site processing would be significantly less compared to the cloud processing, majorly considering the network bandwidth and delays due to the weighting for the processor's time.

Further on, several technological innovations have sped up and facilitated edge processing. The edge devices not only require a simple improvement on the hardware alone; it should be able to scale up to process a large deep neural network model for which it requires powerful software to be able to fit the large data model in a compressed mode into the small hardware devices that have a lower ability with respect to performance and power-related factors.

Different system architectures and strategies bolster model compression, counting Google's TensorFlow Lite, SqueezeNet, Nervana's Neural Organize Distiller, Apple's CoreML, and Facebook's Caffe2Go.

How Are Edge-Based AI Solutions Produced?

It takes little effort to get into edge-based systems, and it cannot be accomplished overnight since it needs system analysis, deployment, and execution of the system at the edge. The system analysis needs an understanding of data collection, pre-processing data, selection of algorithms, and training of the algorithms in a phased manner to get fast and best solutions. The two important key factors, such as processing power and storage capacity, play a vital role in the analysis. The system's implementation can be either decentralized or peer to peer after considering the proposed model's strengths and weaknesses. The algorithm to adopt the model at the edge is as follows:

- Develop either self-designed CNN or the existing pre-trained CNN
- Collect the data set with training and test data for the proposed model
- Train the network to get the expected result
- Find the learning rate, optimize it with different batch sizes and biases, etc., to achieve the desired accuracy
- The trained model can be used for classification and decision making.

Advantages of AI-enhanced decision making at the edge include the following:

1. Since the processing happens at the edge itself with the predefined intelligent algorithms, the results with the insights are speedy in edge-based AI. The response is significantly closer to real-time compared to IoT models deployed centrally until now.
2. The property of receiving data, processing it, and sending it back with the insights is done at the edge itself, acting as the central hub. The security of data in any communication is preserved. This level of protection of data is a big challenge with Internet-connected devices. Edge-based AI-powered devices can include enhanced security features.
3. The large scale of edge-based AI's flexibility is an advantage in making various smart devices in multiple fields from energy management to healthcare management.
4. The solutions produced by the edge-based AI model are independent. The insights out of these solutions are presented periodically wherever needed or presented through platforms with rich GUIs.
5. Customized real-time responses from the edge-based AI gives the customer a sophisticated solution for their problems. The immediate and automated rerouting during travel due to unprecedented events in the planned routes can be achieved because of the quick responsiveness characteristics of edge-based AI.

As we tend towards the profoundly associated digital economy, insights must move to the edge. In this way, the capable blend of AI and the IoT opens up new landscapes for industries to sense and react to occasions and openings around them. Remote and rough locations such as countryside farms, forest areas, oil fields, etc., can benefit immensely from the cutting-edge AI technologies. As IoT moves into more unpredictable and disengaged situations, the need of edge or fog computing will end up more predominant.

Applications of Edge Devices

There are certain kinds of applications that can be achieved on edge devices.

Computer Vision on the Edge

Machine vision through computer vision approaches and algorithms is seeing the reality. The field of computer vision has grown up with the maturity of deep learning algorithms. Edge devices are being empowered to view, perceive, understand, and act.

The model optimization procedure can be used for achieving this. Model optimization is the most acceptable method to make a significant learning model work on a computation contraption even with low power. We can run a deep learning model on edge devices by implementing the model optimization strategies. These methods use the combination of optimizing hyperparameters such as input size, gradient descent, momentum, etc. We will apply distinctive optimization strategies like Adam optimization, which may be a technique that can optimize model performance and loss value during training the model. It computes one's learning rate with unique parameters. The Adam optimization algorithm is a combination of gradient descent with momentum and RMSprop algorithms. There is a practical implementation and its details on this page (https://medium.com/datadriveninvestor/edge-ai-computer-vision-on-the-edge-dfa4ad604651).

Machine Learning (ML) on the Edge

ML algorithms are extensively used in enterprise and cloud environments in order to empower accurate and strategically sound prediction. Now, ML-based prediction moves to the edge. As discussed earlier, healthcare is one of the most technology-demanding areas where ML algorithms are effectively used for diagnosis. In intensive care units, the need for ML-embedded edge is benefits from the real-time data processing and accurate and immediate decision making. The constant and spontaneous inflow of the vital parameters such as blood glucose level, blood pressure, heart rate, SO_2 levels, along with the other parameters related to neurological activities, can be received and analyzed by the ML-edge devices.

Machine learning across multiple edge devices in the connected home – It is not necessary that edge devices independently run the applications to receive and process the data. We can get the most out of it in edge devices where multiple edge devices can be connected and efficiently apply the ML algorithms to get the best insights and decisions collectively. We can consider the example of a smart home environment where multiple devices of the home, such as thermostats, door locks, smart lights, and the smartphone's GPS data, can be linked together to respond to each other without any latency and promptly. With GPS data, thermostats, such as air conditioners and water heaters, can be switched on based on the distance of the owner from the home. Similarly, smart doors can open and lights can be illuminated. Exclusively, none of these events are especially troublesome, but the combination ML with these devices and coordination among these distinctive edge gadgets makes for a transformative experience.

Surveillance and Monitoring – Edge AI is also beneficial for security cameras as these no longer have to upload raw video signals to a cloud server for processing. Edge AI–capable security cameras can use machine learning (ML) algorithms to process captured images and videos locally. This process allows the devices to track and monitor several people and items directly. Footage would only be transmitted to a cloud server when necessary, thus reducing remote processing and memory consumption.

Model compression is another technique used to execute models at the edge device. A compressed model may lose some accuracy compared to the original model but in many cases this is acceptable. Using several compression techniques and caching intermediate results to reuse iteratively, researchers have improved the execution speed of deep neural network models. DeepMon is one such machine learning framework for continuous computer vision applications at the edge device. Similar techniques are being used by TensorFlow Lite to run models at the edge. A wide range of IoT applications can benefit from having local AI processing available.

Approaches for Analytics in Edge Devices

Many organizations are in the process of deploying thousands and thousands of sensor devices and tend to constantly monitor the sensed data at a rapid speed. These operational data that are sensed by those devices are huge, and continual scaling up will create huge managerial issues. Edge analytics offers a key solution by analyzing the data locally, either at the sensor itself or close to those sensing devices, such as a network device.

Edge analytics is considered to be a potential alternative for centralized data analytics, but both models have their own place in any organization. Edge analytics can happen on a subset of data and the decisions and results are stored in the centralized servers for backup and reference purposes, whereas the sensed raw data is not stored anywhere. Applications that require all data for future reference cannot opt for edge analytics. If the application is critical and cannot afford latency, then such applications should opt for edge analytics.

Edge analytics have an advantage for many automated industries and services such as aircraft navigation, manufacturing services, logistics, and security industries by helping them with instant decision making. For instance, if the aircraft faces a sudden turbulence, edge analytics enables the preferred instant actions without delays in providing the directions.

It is not only is applicable for instant decision-making real-time models, but is also useful in scenarios where there is huge amount of data being created at every time interval but due to limited network bandwidth, the required speed of data transfer cannot be assured between the client and server; edge analytics is a better option. In all cases, the edge devices send the data and the decision to the cloud storage also so as to view the big picture of the organization.

Businesses can adapt to edge analytics in any of the following circumstances:

- Analyzing the live data enhances the business productivity
- In need of distributed scalable capability

- Whenever unpredicted change happens in the business in need of quick decisions

Microservices

Microservices or microservice architecture models are an application as a set of many small services, which have the following properties:

- Loosely coupled software
- Individual deployability
- Independent testability and maintainability

Complex, gigantic applications are delivered as a pack of simple, reliable, and reusable microservices. The application logic is divided into classes and objects, methods, and namespaces. These services are easily scalable by simultaneously having a number of instances with the help of a load balancer process.

Microservices Pattern Language

Microservices pattern language comprises a number of patterns that enable to smooth the process of microservices architecture. Once the architecture for microservices is built, it has to undergo testing and assessment to find out the risks and eliminate architectural issues.

Earlier to microservices, the application used to be a single unit of a large logical structure; as the technological solutions easily become obsolete often, it is not really feasible to make the required changes that need to be released as a new version instead. When these monolithic solutions are deployed on the cloud, and when the changes are incorporated, the entire application is required to be rebuilt and should undergo cloud deployment once again. Even scalability is not flexible as the entire application has to go through a scaling process rather than the small parts where scalability is encountered.

Microservices on the other hand are flexible in deployability and independently scalable. They also have the capability for each microservice to be written in different programming languages, though these services are basically designed on the Unix principles. They may also follow different databases and storage structures.

5G Technology at the Edge

The fifth generation of mobile networks (5G) essentially transforms the telecom technologies for the entire globe. It not only provides economic benefits by assuring a persistent, connected digitalization, but many other things and devices stay connected through 5G, creating a virtual society of all things connected through it, such as the Internet of Everything. It ensures global communication and also assures drastic scalability as many smart devices and network equipment increasingly join it. 5G offers flexible configurability as its key design factor for enabling the mobile service providers to deliver the IoT use cases with ultra-reliability. Projects such as smart health care, agriculture, smart societies, logistics, and public services will obtain the benefit of 5G to transform our lives for the better.

Network Function Virtualization (NFV)

Virtualization enables the simulation of hardware platforms like storage devices, servers, and network resources into software. Functionalities of those platforms are decoupled from the hardware and are simulated in the form of virtual instance that exactly works and continue to provide the service as the basic hardware solution itself. Gigantic hardware can now be used as flexible solutions that support various virtual machines and can be easily scaled up or down as and when required.

When this virtualization idea is incorporated on a hardware network, a software-based logical view of networking resources like routers and switches are created while the physical components of these devices continue to provide packet forwarding, and the virtual instances help in easy deployments and in abstraction of these lower-level networking resources intelligently [1–5]. It allows overlying the virtual networks on the underlying physical hardware with the help of white box switching. These white box switches are off-the-shelf switches on the software defined networks (SDN); they depend on the operating system to support the basic networking capability. They can be customized based on the business needs and networking solutions. Virtual networks are built on virtual infrastructures to separate them from the other networking components so that the traffic does not combine with other data communication and confuse the functions of hardware resources.

The ability to make virtual networks that are meaningful and logical, which are dissociated from the underlying network hardware, is known as network virtualization. It helps in better support and integration with virtual environments which are increasing in this 5G era. It also has a good abstraction of network connections and services so as to run the applications independently on the physical hardware, without leaking the minute details of which hardware they are connected to. 5G neural host utilizes network function virtualization (NFV) to enhance the flexibility features and also to reduce the network operations and deployment costs for the domain of edge computing and edge analytics frameworks. This NFV needs to address the infrastructural requirements in multi-access edge computing (MEC) environments. There are many organizational issues addressed by ETSI while merging MEC and NFC, which makes the NFC an edge-aware NFC for 5G neural hosts. G Baldoni et al. [x] proposed the 5GCity architecture, especially for edge computing devices with multi-layer orchestration for the development of edge virtualization security and trust for a smart city project. The citizen data received from healthcare devices, mobility services, and CCTV cameras are need to be sealed from data leakages, which otherwise would be used by attackers for commercial benefits.

As edge computing brings the resources of IT to the edge devices in the network, NFC enables the edge functionalities to run on the software rather than the hardware component. This also helps in enhancing the scalability of edge nodes, which is much better if the same was done on hardware-oriented environments. Bandwidth allocation is also consistent as the edge devices are closer to the user, which brings low latency.

Network Slicing in 5G Core (5GC)

The amalgamation of 5G technology with edge computing enhances the digital and user experience and also improves the performance [6]. While 4G uses LTE radio technology, 5G tends to use new radio (NR) technology with a base station known as gNodeB (gNB).

ML Models for Edge Devices

The key idea by many researchers is to have efficient DNN models to eliminate the unnecessary parameters so that computational resources can work better for model inferences. There are many such DNN models that use this technique, such as YOLO nd Squeezenet. These are pre-trained models that are freely available for research purposes that can be used in TensorFlow, PyTorch, etc.

Model compression is another technique used to execute models at the edge device. A compressed model may lose some accuracy compared to the original model, but in many cases this is acceptable. Using several compression techniques and caching intermediate results to reuse iteratively, researchers have improved the execution speed of deep neural network models. DeepMon is one such machine learning framework for continuous computer vision applications at the edge device. Similar techniques are being used by TensorFlow Lite to run models at the edge. A wide range of IoT applications can benefit from having local AI processing available.

Deep Learning at the Edge

The edge device is an electronic device dedicated to providing connections to the other edge devices and service providers. It has limited resources and inclusion of analyzing algorithms and methods on edge devices is a real challenge. [7–9]

Edge-Based Inferencing

This will become a new normal. IoT sensors and devices generate a lot of data and powerful ML and DL models are being trained, tested, and used in powerful and scalable cloud environments. The refined, curated, and refreshed models can, then, be used in edge devices to make accurate inferences on fresh data. Today, the focus is mainly on the shifting of the AI's inference task to the edge devices from the cloud architecture. The newly captured data resides in edge devices only and it does not travel to the cloud and hence the data privacy and security are fully guaranteed through this futuristic approach.

In 2018, Google declared its "Learn2Compress" model in its machine learning kit to enhance its automatic compression technique. Its model helps to reduce larger AI designs to small forms of hardware for having a device ML for training and presumption in a simplified manner. This model provides the deep learning processing on the mobile edge devices and IoT edge devices. This idea not only does the processing instantly but also maintains the privacy of data and can work even without Internet connectivity. Here, the data processing happens at the edge itself in contrast to the traditional way of a cloud-based centralized processing environment. With edge device clouds, even the training part may move to the edge in the days to come.

Natural Language Processing (NLP) at the Edge

Artificial intelligence's resurgence is widely credited to the significant advancements in computational power that have typified the past several years of IT. When paired with graphic processing units (GPUs) and the elasticity of cloud computing resources, the computational demands of AI are much more viable to the enterprise for instances of ML and NLP. Edge devices are being stuffed with powerful processors and hence all the innovations happening in the enterprise and cloud spaces are being replicated in the edge space also.

Apple's Siri and Alexa from Amazon, Google assistance, etc., demonstrate the potential use of NLP for bettering human life with smart human computer interfaces. But they usually consume or utilize powerful cloud connectivity, servers, processors, and lavish memory for their continuous monitoring and assistance; edge devices cannot afford such powerful resources and so scientists proposed energy-efficient resources for processing speech and text. Many times there is a myth that accuracy is compromised with edge devices when embedding a speech recognition system on it, due to the low level resource usage and low-level algorithms; the reality is that, instead of keeping the complete assistance module, developers create a specialist or a domain-based assistant. Due to this domain-specific assistance, these devices are more powerful compared to the general assistant that lacks the context while trying to understand the meaning of certain overlapping commands.

The freshly attached human-machine interfaces (HMIs) empower edge devices to interact with humans in an intelligent and intimate manner. Edge devices are being enabled to understand human instructions and act upon them with all the alacrity and clarity. In short, edge devices are also made to have natural interfaces through the incorporation of the NLP capabilities.

5G for Edge Computing

The upcoming 5G communication infrastructure will be a great value for enabling edge computing. 5G can handle millions of edge devices per square kilometer. The last mile connectivity will be robust, dependable, and really fast.

Edge AI Use Cases

As populations grow, age, and become wealthier, healthcare systems struggle to provide the increasing level of continuous care that patients need. Digital health is therefore essential to meet the need for better resource efficiency and collaboration across the healthcare industry. A key driver of digital health will be leveraging capabilities at the edge. Edge computing has been rapidly gaining traction and tangible edge deployments have been increasing significantly. Following, we outline some key use cases that could leverage edge computing to help drive the transformation of the healthcare industry and the move towards digital health.

Connected ambulance – In current emergency service systems, paramedics are typically only able to brief emergency doctors, and patients can only receive the diagnostic procedures they require, once the ambulance transporting the patient has arrived at the hospital. This can create inefficiencies and delays in terms of hand-over times and patient transferrals to the correct wards, meaning ambulances are hindered from getting back into the field and patient diagnoses and treatments are slowed down. In an emergency situation, seconds and minutes can be essential. The low latency, mobility, and data-processing capabilities of edge computing at a network edge (alongside 5G) can enable faster and more accurate diagnosis and treatment by paramedics on-site, as well as more granular information at the hospital on the status and location of incoming patients. This can primarily be achieved through

- Livestreaming of processed patient data, such as heart rate from monitors or live video feeds from first responder body cams to the hospital (enabled through 5G).

■ Analysis of patient information and vitals (such as blood pressure, heart rate) at the edge for real-time diagnosis and recommendations by first responders.
■ Augmented reality glasses (rendered at the edge) to display information about patient history and complex treatment protocols to empower paramedics.
■ Haptic-enabled diagnostic tools to enable remote diagnostics by specialists (e.g., remote ultrasounds).

In-hospital patient monitoring – Currently, monitoring devices (e.g., glucose monitors, health tools, and other sensors) are either not connected, or where they are, large amounts of unprocessed data from such devices would need to be stored on a third-party cloud. This presents some level of security concerns for healthcare providers, and limits the adoption of such use cases. An on-premise edge on the hospital site could process data locally to maintain data privacy and compliance, compiling information from multiple sources within the hospital and extracting relevant information. The edge enables right-time notifications to practitioners of unusual patient trends or behaviors (through analytics/AI), creation of 360-degree-view patient dashboards for full visibility, and sending relevant data to be stored securely in a cloud system. This creates significant resource efficiency for clinicians, increasing productivity and decreasing cost per patient.

■ **Google DeepMind/Google Health** – Early prediction of acute kidney injury – a life-threatening condition which, when caught early, can be regulated
■ **CareAI** – Platform for acute and post-acute patient monitoring to enhance quality of care and improve operational efficiency
■ **AWS Outposts** – AWS is targeting the healthcare industry with its on-premise edge technology stack, Outposts. They are looking to bring the power of the AWS core cloud to the hospital/research site, mitigating (some) of the security concerns healthcare providers may have around data privacy

Remote monitoring and care – Life expectancy is increasing globally and populations are increasing in wealth. These two factors coupled together lead to an increase in the treatment of chronic, non-communicable illness such as pulmonary and cardiac complaints, diabetes, fractures, etc. This adds pressure to health care and long-term social care as demands on medical professionals' time increase with a move towards continuous care and chronic disease management. Furthermore, especially in developing or heavily rural markets, there are many patients who physically cannot access the care they need because travel to a medical infrastructure is either prohibitively far or expensive.

Autonomous vehicles – We are all keenly awaiting self-driving cars. These fully automated cars should be highly reactive to the dynamic incidents on real-time roads. If cars are sending their components' data to faraway cloud machines to get the insights out of the data, it may not work as we want. The network latency can damage the whole concept. Therefore, involving edge devices for analyzing edge data is the viable and venerable way forward. Quick and instant capturing and processing of data brings out useful inferences for automatic cars and vehicles to maneuver to reach the destination without any flaw.

Due the independent execution of data recognition of user's authenticity and videosteam analysis, edge device manufacturers give scalable insights that are scalable. Hence, edge computing devices help the business by local processing of user inputs and image processing to make instant decisions to retain the customers and increase their visibility and profit.

Ambient Intelligence (AmI)

A key area of edge-based information processing is ambient intelligence, which refers to the edge analytics that are sensitive to the presence of human beings and are responsive. It is usually used in environments where people's interaction with others or objects are monitored. Important applications of this AmI are to make a smart environment for daily activity monitoring for children, patients, and elderly adults who are home alone, to give assisted living that intelligently detects the existence of a thief or a stranger, fire, and falls to take critical action by calling the police or emergency services. There are many instances of this kind, such as smart bands, watches, smartphones, cameras, triple axes gyroscopes, and accelerometers.

Industry 4.0 – The industrial IoT (IIoT) highly depends on automating manufacturing and operational processes to increase productivity. Using edge AI allows IIoT devices to do visual inspections and carry out robotic control faster and at lower costs.

Conclusion

Distributed computing facilitates edge computing with storage and computation close by to the location where the data is captured and the decisions to be executed. It gives the advantages of improved data privacy and security, low latency with an quick response times, along with the benefit of bandwidth saving. Real-time processing is a highlight of the most robust features of Eedge AI. It allows users to collate, process, and analyze data and then implement solutions in the fastest way possible, making devices highly useful for time-dependent applications. Even though there are better connectivity and models proposed to address scalability and latency issues for edge computing, it is difficult to achieve the computational requirements in the tiny edge devices.

On the other hand, real-time applications with a huge data size, such as automatic cars, industry automation models, and video processing, require low latency, high reliability, and instant decision making. Centralized AI models could not satisfy those requirements due to network bandwidth, high latency, and network issues, which edge devices never face. If each device has high-performing computing power and decision making with the help of interconnection among the edge computing devices, then together they will have advanced computing skills that monolithic cloud computing cannot accomplish.

References

[1] S. V. Simpson and G. Nagarajan. "An Edge Based Trustworthy Environment Establishment for Internet of Things: An Approach for Smart Cities." *Wireless Networks* (2021): 1–17.

[2] J. Chen and X. Ran. "Deep Learning With Edge Computing: A Review." *Proceedings of the IEEE* 107, no. 8 (Aug. 2019): 1655–1674. 10.1109/JPROC.201 9.2921977.

[3] N. Harth, C. Anagnostopoulos, and D. Pezaros. "Predictive Intelligence to the Edge: Impact on Edge Analytics." *Evolving Systems* 9 (2018): 95–118. 10.1007/ s12530-017-9190-z

[4] https://www.gsma.com/futurenetworks/wp-content/uploads/2018/04/Road-to-5G-Introduction-and-Migration_FINAL.pdf

[5] S. Voghoei, N. Hashemi Tonekaboni, J. G. Wallace, and H. R. Arabnia. "Deep Learning at the Edge." In *2018 International Conference on Computational Science and Computational Intelligence (CSCI)* (2018): 895–901. 10.1109/CSCI46756.201 8.00177.

[6] G. Nagarajan, R. I. Minu, and A. Jayanthiladevi. "Cognitive Internet of Things (C-IOT)." In *Sensing Techniques for Next Generation Cognitive Radio Networks*, pp. 299–311. IGI Global, 2019.

[7] https://www.sdxcentral.com/networking/virtualization/definitions/whats-network-virtualization/

[8] G. Baldoni, et al. "Edge Computing Enhancements in an NFV-based Ecosystem for 5G Neutral Hosts." In *2018 IEEE Conference on Network Function Virtualization and Software Defined Networks (NFV-SDN)*, Verona, Italy (2018): 1–5. 10.1109/ NFV-SDN.2018.8725644.

[9] R. I. Minu and G. Nagarajan. "Bridging the IoT Gap Through Edge Computing." In *Edge Computing and Computational Intelligence Paradigms for the IoT*, pp. 1–9. IGI Global, 2019.

Chapter 3

Big Data Driven Edge–Cloud Collaboration for Cloud Manufacturing with SDN Technologies

M. Vijayalakshmi and R.I. Minu

SRM Institute of Science and Technology, Chennai, India

Contents

DOI: 10.1201/9781003145158-3

Introduction

The Internet of Things is a concept that enables any physical object to be linked to the Internet. The World Wide Web sensor technology, along with the Internet of Things, is used in all technologies and areas of our day-to-day lives. The introduction of cloud infrastructure for IoT-enhanced systems by allowing for the permanent collection of tracked data as well as cloud connectivity at any time from any location [2]. However, due to the time delay incurred by information processing in a cloud that is located far away, edge computing, which takes cloud resources closer to the customer, is strongly favored in time-sensitive IoT applications.

Fog and intracellular concentrations allow timely and fast access to resources, making them well tailored for the time-sensitive data produced by the Internet of Things. The edge design is a promising framework for systems that need a lot of computation and have a lot of time restrictions. In evolved WiFi communication, cloud computing with big data analytics and context awareness pave the way for significant changes in handheld devices. Fog and edge systems both represent exciting paradigms for delivering computational resources at the user end while reducing the use of cloud services [10]. Fog processing is used to process or compute data within a cloud environment or an Internet of Things gateway.

An edge network processes data using a computer that is either closer to the sensors or a portal device that would be even closer to the sensor, minimizing the time it takes for data to pass and the amount of power it consumes during communication. Only with advancement of sensing devices for smaller scale, reduced cost, better battery life, and higher accuracy, efforts were made in the industrial sector to develop and implement a wide range of smart sensors, computers, and facilities to create what is known as business processes. One of most critical advantages of cloud computing, aside from the decrease in cost and power usage, is that data is more reliable because it is not transmitted somewhere. As a result, the IOT edge paradigm takes precedence over other application domains, but it still depends on the cloud for prolonged trips in configurations [4]. The edges are analogous to a cloud environment; however, unlike private clouds, it does not target a

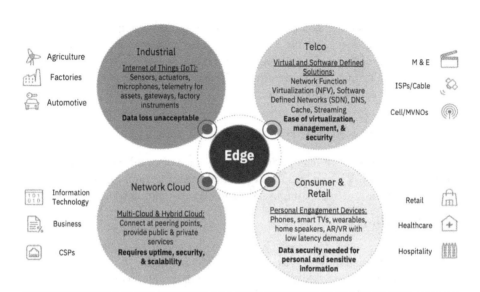

Figure 3.1   Edge Computing Architecture.

Source: https://www.ibm.com/cloud/architecture/architectures/edge-computing/

single entity, but rather serves a community of organizations, businesses, or some other business within its realm. Edge computing makes use of powerful computing infrastructure and enabling equipment as edge servers to provide facilitate easy access to process automation.

Developed research properties with incorporated identifying (ID), detecting, and acceleration capabilities are typically linked via cloud computing (IoT) and 5G technologies, and easily incorporated into highly automated networks such as cloud fabrication systems and connected cars. Figure 3.1 elaborates the general architecture of edge computing.

Manufacturing plants, telecommunications digitized network feature (VNF), and smart manufacturing are examples of edge or reduced applications, as are content creation and gaming, as well as real-time prediction, or manipulating tracking devices. Communications systems, industrial, and retail are the various systems that push IBM edge technologies, as seen in the edge computing architecture [16].

The four viewpoints of edge computing are depicted in this diagram. Edge networking, from any angle, decentralizes and expands campus networks, wireless networks, data center channels, and Internet networks. Edge applications come in a variety of shapes and sizes. They may be on the go, such as in wired vehicles, trains, or smartphones. Until they are part of a smart home, a production facility, they can be fixed.

The reliability of the system on a network is indeed a major issue with the development of gadgets and the range of available base stations. Not all smart objects have enough computing energy to function antivirus software that is reliable. As a result, much of the security burden is shifted to the network edge or firewall that is the next nearest physical layer [6][12].

Classifications of Edge Computing

The literature on pervasive computing concepts, such as cloud services, fog nodes, and portable network virtualization is examined in this section. Figure 3.2 depicts the characterization of edge computation and related terminology.

Fog Computing

Cisco coined the word *fog computing* to describe a cloud technology solution. Through positioning those services and interactions at the channel's edge, this solution capitalizes on the dual issue of the abundance of smart devices and the potential provided by the data those devices produce [1].

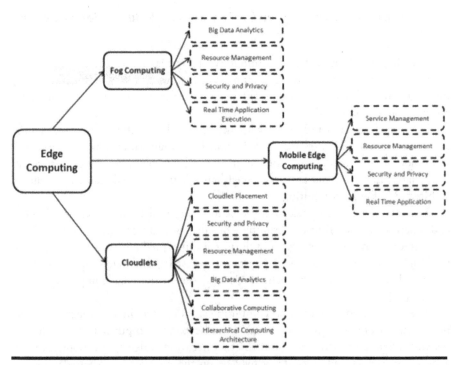

Figure 3.2   Edge Computing Classifications.

Source: https://www.sciencedirect.com/science/article/abs/pii/S0167739X18319903

Real-Time Application Execution

All fog servers function as a data center and signal processor. Aside from that, the server allows for signal classification, source recognition, and vector autoregression model fitting. The presence of a fog server close to the user, as well as a wearable network, forms a triangular relation between the nodes. The triangular relation can be used to improve the system's stability and efficiency. Machine-to-machine (M2M) advertise protocols are also supported by the proposed scheme. The transport layer security protocol is used to enforce device security, which is a critical aspect of the ubiquitous computing system [8].

Resource Management

Edge computing, which allows proper analysis capable of diagnosing system faults, can provide a host of resources in smart manufacturing. The computers that are used in manufacturing send large capacities of data to fog nodes. Fog nodes, on the other hand, have limited computational and storage capacity, necessitating effective resource allocation mechanisms [18].

The virtualized environment offers hosting facilities for VMD applications. The thesis concentrated specifically on productive energy management issues with the aim of ensuring QoS in FC-MCPS.

In the field of fog computing, flexible mobile device unloading and portable storage established development to aid mobile application execution. The planned unloading judgment necessitates active resource management.

The orchestration of extremely complex heterogeneous services at different hierarchical levels makes developing fog computer technology technologies difficult.

An increased fog system design as well as a number of supporting technologies are essential for achieving the cloud computing vision. Fog architecture allows multiple users' programs to coexist when each user is given the impression of having resources allocated.

The fog-based system resource management paradigm attempts to distribute capital in an equal and optimal manner. The authors divided IoT devices into three categories based on their mobility and design, and then managed the available resources.

The research primarily focused on asset prediction, estimate, reservation, and pricing, taking into account the system and consumer type. The following formula resources the assessment model:

$$M = \sum \left(\left(U_i * \left((1 - x\,(P_i\,(L|H)_s)) \right) - \sigma^2 \right) * (1 - \omega_i) * \phi \right) \qquad (3.1)$$

where M, Ui, x(Pi(L|H)s), 2, I and reflect necessary services, specific price of example involved I average of customer-based abdicate chances of particular consumer, variability for customer centric relinquish risks, constant solution variables value, and accessing system form, respectively.

Requirements of enabling Edge computing

In order to use edge computer systems, this section outlines the main specifications that must be fulfilled. Edge computing includes features such as smart pricing, real-time network management, a shared operating model for administration and installation, strategic planning, flexible architecture, redundant and failure capabilities, and security [7].

■ Dynamic Billing Mechanism

A mobility pattern, along with multi-vendor schemes (multi-service providers and operators), creates a difficult user tariff process. When an effective photo is facilitated by their traveling charge estimation, a complex billing process is expected by multiple providers of edge software applications. The amount of different phone devices who may request particular services (e.g., CPU and memory specifications) with wired and wireless parameters (e.g., capacity demand and availability for data transfer, latency, delay, and degree of protection as per device requirements, etc.) from the cloud by edge-based programs is the key motivation underlying the dynamic billing process. Service supply (e.g., billing charges which differ in case of multiple users present, resulting in high resource demand), intensity of service use (e.g., how often a single consumer uses resources), and length of service use are three variables that should be addressed when developing the complex billing system.

■ Real-Time Application Support

Fog computing is designed to offer a variety of services, with a focus on real-time applications [19]. Edge computing will play a key role in improving the learning environment in higher education by e-learning and gamified, for example.

■ Business Model for Management and Deployment

Multiple users own edge computing networks, which operate under various business models. Every company practices different business strategies and management procedures, as well as different legislation and standards, depending on how it is organized. Edge systems, likewise, are built by various manufacturers and have their own implementations, affecting service efficiency and incurring high costs. To address the above concerns, a collaborative administration and implementation business plan is needed to maintain high recital while still providing low-cost amenities to end users.

■ Resource Management

An specific edge of the network provider's technology investment is dependent on the planned service demands of customers. As a result, only a limited amount of services are available to support a specific number of people. Low distribution demand on the other hand means lower sales. Network operators can maximize their sales by combining their available services with other wireless carriers with increased product demands. Enhanced offloading and strong efficiency between variable cognitive and network allocating resources could benefit from increased new system needs [5].

■ Scalable Architecture

The range of phones in the edge network has grown dramatically as a result of rapid advances in IoT, as has the need for edge-based applications and resources. Despite the increased load, edge cloud apps are expected to work reliably.

A scalable network virtualization architecture is important for meeting this efficiency expectation because it can reduce costs. Various features such as resource virtualization, cryptocurrency trust institution, and automatic edge-IoT orchestration can be used to construct a modular architecture for the edge software platform.

These IoT tools (such as device-based simulators, Internet connectivity to concepts via concept, and so on) could be shared using software abstraction and free application module interfaces (API). The IoT framework is installed as an autonomous "slice" that segments the similar detecting tools and facilitates multi-application founder by integrating resource virtualization.

■ Redundancy

Dual crucial considerations for the efficient operation of edge computing systems that serve multiple sensitive software products with low dormancy and nonstop information transfer facilities are reliability and fail-over capability.

■ Security

Because of the diverse existence of edge computing networks, protection is a must for network and device operation. Consumers are still being influenced by security concerns when it comes to adopting these modern edge computing technologies [20].

Edge Computing in Big Data

Gigabytes of data are collected from businesses, organizations, and academic agencies from a variety of outlets, like social networks, user messages and survey results, phone conversation reports, Internet assists in monitoring, web server logs, and sensors.

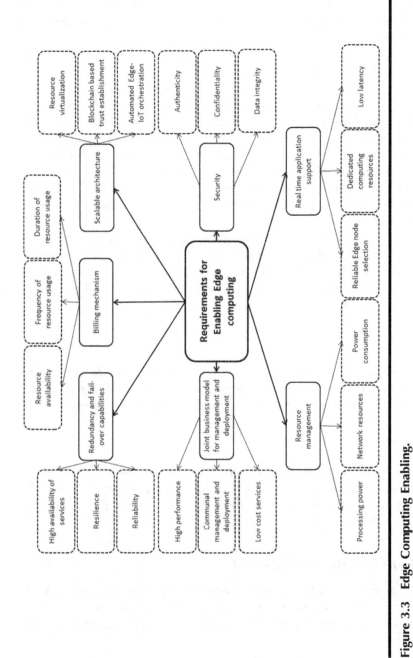

Figure 3.3   Edge Computing Enabling.

Huge volumes of unstructured, semi-structured, or structured data flow constantly across and through organizations are referred to as big data. Big data has been here for a long time, and most businesses now realize that they're using insights to extract actionable information from their data. Big data analytics is a major influencing factor analytic that includes complicated functions with factors including such predictive modeling, while business analytics answers simple questions regarding business activities and results.

Big data looks at a lot of data to find secret trends, associations, and other details. Batch or streamline computing may be used to process large amounts of data. This means that data is processed for certain purposes and the output is obtained using a super market paradigm [10].

Big Data Analytics

The method of conducting various analysis activities on data, such as sorting or feedback effects, is referred to as big data analytics. Figure 3.3 depicts a standard big data analysis flow. (Figure 3.4)

The very first step is to gather and integrate data from various sources. The next step, data cleaning, can take a long time to complete, but it may dramatically minimize the data size, requiring less work and attention for data analytics. Raw

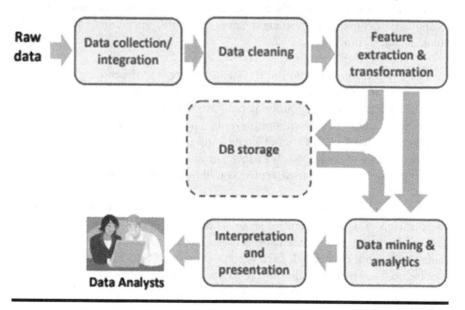

Figure 3.4   Flow of Big Data Analytics.

Source: https://www.researchgate.net/publication/330329179_Fog_Computing_Realization_for_Big_Data_Analytics

data is typically informal, meaning it lacks a predetermined data model and is not ordered in any particular way. In the next stage of the flow, the data is converted into semi-organized or structured data [22].

To boost data accuracy, data cleaning entails finding and eliminating errors and contradictions. Because many data sources must be combined (for example, in database systems), the need for information collection increases dramatically. This is due to the fact that the references often contain duplicate data in various forms. Verifying that the data is correct is one of the most critical stages of any data processing mission.

The measured values are accurate or, at the very least, follow a series of guidelines. Inaccurate inventory entry, incomplete records, or other potential contamination may all lead to data quality issues. For example, a variable like gender can only have two points (M or F), and a variable like pulse rate will only have one value.

Artificial Intelligent in Edge Computing

The device model of machine learning in edge computing, in order to provide a talented and capable edge computing in handling the immense data flow in IoT-based applications, has four levels, with the bottom level being the intellectual elements used within sensing; the next-highest layer, layer one, integrating the IoT technologies design; and the highest layer, layer two, integrating the IoT technologies architecture [16].

The tier with the collection of tools and parameters for handling the arriving massive data stream is at the very top. The AI integration of edge computing is depicted in Figure 3.5. The autonomous instruments that are an abstraction of sensors are found in the lowest layer, layer 0. The sensor, which is the central and foundational part of the Internet of Things, aids in the collection and processing of massive amounts of data. Devices include portables, wearable tech, speech sensors, positioning sensors, motion detectors, equilibrium sensor systems, and velocity sensors, among others.

The IoT infrastructure for the different technologies focuses on the transmitting and receiving of data from and to smart objects is used in the next layer, layer 1. The various networking methodologies facilitating the information distribution include the network connection, fixed wireless connectivity (LTE), and Wi-Fi, either over the phone. The reserves in the IoT are used to save the data from the network's regularly input and output computers. The reserves in the IoT framework assist with data centers as required.

The perception engine in layer 2 is what allows the edge cloud to improve. Since it offers data extraction and data analysis tools for the knowledge collected,

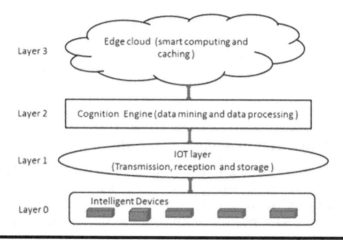

Figure 3.5 AI and Edge Computing System Model.

the computational engine is referred to as the autonomous intelligence's core. The perceptual engines are made up of two engines: including one for data management and another for resource management. The conceptual engine organization is seen in Figure 3.5 [14].

The interface cloud is the highest position, which essentially computes data in a smart way, closer to the consumer computers. Machine learning is made up of the necessary hardware and frameworks for efficiently processing data at a remove from the mobile networks. Some of the modules used in artificial intelligence are entry points, ground stations, connectors, and path servers. Although fog computing is a cost-effective solution to cloud services, data that requires complicated calculations is often sent to the cloud.

So, using machine learning, the suggested approach calculates the delay in both edges and cloud-based applications and assigns delay-sensitive mathematical calculations to the edge and complicated calculations that require more computational time to the cloud technology. To increase the efficiency of edge devices, encryption is also used at the edges for quick access to knowledge from the edge.

Benefits of Big Data Analytics in Fog

a. **Improved business**: Big data analytics enables businesses to make more use of their data, and use it to find new markets, allowing for strategic management decisions, new sales opportunities, more aggressive marketing, greater customer support, increased operating performance, and higher profitability.

b. **Cost savings**: Big data analytics can save a lot of money when it comes to managing vast volumes of data and running a company more efficiently.

c. **Quicker and improved decision making**: Companies are able to interpret data quickly, make decisions, and remain flexible.
d. **Latest offerings**: With the ability to use information to evaluate consumer preferences and loyalty comes the possibility of providing customers with exactly what they want [9].

SDN Perspective of Edge Computing

Program-based networking is a modern concept of networking that distinguishes logically centralized data (traffic) propagation. It brings all traffic control under one roof.

The main advantage of this strategy allows for real-time and dynamic modification of mass transfer policies in system fabric architecture, as well as the ability to adjust the position of specific connected devices due to SDN's actual modifiability.

Related to the concept of real-world portability provided by software-driven networking, the spectrum of SDN has also extended to network environments, including 5G cell messaging and campus-based networks. By dividing a computer network into two structures, SDN aims to create a network.

Software-Defined Networking

Program has two purposes. The transport layer is responsible for forwarding frames to their final destination. However, in order for the control plane to work, we need a method of computing each router's condition, which enables the routes to make the best decision possible when passing data to the destination [15].

The SDN controller in SDN is organized logically in a centralized management system. In addition, the trigger usually manages a network's various routers and, in many cases, the control software is in charge of all of the routers in the network.

SDN is a modern technology that aims to make the Internet a more effective and more adaptable network. Traditional networks are often very crowded. Static, slow-changing, and devoted to a single service using SDN, we can create a network that can support a large number of users. A variety of services in a diverse manner allows one to converge various services into a single platform. Both content providers and carriers may benefit from this (Figure 3.6).

Advantages and Disadvantages of SDN Model

a. SDN does not necessitate high-end switches and can be implemented with low-cost hardware and switches. Instead of the pricey high-end switches, it

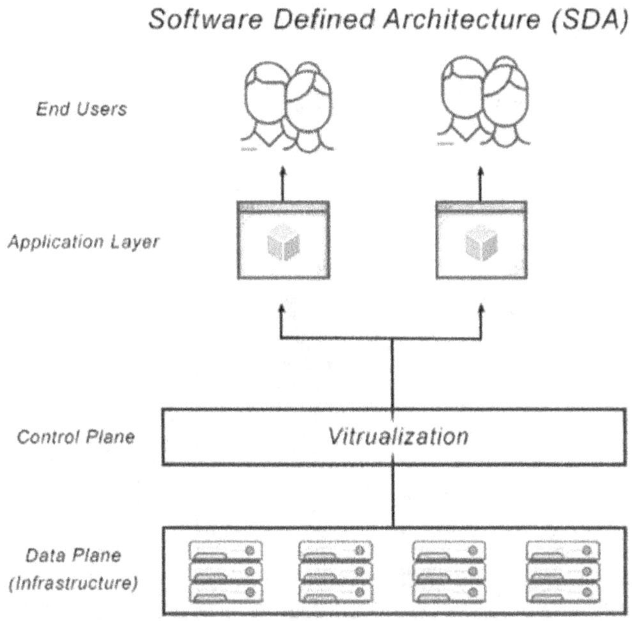

Software Defined Architecture (SDA)

Figure 3.6 SDN Architecture.

Source: https://avinetworks.com/glossary/software-defined-architecture/

doesn't have a lot of computing power. It aids in the management of an organization's operational costs. Because the operator can be efficiently controlled by management, SDN also provides a central control system that aids in determining network data stream.

b. According to SDN, both switches now serve as firewalls, filtering packets as they reach the network. This aids in the monitoring of all malicious operations as well as the data security. We can also simulate the controller by using SDN to monitor such unusual traffic for thread identification and data loss reduction fault tolerance handling [13].

c. SDN allows for effective handling and preparation of networking, computation, and storage services. Because there is a network address, we have more freedom in making up the rules and modifying the path from a single venue.

d. SDN has a consistency problem of scalability. It's difficult for a single controller to handle all of the tcp connections and decision making. This is accomplished by copying the controller, but this control system must then be synchronized, posing additional difficulties.

e. A further disadvantage is the focal point of loss. If the operating system is hacked, the entire network is compromised, even whether a problem occurs with this device or the system in general. The network is in difficulty due to the replication of a few controllers [17].

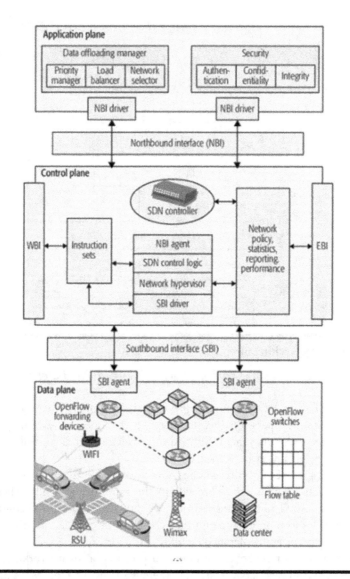

Figure 3.7   SDN-Based Control Scheme Architecture.

Source: https://www.researchgate.net/figure/Proposed-SDN-based-controller-a-architecture-of-an-SDN-based-controller-b-flow-table_fig2_318993172

Data-Intensive Applications for the Workload Slicing Approach

The initial workload (W) is divided into binary types in this scheme:

- delay-sensitive (X) and
- delay-tolerant (Y)

Workload X is now focused on real-time claims that demand the fastest possible response time. Furthermore, Y is a workload that takes the longest to complete and necessitates a lot of computational power. However, it must be done by a certain deadline. Currently, X is a high-priority workload that is planned ahead of Y. The workload (Y) necessitates a lot of processing power and is sent to geo-distributed cloud DCs. However, the dynamic assignment (X) is different. As seen below, it has been subdivided into two sections [21].

However, as seen below, the real-time workload (X) is split into two sections. A portion of the workload (Xe) is planned to be executed on existing edge DCs. However, certain workloads (Xc) can necessitate high computational resources that aren't always available at edge DCs. This kind of workload is redirected to fog DCs. Figure 3.7 depicts the workload slicing scheme's design. Algorithm 3.1 depicts the operation of the suggested slicing system, which uses ordered preemptive round robin (PPRR) to list jobs in DCs or edge machines.

Algorithm 3.1 Workload slicing and scheduling algorithm

Input: Workload W

Output: Cloud DC or ED

1: Slice workload W into X and Y

2: if W = Y then

3: Check for type of jobs

4: Compute F : (atype, breq, creq)

5: if F : (atype, breq, creq) are available with DCi then

6: Add workload → QN : (Q1, Q2, ..., Qn)

7: Select flow path using Algorithm II

8: Schedule job F→ DCi → PPRR

9: else

10: Schedule job → DCi* → PPRR . i /∈ i *

11: end if

12: else

13: Check for available EDs

14: Map X with available EDs

15: if Required resources are available with EDi then

16: Add workload → QM : (Q1, Q2, ..., Qm)

17: Select flow path using Algorithm II

18: Schedule job → EDi → PPRR

19: else

20: Add workload → QN : (Q1, Q2, ..., Qn)

21: Schedule job →Cloud DCs

22: end if

23: end if

Source: https://www.researchgate.net/publication/319072171_Optimal_
Decision_Making_for_Big_Data_Processing_at_Edge-Cloud_
Environment_An_SDN_Perspective

SDN Controller

The fundamental web organization is derived from the controller in the SDN system. Unlike conventional networks, SDN allows all forwarding devices (FDs), such as routers, entries, and adjustments, to conform to new functionalities and network policies with ease. The free flow protocol is used in SDN's networking infrastructure.

The data plane's operation is broken down into several stages, which are detailed below:

- Step 1: The root DCs that need the job to be migrated to another DC submit a submission. The scheduler receives DC's request and places it in a queue for further processing.
- Step 2: The proposed structure an instruction set to align the input parameters with the SDN controller's rules. Source Internet address, origin MAC address, on escapable address, port number, and communication protocol are all included in the flow id are all part of the matching rule. Reasonable behavior is decided based on matching rules. Forwarding, updating, discarding, and replication are some of the acts that FDs can take.
- Step 3: The appeal is sent to the flow planner until the required action has been determined. The action is then completed by selecting a suitable flow table.
- Step 4: After selecting the required flow table, the packets are migrated to the destination DC.
- Step 5: This step entails providing feedback to ensure that the flow direction is reliable. This is accomplished by the use of figures that provide a counter for reporting to the dispatcher.

When picking a fluid flow (j) for circulation, the method below exhibits least power usage and assured spectral efficiency (f).

Algorithm 3.2 Energy-aware flow scheduling algorithm

Input: f, sf , t d f , t r f , G, f a , f q , and f s

Output: path p, rf

1: Calculate guaranteed flow rate (rf) using Eq. (37)

2: j ← FindPath(G, f a , f q , f s , f, gf)

3: if valid path exists then

4: if physical path j exists then

5: Schedule fp over p

6: for Each flow path J do

7: Divide J into flow sets fset with no shared links

8: for fset ∈ J do

9: Calculate tact = activetime(fset)

10: Compute energy consumption using Eq. 14

11: if (tact is minimum) then

12: f q ← f q + f

13: Schedule f

14: end if

15: end for

16: end for

17: else

18: Check for virtual path j v

19: if (j v exists) then

20: Schedule f

21: end if

22: end if

23: else

24: Suspend fp till a valid path is available

25: f s ← f s + f

26: Report to controller

27: Controller rebuilds flow table to provision valid flow path

28: Repeat steps 1-16

29: end if

30: if flow f finishes then

31: Update f a ← f a - f

32: Move next flow in queue to the top

33: else

34: Repeat steps 1-16

35: end if

Source: https://www.researchgate.net/publication/319072171_Optimal_Decision_Making_for_Big_Data_Processing_at_Edge-Cloud_Environment_An_SDN_Perspective

Formula for energy consumption:

$$E_{dc}^n = \sum_{p \in S} D_q \times \frac{Tq}{b_c \Theta_q |R_q|} + \sum_{r \in P_q} D_r^q \times \frac{T_r^q}{b_c \Theta_r^q} \tag{3.2}$$

Guaranteed flow rate equation:

$$r_f = \frac{S_p}{T_p^d - T_p^r} \tag{3.3}$$

The inbound job queries are sliced in this ecosystem. EDs and cloud DCs are prioritized and scheduled on this basis. Furthermore, an SDN controller for an energy-aware network is proposed. Virtualization networks are used in a flow programming model. Finally, there is a Stackelberg's inter, multi-follower game is designed to choose the best DC or ED to house the migrated workers.

Evaluation

The suggested scheme is tested over a longer time horizon after it has been analyzed for a particular time window (12 hours). The findings reveal that the edge–cloud setting has a distinct advantage over the other two scenarios. The normal SLA defilements for the proposed setting are smaller than the further dual events, as seen in Figure 3.8(a).

Furthermore, the new scheme uses a lot of energy. As seen in Figure 3.7, this case needs less energy than the others. Lastly, as seen in Figure 3.8(c), for the three scenarios, the migration rate is contrasting. The findings suggest that the rate of migration in EDs is increasing due to a scarcity of capital, rather than the other two instances in emergency rooms. The cloud DCs have the lowest surface energy, but the cloud DCs have the highest migration rate. It's almost on par with the proposed climate.

Figure 3.8(d) depicts the total overhead for any of the three scenarios. As a consequence, the edge–cloud system has the lowest latency. In relations of power consumption, SLA breaches, relocation rate, and overhead, the findings demonstrate that the designed edge community cloud outperforms other scenarios.

The suggested ILP problem is actually perceived challenges carried out. In general, ILP concerns are NP-hard, although this is an exception. This isn't valid for any problem. The current issue is a more straightforward example and can be conveniently solved in light of the current constraints [23].

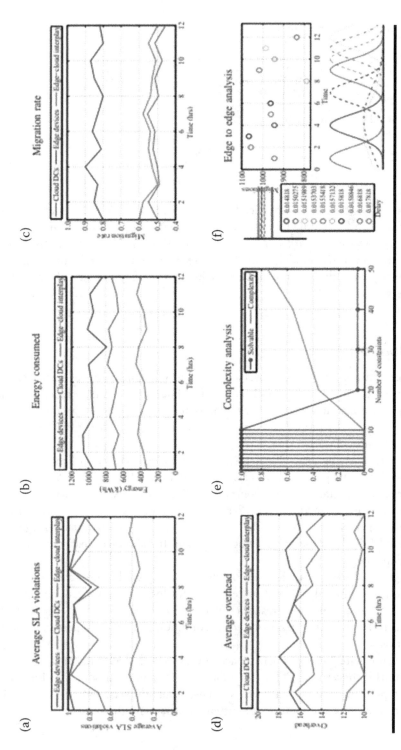

Figure 3.8 Results Obtained for 12-hr Scenario: (a) Average SLA violations; (b) energy consumed; (c) migration rate; (d) average overhead; (e) complexity analysis; and (f) edge to edge analysis.

Figure 3.8(e) depicts the difficulty and optimality of the problem statement as a function of the quantity of limitations. It explicitly reveals that the projected problem is solvable up to ten number restrictions, but then becomes more complicated.

Finally, migrations from edge to edge are investigated. Figure 3.8(f) demonstrates that EDs with insufficient resources exhibit elevated levels of activity in the rate of migration. Edge-to-edge populations are also examined in terms of migrants and delays.

Practical Applications of SDN

The benefits are:

- Enhanced safety
- Compact functioning charges
- A better user experience

Enhanced Safety

SDN can provide security tools that respond quickly to attacks at their origin, as well as simplify user access management and preventing. Through unplugging network connectivity at the danger's origins on a token by token basis, the integration of successful internal network monitoring and straight software management of both the wired and wireless access levels of the network allow accelerated threat identification and instant threat vaccinating.

Compact Functioning Charges

Minimizing an industrial network's operating costs can be accomplished by doing something like:

- facilitating user onboarding
- applying business rules consistently from centralized apps
- simplifying troubleshooting

Bring Your Own Device (BYOD) and "Choose Your Own" services have contributed in a more flexible population and more options in terms of consumer equipment. In enterprise networking, achieving unified control of user and system identities has been a major obstacle.

When user and device databases are paired with user access control guidelines, and the resulting information is immediately converted into network equipment operating orders, significant productivity gains, cost benefits, and improved network availability and privacy are achieved.

Better User Experience

- Achieve better flexibility and remote access to enterprise data and software.
- Use the products that are most appropriate for them.
- You'll have access to a wider variety of software. Combine several contact tools at the same time, such as audio, video, and data – all in high quality.

Role of Big Data in Decision Making

Company executives are confronted with strong consumer demands and fierce competition. In today's environment, there are rising labor and commodities prices, as well as quicker delivery life spans. As a global economy, the borders between countries have become fragmented. Entry to the marketplace is no lengthier, limited by location or distance from the market. Companies must recurrently pursue challenges and vulnerabilities in such a competitive world and make strategic decisions quickly based on available data. In this segment, we'll look at how conventional "small data" and "large data" will help you make informed commercial verdicts [3].

Earliest DSS

Classic decision support systems facilitated internal management decisions based on data provided by transaction dispensation systems such as ERPs. As time went on, similar mechanisms on both the upstream and downstream sides were added (SRM and CRM) (Figure 3.9).

Data warehousing and data gathering processes used traditional data sets as inputs. Figure 3.10 depicts the general work flow of a conceptual framework on big data and decision making. The overall design featured a main development in data storage that saves retrieved data and divides it into smaller databases, and a storage server that stores and categorizes that data [11].

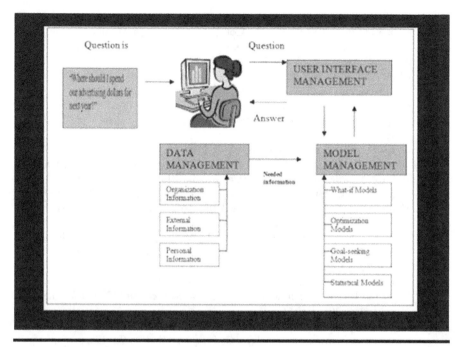

Figure 3.9   Decision Support System.

*Source: https://www.google.com/search?rlz=1C1SQJL_enIN937IN937&source=
univ&tbm=isch&q=Traditional+Decision+support+system+diagram&sa=X&ved=
2ahUKEwiXvouj3drwAhXP7nMBHeAADZEQ7Al6BAgDEFY&biw=1366&bih=568#
imgrc=YozL7va4Qjlc6M*

Figure 3.10   Conceptual Framework on Big Data and Decision Making.

*Source: https://www.researchgate.net/publication/326408012_Role_of_Big_Data_in_
Decision_Making.*

References

[1] A. Al-Fuqaha, M. Guizani, M. Mohammadi, M. Aledhari, and M. Ayyash. "Internet of Things: A Survey on Enabling Technologies, Protocols, and Applications." *IEEE Communications Surveys and Tutorials* 17, no. 4 (4th Quart., 2015): 2347–2376.

[2] Y. Shi, Q. Han, W. Shen, and H. Zhang. "Potential Applications of 5G Communication Technologies in Collaborative Intelligent Manufacturing." *IET Collaborative Intelligent Manufacturing* 1, no. 4 (Dec. 2019): 109–116.

[3] B. Li, L. Zhang, S. L. Wang, F. Tao, J. W. Cao, X. D. Jiang, X. Song, and X. D. Chai. "Cloud Manufacturing: A New Service-Oriented Networked Manufacturing Model." *Computer Integrated Manufacturing Systems* 16, no. 1 (2010): 1–7.

[4] A. Gilchrist. *Industry 4.0: The Industrial Internet of Things.* New York, NY, USA: Apress, 2016.

[5] G. Q. Huang, P. K. Wright, and S. T. Newman. "Wireless Manufacturing: A Literature Review, Recent Developments, and Case Studies." *International Journal of Computer Integrated Manufacturing* 22, no. 7 (Jul. 2009): 579–594.

[6] Y. Zhang, G. Q. Huang, T. Qu, O. Ho, and S. Sun. "Agent-Based Smart Objects Management System for Real-Time Ubiquitous Manufacturing." *Robotics and Computer-Integrated Manufacturing* 27, no. 3 (Jun. 2011): 538–549.

[7] C. Yang, S. Lan, W. Shen, G. Q. Huang, X. Wang, and T. Lin. "Towards Product Customization and Personalization in Iot-Enabled Cloud Manufacturing." *Cluster Computing* 20, no. 2 (Feb. 2017): 1717–1730.

[8] C. Yang, W. Shen, and X. Wang. "The Internet of Things in Manufacturing: Key Issues and Potential Applications." *IEEE Systems, Man, and Cybernetics Magazine* 4, no. 1 (Jan. 2018): 6–15.

[9] D. Mourtzis, E. Vlachou, and N. Milas. "Industrial Big Data as a Result of IoT Adoption in Manufacturing." *Procedia CIRP* 55 (2016): 290–295.

[10] C. Yang, W. Shen, T. Lin, and X. Wang. "IoT-enabled Dynamic Service Selection Across Multiple Manufacturing Clouds." *Manufacturing Letters* 7 (Jan. 2016): 22–25.

[11] R. Deng, R. Lu, C. Lai, T. H. Luan, and H. Liang. "Optimal Workload Allocation in Fog-Cloud Computing Toward Balanced Delay and Power Consumption." *IEEE Internet of Things Journal* 3, no. 6 (Dec 2016): 1171–1181.

[12] F. Jalali, K. Hinton, R. Ayre, T. Alpcan, and R. S. Tucker. "Fog Computing May Help to Save Energy in Cloud Computing." *IEEE Journal on Selected Areas in Communications* 34, no. 5 (May 2016): 1728–1739.

[13] P. Borylo, A. Lason, J. Rzasa, A. Szymanski, and A. Jajszczyk. "Energyaware fog and Cloud Interplay Supported By Wide Area Software Defined Networking," in *IEEE International Conference on Communications (ICC)* (May 2016): 1–7.

[14] B. Wang, Z. Qi, R. Ma, H. Guan, and A. V. Vasilakos. "A Survey on Data Center Networking for Cloud Computing." *Computer Networks* 91 (2015): 528–547.

[15] A. Blenk, A. Basta, M. Reisslein, and W. Kellerer. "Survey on Network Virtualization Hypervisors for Software Defined Networking." *IEEE Communications Surveys Tutorials* 18, no. 1 (2016): 655–685.

[16] G. Xu, B. Dai, B. Huang, J. Yang, and S. Wen. "Bandwidth-Aware Energy Efficient Flow Scheduling with SDN in Data Center Networks." *Future Generation Computer Systems* 68 (2017): 163–174.

[17] S.-H. Wang, P. P. W. Huang, C. H. P. Wen, and L. C. Wang. "EQVMP: Energy-Efficient and Qos-Aware Virtual Machine Placement for Software Defined Datacenter Networks," in *International Conference on Information Networking* (Feb 2014): 220–225.

[18] Y. Guo, Y. Gong, Y. Fang, P. P. Khargonekar, and X. Geng. "Energy and Network Aware Workload Management for Sustainable Data Centers with Thermal Storage." *IEEE Transactions on Parallel and Distributed Systems* 25, no. 8 (Aug 2014): 2030–2042.

[19] A. Beloglazov and R. Buyya. "Optimal Online Deterministic Algorithms and Adaptive Heuristics for Energy and Performance Efficient Dynamic Consolidation of Virtual Machines in Cloud Data Centers." *Concurrency and Computation: Practice and Experience* 24, no. 13 (Sep 2012): 1397–1420.

[20] G. S. Aujla, M. Singh, N. Kumar, and A. Y. Zomaya, "Stackelberg Game for Energy-Aware Resource Allocation to Sustain Data Centers Using RES." 2017. 10.1109/TCC.2017.2715817.

[21] R. I. Minu and G. Nagarajan. "Bridging the IoT Gap Through Edge Computing." In *Edge Computing and Computational Intelligence Paradigms for the IoT*, pp. 1–9. IGI Global, 2019.

[22] G. Nagarajan, R. I. Minu, and A. Jayanthiladevi. "Cognitive Internet of Things (C-IOT)." In *Sensing Techniques for Next Generation Cognitive Radio Networks*, pp. 299–311. IGI Global, 2019.

[23] S. V. Simpson and G. Nagarajan. "An Edge Based Trustworthy Environment Establishment for Internet of Things: An Approach for Smart Cities." *Wireless Networks* (2021): 1–17.

Chapter 4

Artificial Intelligence in 5G and Beyond Networks

Dimitris Tsolkas and Anastasios-Stavros Charismiadis

Department of Informatics & Telecommunications, National and Kapodistrian University of Athens, Panepistimiopolis, Ilisia, Greece

Harilaos Koumaras and Andreas Foteas

NCSR "Demokritos", Institute of Informatics and Telecommunications, Paraskevi, Greece

Contents

DOI: 10.1201/9781003145158-4

Introduction

The last three decades, mobile networks have evolved rapidly and, currently, they have reached the point where multiple technologies have been integrated, e.g., WiFi and IoT technologies in the radio access part and cloud technologies in the core/control part. Those integrations have transformed the conventional monolithic network paradigm to a powerful software platform. Network slicing, flexible service deployment, end-to-end network performance monitoring, and dynamic network tenancy are only a few of the services that those software platforms can provide.

In the era of 5G and beyond, the potentials emerged due to the previously mentioned paradigm shift, and are being studied extensively, with a major objective to incorporate automation functions in network management and service provisioning, which, in combination, can realize a second paradigm shift towards intelligent software platforms.

The key toolset towards intelligence lies in the field of artificial intelligence (AI), referring to the network capability for autonomous human-like behavior. The AI toolset exploits automation mechanisms, which are mainly borrowed from the machine learning (ML) theory.

The challenges toward applying AI in 5G and beyond networks, refer to:

- ■ *The operations of the mobile networks that can take advantage of the various types of ML functions/algorithms.* This assists in clarifying which level ML can be incorporated in 5G and beyond systems. To adequately address this aspect, the fundamental aspects of the major types of ML mechanisms, namely, supervised, unsupervised, and reinforcement learning, should be studied and mapped to key algorithmic functions of the mobile networks, such as network planning decision algorithms, radio/computation resource allocation and management schemes, network slice management, network handover decision algorithms, etc.
- ■ *The pathways toward a market and business ecosystem where mobile networks are transformed to intelligence software platforms exploitable by third parties/vertical industries.* Based on the previous aspect, the major challenge in enabling ML capabilities in any network operation is the collection of data in a secure and standardized way. In this framework, the openness of network data and measurements for enabling ML mechanisms as well as the level of trust in AI decisions, with regard to the roles of the stakeholders (operators, vertical industries, etc.) should be studied. On the one hand, the capabilities for data collection and measurements through open APIs that reside at the network core and edge will be the key enablers that will set the directions for addressing privacy and trust issues that emerge from the previously mentioned openness.

The structure of this chapter, following this introductory section, is as follows: Section 2 discusses the AI applicability in 5G networks, providing the fundamentals on ML and discussing the types of problems in 5G network functionality. Also, a state-of-the-art analysis of the AI methods and techniques is presented. In Section 3, the AI ambition for 5G technologies is presented, focusing on the most representative 5G features, which will have the highest impact when it becomes available, and where the AI is expected to play a major role. In Section 4, the vertical industries of a 5G ecosystem are considered, especially the ones where the AI use will have an impact, such as the entertainment market. Section 5 addresses the potential impact and the business opportunities of the AI use in 5G networks, discussing the various areas that will be positively impacted. Also, novel business models are discussed. Finally, Section 6 briefly presents the future directions and perspective of AI in 5G, while Section 7 concludes the chapter.

Applying AI in 5G Network Functions

Fundamentals on ML

AI can be considered an amalgam of multi-disciplinary techniques such as machine learning, optimization theory, game theory, control theory, and meta-heuristics.

Among them, machine learning (ML) is having a pivotal role with vast usage in optimization, detection, and estimation techniques. Depending on the nature of the learning objects and signals to a learning system, machine learning is typically classified into three broad categories.

Supervised Learning

A supervised learning agent is fed with sample data as inputs and their desired outputs, and the goal is to learn a general rule that relates the inputs to the outputs. After the training period, the agent will be able to predict the outputs given unknown future inputs. Popular algorithms used for supervised learning are regression, decision trees, random forest, gradient boosting, support vector machines, k-nearest neighbor, and neural networks. Supervised learning is commonly used in applications where historical data with patterns are repeated and can be found also in the future data. Supervised learning has been widely applied to solve channel estimation issues in cellular networks.

Unsupervised Learning

Compared to supervised learning, in unsupervised learning no labels are provided to the system. Therefore, the agent must determine the structure in its input on its own. Usually unsupervised learning aims to discover hidden patterns and find the suitable representation in the input data. Popular algorithms used for unsupervised learning are K-means, Apriori algorithm, principal component analysis (PCA), singular value decomposition (SVD), and independent component analysis. In the field of AI, unsupervised learning is applied to estimate the hidden layer parameters in neural networks and plays an important role in deep learning methods. Unsupervised learning can be considered the most widely applied AI category in cellular networks. For example, PCA and SVD methods have been used to manipulate the receiving matrix of massive Multi-Input Multi-Output (MIMO) to reduce the computational complexity. Moreover, 5G NoMA receivers also adopt some factor graph-based methods such as expectation-maximization and message-passing algorithms to achieve a lower bit error rate. On the other hand, some classifiers, such as the K-means algorithm, are also useful to detect network anomalies.

Reinforcement Learning

This technique is based on a learning system often called *Agent*, that reacts to the *Environment*. The *Agent* can perform certain actions and, based on these actions, the Agent's state will change, leading to either a reward or a penalty. The Agent does not have explicit knowledge of whether it has come close to its goal and take actions in the Environment so as to maximize the cumulative reward in a Markov decision process (MDP). By iterating the action and reward/penalty process, an Agent learns the Environment. Therefore, reinforcement learning demonstrates strong pattern recognition ability. Reinforcement can be used in the field of cognitive radio and usually model the dynamic transition of spectrum availability as a Markov chain, and extensively apply reinforcement learning methods to make the decision whether or not it is suitable for secondary transmission in one primary licensed spectrum, in terms of least interference to the primary spectrum.

In the following table (Table 4.1) is a summary of example usage of the ML schemes in the 5G mobile and wireless communication technology [1].

Types of AI-Related Problems

The nature of the problems that can be solved with the use of ML and, in general, AI, can be categorized into three main areas [2].

Optimization

Optimization is the process of setting decision variable values in such a way that the objective in question is optimized. One typical example of the combinatorial optimization problem in 5G NR includes network resource allocation. In a resource-limited network, an optimized scheme must be considered for the allocation of resources to different users who share the network such that the utilization of the resource achieves maximum efficiency. As an application of the HetNet architecture in 5G NR with features like network virtualization, network slicing, and self-organizing networks (SON), network resource allocation problems are growing in complexity and require more effective solutions.

Detection

Anomaly detection refers to identification of items or events that do not conform to an expected pattern or to other items in a dataset that are usually undetectable by a human expert. The design of the communication receiver is an example of the detection problem. An optimized receiver can recover the transmitted messages based on the received signals, achieving minimized detection error rate. Detection will be challenging in 5G within the massive MIMO framework.

Estimation

The estimator is the formula that evaluates a given quantity (the estimand) and generates an estimate. This estimate is then inserted into a classifier system to determine what action to take. The typical example is the channel estimation problem. 5G requires accurate estimation of the channel state information (CSI) to

Table 4.1 ML Techniques in Mobile Networks

AI Technique	Learning Model	5G-Based Applications
Supervised Learning	Machine learning and statistical logistic regression techniques	Dynamic frequency and bandwidth allocation in self-organized LTE dense small-cell deployments
	Support vector machines (SVMs).	Path loss prediction model for urban environments
	Neural-network-based approximation.	Channel learning to infer unobservable channel state information (CSI) from an observable channel
	Artificial neural networks (ANN), and multi-layer perceptrons (MLPs).	Modeling and approximations of objective functions for link budget and propagation loss for next-generation wireless networks
Unsupervised Learning	K-means clustering, Gaussian mixture model (GMM), and expectation maximization (EM).	Cooperative spectrum sensing. Relay node selection in vehicular networks
	Hierarchical clustering.	Anomaly/fault/intrusion detection in mobile wireless networks
	Unsupervised soft-clustering machine learning framework.	Latency reduction by clustering fog nodes to automatically decide which low power node (LPN) is upgraded to a high-power node (HPN) in heterogeneous cellular networks.
	Affinity propagation clustering.	Data-driven resource management for ultra-dense small cells

(Continued)

Table 4.1 (Continued)   ML Techniques in Mobile Networks

AI Technique	Learning Model	5G-Based Applications
Reinforcement Learning	Reinforcement learning algorithm based on long short-term memory (RL-LSTM) cells.	Proactive resource allocation in LTE-U networks, formulated as a noncooperative game which enables SBSs to learn which unlicensed channel, given the long-term WLAN activity in the channels and LTE-U traffic loads
	Gradient follower (GF), the modified Roth-Erev (MRE), and the modified Bush and Mosteller (MBM).	Enable femto-cells (FCs) to autonomously and opportunistically sense the radio environment and tune their parameters in HetNets, to reduce intra/inter-tier interference
	Reinforcement learning with network-assisted feedback.	Heterogeneous radio access technologies (RATs) selection

achieve communications in spatially correlated channels of massive MIMO. The popular approach includes the training sequence (or pilot sequence), where a known signal is transmitted, and the CSI is estimated using the combined knowledge of the transmitted and received signals.

AI-Enabled 5G Network Management

From the 5G network perspective, a possible AI-empowered 5G network management is depicted in Figure 4.1 [3].

In this model, an AI controller acts as an application on top of ONOS or an independent network entity, and communicate with RAN, CN, or global SDN controllers using open interfaces. The AI center will have access to the service-level agreements (e.g., requirements on rate, coverage, failure duration, redundancy, etc.), monitor UE-level information (e.g., receiver category, battery limitation), network-level information (e.g., spectrum, number of serving subscribers, QoS (quality of service), key performance indicators of network functions, scheduled maintenance period, etc.), and infrastructure-level information (e.g., server type,

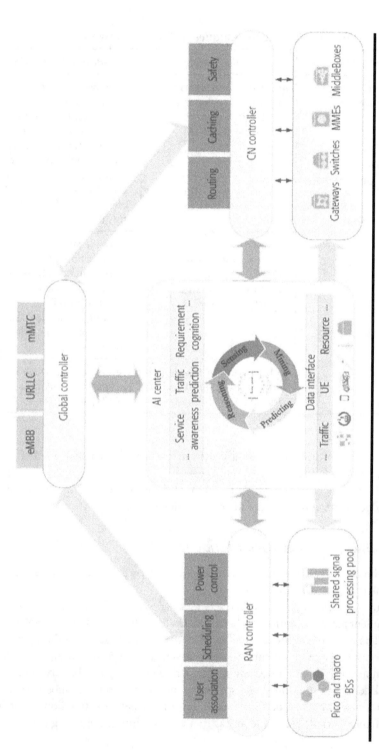

Figure 4.1 AI-Enabled Architecture for 5G Network Management [3].

CPU, memory, storage, network standard) from the SDN controllers, so as to get in touch with cellular network data such as traffic information, UEs, and network resources. Afterward, the AI center will utilize its embedded modules (e.g., sensing, mining, prediction, and reasoning) to process the obtained information, and feedback learning results, which may include traffic characteristic analysis reports, UE-specific controlling information, and network configuration notification, to the SDN controllers.

State of Play on AI-Enabled 5G Functionality

In the context of introducing machine learning (ML) techniques in new generation networks, many research studies have been conducted in recent years. Organizations such as ITU and ETSI, have paved the way towards enabling ML in 5G by establishing groups that focus on studying and standardizing the implementation of ML in the future network's ecosystem. Such groups are ITU-T Focus Group on Machine Learning for Future Networks including 5G (FG-ML5G) [4] and ETSI Experiential Networked Intelligence (ENI) group [5]. The work from these groups was a "kick off", but also served as a guideline, from academia and industry in order to conduct their own studies on integrating ML in next-generation networks. Especially in the last three years, ML is proposed from many researchers as a great tool towards more agile, flexible, and adaptive networks. In [6] the authors perform a comprehensive survey of the applications of deep learning (DL) algorithms for different network layers, including physical layer modulation/coding, data link layer access control/resource allocation, routing layer path search, and traffic balancing. A short review of ML is done in [7] and a possible match is proposed between some ML techniques and specific automation problems in new 5G networks. The paper [8] presents artificial intelligence (AI)–based solutions concerning three problems in new generation wireless networks, namely radio access network (RAN) slicing, radio access technology (RAT) selection, and mobile edge caching and content delivery. Most of the solutions include reinforcement learning (RL) and neural network (NN) algorithms. The authors in [9] propose the integration of AI to automate and control next-generation networks in their intent-based networking (IBN) platform for provisioning of network slicing. The research study [10] presents general proposals on how ML methods, and especially NN, could be applied in a network slicing concept (data analytics, traffic prediction, resource allocation, etc.).

Apart from surveys and reviews in the specific field, many researchers have implemented their own frameworks and testbeds to experiment on ML for solving different requirements in 5G networks. For that reason, next we have tried to categorize the selected references according to the domain of 5G they are focusing on.

For traffic-type detection and automated allocation of traffic in slice we distinguished the following works. Paper [11] presents a ML-based model for predicting traffic type on vehicular networks using a combination of convolutional NN (CNN) and long short-term memory (LSTM), and a resource allocation scheme based on the previous prediction model. The authors in [12] study the allocation of different services to three network slices (Enhanced Mobile Broadband (eMBB), Critical Communication (CriComm), Massive IoT (mIoT)). Specifically, four ML methods are implemented and compared, namely random forest, K-nearest neighbor, support vector machines, and decision tree, for allocating new services to the above slice categories. DeepSlice, presented in [13], is a NN approach for predicting the slice a traffic should be allocated. NN is preferred due to the unstructured and huge data of the problem. Random forest is also proposed for well-structured data. DeepSlice is tested for three use cases: allocate an unknown traffic type, load balancing, and slice failure. In [14] the authors present DeepCog, a new mobile traffic data analytics tool that is explicitly tailored to solve the capacity forecast problem, using NN, and in [15] again NN is used to predict traffic volume in a 5G optical transport layer.

Concerning resource allocation in 5G, the authors in [16] propose, implement, and test a multi-agent deep reinforcement learning (DRL) algorithm that allocates resource blocks in RAN independently of the number of slices awaiting to be deployed. In [17], a resource allocation scheme for network slicing is proposed using a combination of a generative adversarial network (GAN) algorithm and a distributional RL algorithm to take the decisions of allocation, while the simulations experiment with bandwidth allocation to each slice. The authors in [18] formulate the problems of mode selection and resource allocation in fog RAN as MILP. With performance requirements and limited resources considered, a system power minimization problem is formulated, and two RL-based approaches are developed for the mode selection problem. To guarantee the slice isolation, both orthogonal and multiplexed sub-channel allocation strategies are presented. A dynamic resource allocation scheme for network slicing is presented in [19]. The DRL-based algorithm learns by experience, focusing on three parameters: performance, SLA violation, and network utilization.

An important sector that the use of ML may also be decisive is the fulfillment of service level agreements. Three interesting papers are referring to SLA optimization aspects. Firstly, in [20] end-to-end SLA decomposition to different network's domains is issued, and ML methods are proposed for regression in SLA parameters as latency, bandwidth, etc. Secondly, in [21] a DRL algorithm is proposed for radio resource management to decide whether to apply changes to control parameters of a slice or not. Last but least, the authors in [22] propose recursive NN (RNN) with LSTM to predict if a new network slice request will violate the SLA if accepted.

Some researchers have also proposed ML-based methods to jointly solve the previous aspects. The short paper [23] proposes an ML framework for network slicing resource allocation with a DL method for traffic detection and a RL method for optimizing resource allocation, and similarly in [24] the authors present a DRL method for provisioning mobile service provider (MSP) and the CSP (cloud service provider) services and a regression model for traffic prediction. Furthermore, a framework to jointly solve traffic detection and SLA fulfillment is presented in [25]. Specifically, the framework introduces a self-organized network concept in which various ML algorithms, such as K-means, naive Bayes, support vector machines, neural networks, gradient boosted tree, and random forest, are tested for traffic detection and assignment of appropriate QoS parameters e.g., bandwidth, from an SDN controller.

The AI Ambition for 5G Technologies

Network Slicing beyond MANO

Network slicing [26] is set to be a prominent feature of 5G to allow the partitioning of a single network into a number of segregated logical networks, each optimized for a particular type of service, or dedicated to a particular customer or application [27]. Network slicing requires complex control operations over the end-to-end network and IT resources, extending well beyond the NFV MANO scope, which focuses on the virtual network appliances [28].

The necessary capabilities for network slicing support in 5G systems have been already defined in the latest 3GPP Release 15 specifications approved in June 2018, which include the definition of the network slice identifiers, denoted as single network slice selection assistance information (S-NSSAI) as well as the signaling procedures and functions necessary for network slice selection between the UEs, the next generation RAN (NG-RAN), and the new 5G core network (5GC). 3GPP has also defined a set of three standardized slice service types (SSTs) to refer to an expected network slice behavior in terms of features and services (i.e., MBB, URLLC, and mMTC), though remarkably 3GPP does not specify the characteristics of these SSTs.

In this context, regardless of the specific network slicing services (e.g., automated provisioning of slices) and of the underlying technologies for implementing network slicing supported in the ICT-17 experimental platforms [29] to be leveraged by 5G/B5G, it is essential

■ To have a *common method that the industry can refer to in order to describe the characteristics of any slice* since network slicing will be relevant for numerous use cases from vertical industries [30]. In this way, by establishing a common method for slice characterization: (1) the slice customer knows how to express the service requirements and is assured that such requirements can be met; (2) the slice provider knows what to deliver; (3) there is a sound basis for a contractual agreement between the slice provider and the slice customer; and (4) UEs can roam into another network, but maintain access to the services that require particular network capabilities e.g., by allowing a home network operator to buy a slice in a visited domain or by having commonly defined slices available in each network. To progress towards such an ambitious goal, GSMA has created the network slicing task force (NEST) addressing the characterization of network slices for vertical industries. NEST is expected to define a generic slice template (GST) with a set of attribute names, definitions, and units that could be filled with values and/or ranges based on specific vertical industry use cases.

■ To demonstrate and assess the end-to-end slicing mechanisms, as well as the performance of the network slices themselves, *in multi-service/multi-slice usage scenarios, under realistic conditions*, extending well beyond in-lab trials.

Ambition

In 5G, it is foreseen that sophisticated radio transmission, resource allocation, and network slicing techniques will be used. To meet these advances, it becomes more and more challenging since network infrastructure becomes complicated and heterogeneous. One promising arrangement is to use the extraordinary potential of manufactured insights (AI) innovation, which has been investigated to supply arrangements extending from channel expectation to independent arrange management, as well as network security. Network intelligence and automation are pivotal to the advancement of 5G, IoT, and mechanical digitalization. For illustration, the creators of [31] proposed X-LSTM to foresee future utilization to oversee 5G cutting. A metric called REVA is created, and to figure REVA the following 30 seconds with forecast interims of 5 seconds. The creators created X-LSTM, which is built upon LSTM and ARIMA, which a well-known measurable strategy. This methodology enables an improvement of X-LSTM over ARIMA and LSTM for X-LSTM.

Radio Technologies and Spectrum

In the 3GPP 5G Release 15, a number of new or extended frequency bands are specified. For radio access, these are namely frequency bands around 700 MHz, 3.4 GHz to 3.8 GHz, and the low mmWave frequencies around 26 GHz and 28 GHz in Europe and the United States, respectively. For the transport network, radio links in the mmWave bands at 60 GHz and E-band (70/80 GHz) are considered most suitable. Thereby, the 60 GHz band will be mainly considered for small cell deployment in dense urban areas because of the limited range of about 250 m, whereas E-band links appear more suitable for larger distances (up to about 2.5 km), usually needed in rural areas. The main reasons for the difference in range between 60 GHz links and E-band comes from the oxygen (O_2) attenuation that affects radio propagation at 60 GHz [32].

Another interesting scheme that is being considered in the context of 5G is self-backhauling. This means that the very same radios are used both for mobile access and for fronthaul/backhaul. For self-backhauling systems, operating in the mmWave bands at 26 GHz and 60 GHz are particularly well suited. Self-backhauling is a cost-efficient means for small cell deployment avoiding expensive optic fiber connectivity and dedicated radios for the transport link. To further increase the data rate of wireless fronthaul/backhaul links, techniques like line-of-sight (LOS) MIMO can be deployed. LOS-MIMO requires optimal antenna spacing of the transmit antennae and the receive antennae for a given distance. Since this is wavelength dependent, mmWave systems are most suitable for LOS-MIMO transmission. With tolerable separation of the antennae of about 40 cm, orthogonal channels and independent MIMO streams can be achieved over a distance of about 100 m. LOS-MIMO can be further enhanced using hybrid beamforming. This way an even larger number of MIMO streams can be achieved, facilitating ultra-high data rate transport connections for base stations in dense urban areas.

Ambition

There is concern at present that the rising use of wireless technology would overcrowd the airwaves that our devices use to connect with each other. One suggested way to solve this problem is to create communication devices that don't always transmit on the same frequency. By allowing intelligent knowledge of RF operation that was not previously feasible, AI algorithms can then be used to find available frequencies. A promising function for resource allocation in 5G wireless communication networks could be machine learning/deep learning. For interference management, spectrum management, multi-path use, connection adaptation, multi-channel connectivity, and traffic congestion, deep learning can be a good alternative. Machine learning within the RAN increases efficiency significantly by:

- Reducing energy consumption
- Exploiting channel data to support better connections
- Usage of massive MIMO systems
- Make better use of feedback and reactions from the real world to compensate for hardware, distortion, non-linearities, and impacts

Core and Edge Computing and Networking

Cloud and virtualization technologies are transforming the communications industry with the introduction of new paradigms like Telco Cloud and network functions virtualization (NFV) which, by decoupling hardware and software, are allowing applications to be deployed and run on top of platforms in a flexible, efficient, and scalable way. Combined with the vastly increased number of data processing devices at the edge and the evolving 5G networks, the emergence of the concept of edge computing leads to a distributed mobile edge computing (MEC) ecosystem that will enable the efficient deployment of 5G use cases in vertical markets. As it turns 5G mobile communication networks into distributed cloud computing systems, the MEC has recently gained considerable traction. Located in close proximity to edge devices, MEC allows low latency service delivery to/from mobile users in the order of microseconds, through the radio access network (RAN). MEC provides IT and cloud-computing capabilities within the radio access network (RAN) near mobile subscribers, providing a low latency and high-speed context-aware service environment with direct access to real-time radio network information. By processing data locally, MEC applications can also significantly reduce data transfer costs [33].

Ambition

The anticipated future requirements for the implementation of edge device intelligence would contribute to MEC's evolution into an AI-enabled platform that will be able to provide edge devices with intelligent services provided over a fixed or mobile access network. AI capabilities will proliferate, bringing them out of the cloud, and they will be the fundamental technology that enables future hybrid computing where local, cloud, or device-based computing decisions can be made in real time based on latency needs, power needs, and overall storage and efficiency needs.

Such AI-enabled edge systems, which include computationally efficient dedicated hardware capable of running ML/AI algorithms, are deviating from the classical ML/AI concept; the latter focuses primarily on offline and centralized AI/ML and is implemented by a cloud computing model in which the entire data set is provided a priori and used for the training process centrally. Recent research studies have sparked a huge interest in collaborative, distributed, low-latency, and stable ML, in comparison to cloud-based architectures, calling for a significant departure from cloud-based and centralized training and inference towards a novel device design coined by the words "AI at the Edge", where a large number of edge devices, such as network base stations (BSs) and/or mobile devices, including phones, cameras, vehicles, drones, etc. are unevenly distributed and respectively the training data are also split to them. Moreover, every edge device has access to a fraction of the data and limited computing and storage capacity, where edge devices share their locally trained models instead of sharing their private data and collectively perform training and inference. Finally, network data abstraction and dimensionality reduction are important, as it is difficult to store the immense amount of monitored data.

This ambition makes it possible to deploy an advanced 5G/6G network [34] that can act as a distributed computer with the objective of providing AI at the edge and which will be deployed between the level of cloud computing (the network core) and the connected end-users/devices (at the wireless access).

The AI Ambition for 5G Vertical Sectors

Innovations for the Media and Entertainment Sector

Media and entertainment are one of the most disruptive vertical markets that will benefit from 5G [35,36]. Slicing offers lots of content delivery mechanisms and the opportunity for greater control over radio resources, which was previously under the control of the mobile operator. So, content providers [37], such as Netflix and Amazon Prime could benefit from new business models and engage as virtual network operators (VNOs) in tighter interaction with the underlying network infrastructure. Besides that, the VR consumer technology achieved a massive breakthrough in 2016 when within a few weeks both the Oculus Rift and the HTC Vive became available to consumers worldwide. The "immersiveness" achieved by these top-end VR systems was hailed as a dawn of a golden age for VR, and it was projected that tens of millions of consumers would buy their own VR systems within a couple of years. Nevertheless, things did not progress as envisaged: although the VR market expanded, aided also by the introduction of very potent mobile VR systems, its growth was not as expected [38].

The reasons are probably a combination of factors, such as lack of killer apps, low quality of HMD displays, content which has not adapted to the production needs of VR, and most of all lack of the social factor [39]. Among these factors, the shortcomings of current network infrastructures are critical [40,41]. The networks do not support true immersive, online, multiplayer VR content. Latency is a major bottleneck: in order to achieve an immersive experience and avoid motion sickness MTP latency should ideally be below 5 ms. Moreover, current bandwidth does neither support increase of the FOV (field-of-view) of the HMDs, nor high-resolution video, which for VR is above 8K. Removing the bottlenecks of network bandwidth and latency will allow the VR content creators to develop content that can be shared by people using VR in different places, as well as VR manufacturers to develop hardware that can utilize the expanded capabilities.

Ambition

5G identifies use cases with today's latency of less than 10 ms, and 6G is already considering to 10 microseconds (μs). The bandwidth for networking is increasing by 5G and Wi-Fi 6. 5G expects to expand to 10 Gbps and 2 Gbps is already enabled by Wi-Fi 6. Edge thus makes it possible for media and entertainment businesses to produce content and digital experiences quicker and with lower latency. Since some data is centrally processed while other data is processed at the edge, output is improved by MEC. At the same time, multiple applications requiring large bandwidth will run. The interaction of content users can be improved by an infrastructure based on a 5G network and mobile edge computing.

Innovations for the PPDR Sector

5G/B5G will explore the combined usability of the recently defined 3GPP Mission Critical Services specifications and situational awareness technologies [42], such as wearable cameras, video analytics, IoT devices collecting bio-signals, and information of the environment and blockchain applied on first-responders' safety, coordination, and communication on the field, sustained by 5G technology. While 3GPP MCS protocols are designed to generally cope with the requirements of different mission critical communications verticals (e.g., public safety, public transport, maritime communications), there is still a need for evaluating the current specification for specific scenarios such as those proposed in 5G/B5G. 3GPP MCS are defined taking into account that the underlying 4G and 5G networks support a series of features such as QoS handling, direct communications, and multicast/broadcast services. 5G/B5G will evaluate the usability of modern communications systems (e.g., 5G-ready Malaga platform inherited by H2020 ICT-17 5GENESIS) and the synchronization and real-time operation of aggregated awareness technologies as an early warning system (EWS).

5G/B5G envisions that the location of PPDR services may have an essential role due to the constraints that the synchronization of components or communications themselves may well have according to the overall experienced delay. Therefore, 5G/B5G will cover the deployment of required PPDR network slices and VNFs in different locations depending on the monitored network and emergency conditions. To achieve this goal of flexible PPDR service deployment, the entire PPDR service stack will be handled either using 5G-ready MEC-based servers close to the first-responders field or ordinary servers behind the EPC. Thus, according to the tracked conditions, the entire PPDR service will be switched to the other deployment site, enabling load balancers, service-level KPI improvement and availability to respond to emergency conditions with isolated network areas where the work, safety, coordination, and communication of first responders is of utmost importance.

Ambition

The productivity of joint public protection and disaster relief (PPDR) missions would benefit from the use of advanced AR/VR applications by providing greater situational awareness and deeper immersion in real time. However, the violation of privacy and data in the field remains a concern addressed at the edge by 5G and AI. By bringing processing and collection into the environment(s) where the data is generated, instead of centralizing and storing the data at a remote location, edge computing helps to mitigate some of these concerns. In addition, AI at the edge can provide first responders with voice-driven interfaces, maximizing their mission capability and productivity under different conditions.

Innovations for the Automotive Sector

In recent years, the need of intelligent systems within the vehicle has gradually generated a more complex and more distributed electronic architecture, with increasingly powerful "smart centers". This complexity will be further increased with the arrival of the connected and the autonomous vehicle: information of online services is needed to be integrated in the own motor control calculations, and artificial vision, data fusion, and AI will increase the computing power of the processors, which is needed.

Unlike other computer systems, all the intelligence of the vehicle has always been on board due to its need for real-time calculation and the criticality of the driving-orientated functions. This leads to an increase in the cost of the electronics of the vehicle, which at the same time become more and more critical. Likewise, the distributed on-board electronics greatly limits the synergies between systems and components and the introduction or enhancement of new features, as well as simple software updates.

Remote intelligence would be a great solution to increase flexibility in the management of the vehicle and its systems, to increase computing capacity without requiring huge hardware upgrades, to drastically reduce the cost of onboard electronics and to allow many more synergies between system control functions and online services.

Ambition

5G is becoming the future of autonomous vehicles, with its millisecond latencies, high-bandwidth and network slicing capabilities, while the mobile edge computing empowers AI-based services, like navigation and connected vehicles that require large amounts of locally relevant data computation, management, and data analysis.

Innovations for the E-Health Sector

Health applications and services rely on IoT devices, wearables that are able to measure physiological parameters. Nowadays, professional athletes and even casual amateurs use monitoring devices to assess their performance levels to better enhance the efficiency of the training sessions and for a better preparation of competitions. In this context, the continuous tracking of physiological parameters in large-scale events introduces high volumes of data. 5G/B5G will explore the engagement of 5G towards increasing safety in the training activities and competitions, as data can be shared with medical centers and sports event organizers to detect risk situations (to provide timely responses in emergency situations) and to coaches (to better assess the runner status and performance). In addition, the high number of devices introduces challenges in the network that can be addressed with the 5G support for massive machine type communications (mMTC).

5G/B5G lays down the foundations for health institutions and sports industry to devise new and tailored products/services according the data available in real time and in demanding scenarios (competitions running in crowded scenarios) within an integrated safety perspective.

Ambition

Edge AI and 5G are important for both patients and healthcare professionals in the healthcare sector. The recording of vital signs can be of enormous benefit to Edge AI. Medical devices intended to record information such as heart rate, temperature, breathing rate, blood pressure, etc. may use AI to detect any abnormality in a moment. In radiology, images from DICOM (digital imaging and communications) are very large. Transmitting these images to the cloud or a central server to process and obtain the machine learning inference can therefore be very expensive and time consuming. Edge AI requires the study to occur locally, however, and this leads to a much quicker diagnosis.

Creating Innovation Potential for AI Applications

Benefits and Impact of 5G/B5G in AI-Enabled Vertical Industries

AI-enabled 5G/B5G is expected to allow verticals and vertical users to obtain benefits in multiple areas:

■ **Strategic and operational benefits:** *Strategic* benefits will arise from greater access to information about the supply chain, internal operations, market characteristics, and consumer utilization of goods and services, while *operational* benefits and enhanced productivity will arise from increased real-time access to information about operations (inside/outside the workplaces and throughout the supply chain);

- **Direct user benefits:** Such benefits should arise for consumers from access to "improved" goods or services. Improvements could include cost, quality, usability, reliability, and longevity;
- **New business models and opportunities for revenue:** 5G/B5G UCs will contribute to enable new business models and create a great opportunity in different vertical sectors to generate a considerable revenue pool;
- **Societal benefits:** Not less relevant are also the second-order benefits arisen from the "knock-on" impacts from the use of goods and services. These are generally more indirect benefits to society such as enhanced productivity (economic), reduced pollution (environmental), and enhanced security (legal/regulatory).

Strategic and Operational Benefits

A complete list of the strategic and operational benefits expected in the 5G/B5G framework is given below:

- *More capacity for more customers*: As venues offer more immersive experiences, the level of connectivity required will certainly increase. 5G offers up to 40 times more capacity than 4.5G, enabling operators to meet this demand and provide visitors with a perception of infinite capacity.
- *Make broadcasting simpler*: 5G wireless networks spell the end for the wired connections previously required by high-definition cameras, or the large number of cameras it takes to provide increased user content. The broadcasting of events is more flexible, as cameras can be operated wirelessly. Network slicing provides the dedicated and isolated virtual networks that enable content producers to reliably upstream video content, even if the rest of the network is heavily loaded. It dramatically improves the economics of creating new content for VR, using "bullet-shot" cameras and Nokia OZO cameras for 360-degree views.
- *Increase venue bookings*: Venue owners can attract a wider variety of event types, by providing for a range of IT and communications needs through the flexibility of 5G networks. Live broadcasts for sports events need low-latency communications and ultra-resilient connectivity. Recording for music events needs significant local processing of high-fidelity audio and high-definition video feeds. Smaller corporate events in adjacent conference facilities built into the stands require sophisticated virtual private network capabilities.
- *Cater for corporate clients*: With 5G, event organizers can cater for corporate visitors by creating digital connectivity zones, offering a greater quality of connectivity experience and avoiding congested Wi-Fi frequency bands.
- *Monitoring*: Under 5G and ETSI MANO topology, it is relatively easy to both provide internal PPDR service stats (e.g., current ongoing calls, type of calls, past calls, RAM and CPU consumption, service-level KPIs, etc.) and extract macroscopic consumption of the VNFs (mostly RAM and CPU

consumption of the instance). The former gives complete information, even being able to gather information about the service KPIs in order to deduct its behavior at the protocol level. The latter provides information about the deployed instance so as to know if the VNFs, for example, count with enough resources to run appropriately.

- **Scaling:** Related to the previous benefit, with the performance information being gathered, we could decide in the VNFs themselves whether they have enough physical resources or not. Either if the evaluation prompts that the resources are little or more than enough, the VNF con be scaled, up or down. In case of PPDR and if we need for instance to scale up to increase the service power to handle more simultaneous MCVideo calls, it could be done in two ways: either deploy a new instance of the MCVideo VNF or increase the VNF resources and re-deploy it. In both cases the resources spent in MCVideo calls are greater and the performance constraint is solved.

- **Reduction of integration phases:** As a common technology playground, the use of 5G technology with virtualized services and agile deployments helps establish common technology components that could serve as well-known technological bridges in order to integrate different solutions. These solutions will need to only adjust their interfaces to common interfaces and procedures (e.g., OSM, Open APIs, CAPIF, etc.) and therefore, the technological integration would be seamless.

- **Reduction of contractual constraints:** In the context of two operators negotiating to share their spectrum and provided services to end users, 5G would drastically change the contractual problems and negotiating periods by making easily available and put to work together the most substantial technological goods such as network slices or service VNFs over PNFs regardless of the selected facilities of interested parties. In the same way, the ecosystem reduces the constraints of a new service to be included in the service catalog of a certain operator.

- **Service availability:** Due to the widespread network integration of specific 5G components and integration with legacy 4G networks and vertical-specific devices (e.g., IoT devices, surveillance cameras), the available services would not only be wider, being used seamlessly regardless the access network, but also more complete integrating additional support technologies (e.g., wearable cameras and IoT monitoring devices with first-responders to increase situational awareness).

- **Cloud-enabled benefits:** Drastic reduction of weight and costs of the electronic system shipped in vehicles, after moving the main computing to a remote server. Moreover, as the vehicles can be driven remotely, computing does not depend on onboard hardware any longer, and lays on a remote supercomputer, which leads to much more flexibility and many more features. Also, when computing is done remotely, cloud services could be integrated into functions, enriching their accuracy or improving user benefits.

■ *Synergies between vehicles/"swarm" fleet operation:* Taking the concept to the extreme, in the future, where a whole fleet could be operating with remote intelligence, it would be much easier to manage cooperative driving between vehicles (and improve autonomous driving systems) since all data and calculations are made on remote servers and, therefore, available from the network.

Direct User Benefits

Below, we list the direct user benefits that emerge due to the 5G/B5G approach:

■ *High-quality spectator experience:* The high throughput and low latency of 5G is ideally suited to delivering services that transform event experiences in a number of different ways. With 5G, every visitor can access the same choice of high-quality experiences, regardless of which seat they have. They can select from a choice of cameras on their smart device or VR headset – from 360-degree VR views to player perspectives – to see what's happening from any angle. They can even virtually "beam" themselves into different areas of the venue to experience what it's like to be track-side for critical moments, like pit-stops in Formula One races, or on the goal line to see the winning shot go in. They can be at the heart of the action.

■ *Access to augmented-type of information:* The low-latency capability of 5G, coupled with mobile edge computing, enables visitors to access AR within the stadium. So, they can also request to see instant replays, or access live commentary and behind-the-scenes interviews. They can also further enhance their experience with extra insights, such as player stats, referee decisions, or real-time game analytics. With low-latency AR, it's all effortlessly accessed and presented with seamless integration into the attendee's field of view. AR also makes it easier to get around the venue, with easy-to-access directions to concessions stands and toilet facilities, or real-time information on start times or queues. And it doesn't end there. With increased, always-assured connectivity inside the stadium, visitors can take home a high-definition, 360-degree view as a souvenir clip. They can enjoy seemingly unlimited access to mobile data and networks, so they can upload video clips or update social networks. And they can easily access other value-added services, like pre-ordering food and drink, buying merchandise, or online betting.

■ *Greater available capacity:* End users would have the possibility of having greater available capacities in the network to allow enhanced services that require wider bandwidths. As an easy example, first responders may easily congest a 4G deployment during emergency events in case MCVideo capabilities of MCS are used. The increased capacity of 5G deployments and the easier way to load balance the traffic from one small cell to another makes the whole system more robust to operational errors or required QoS infringement.

- **Greater responsiveness**: First responders would have greater responsiveness due to the evolved network delays and increased information resources. The integrated vertical-specific components would be more under the 5G eco-system, building more powerful technology that in the case of PPDR would respond faster and more efficiently, helping first responders act quickly.

- **Improved KPIs**: Based on the same end-to-end delay reduction, the communications themselves would greatly improve KPIs, impacting on the QoE. It is clear that, the lower the overall delay, the faster communications between first responders or first responders with the emergency control room. Therefore, the improved delay directly impacts the efficiency and accuracy in the field.

- **Cost-effectiveness**: The access to open standards allows the entry of many other parties in the mission critical ecosystem, allowing a wider product portfolio and, therefore, having access to more cost-effective solutions. In this regard, not only the SW and service solutions are cheaper, but the mission critical devices as well, switching from proprietary and closed technology to open and affordable solutions.

- **Enhanced safety in running events**: Professional athletes and individuals participating in running events can be actively monitored in real-time using wearable devices that do not obstruct their movements and hence their performance. These devices allow complete monitoring of their health status at all times, together with their accurate real-time positioning. Such data is shared with events' organizers and medical staff/centers, which receive it live and may send alerts/perform actions whenever needed. For instance, assistance can quickly be dispatched to the location of a runner in distress. Therefore, it can be considered an extra service to be provided by event organizers in coordination with the health sector.

- **Increase participation experience for runners**: The support of consecutive starts and the monitoring of runners through wearables and sensors enhance the experience of participants in several ways. For instance, the waiting times in the stadium are reduced, since multiple starts are performed with the timing applications. Also, athletes will have access to much more data about their performance and health status, which can either be used to ensure their well-being, to assist their coaches or themselves on improving their performance, or simply to be shared in social networks among friends and colleagues.

- **Flexibility to update and upgrade a vehicle**: The system would allow the update and expansion of vehicle functions, just by updating a remote software. This allows, on the one hand, a better maintenance of the vehicles at a technological level, but it would also allow to offer new premium services to the users without requiring a hardware upgrade of the vehicle. The "features" of the vehicles would become mere online updates or software management.

New Business Models and Opportunities for Revenue

5G creates a great opportunity in different vertical sectors to generate a considerable revenue pool. In this direction, 5G/B5G targets a different set of use cases in automotive, media, eHealth, and public safety. Each use case represents a vertical sector specifically customized based on regional needs and with social impacts targeted at corresponding European countries. This rich platform presents a real-life ensemble for the stakeholders (technology providers, vertical service providers/operators, and vertical users) to

- Dynamically engage with each other
- Identify and resolve potential challenges and barriers to enable vertical use cases
- Realize their roles within the evolving value chain via establishing new business models

Technology providers have classically enabled connectivity primarily for human communications in the form of voice, data, and the Internet. Operators have also established their business models based on such services. However, enabling vertical services requires a new set of benchmarking methodologies and applications mainly focusing on tailor-made vertical specific KPIs. Unlike previous generations of networks, this requires closer interaction with local businesses (as vertical users) to better understand their needs and to follow an experimental and iterative testing and optimization process to achieve the required KPIs.

In similar manner, network operators (and vertical service providers) need a platform to verify different business models. This will enable them to transform their value proposition from connectivity provisioning into a new range of B2C and B2B offerings enabling new services and applications.

The above multi-play platform opens up the possibility for new markets and applications within Europe. In particular, small businesses and start-up companies may have a chance to develop new applications that otherwise would be impossible to achieve without direct engagement with key ecosystem players.

Below we list *new business models and revenue potential* that emerge in the framework defined by the selected use cases:

- *New revenue streams*: With a flexible network infrastructure, 5G enables service providers to take advantage of new revenue streams – both online and offline. Operators can offer visitors increased entertainment options, like enhanced views and VR. For such advanced services, 5G offers a take-rate (the percentage of the total audience the operator can support) of up to 30%, compared with just 2% offered by 4.5G. In addition, by offering these services, operators can maximize their brand perception with sports enthusiasts.

- ***Increase fan loyalty to the in-stadium experience***: By meeting their ever-increasing connectivity expectations, and by providing new ways to experience events, stadium owners and event organizers can continue to attract massive demand from fans and more casual attendees for live events. They can further leverage that customer loyalty with pre- and post-event offers and experiences enabled by 5G, to open up new revenue streams.

- ***Increase advertising and retail revenues***: The increased connectivity of 5G creates new ways to offer and sell advertising and sponsorship opportunities, with increased revenues available from moveable, digital advertising spaces. Additionally, independent secure links can be offered to support back-office connectivity and point-of-sale (POS) systems for on-site retail concessions.

- ***Public/Private deployment models***: Due to the system flexibility and agile deployment of new services or physical facilities to run those services, the market will suffer a significant transformation, adopting deployments with a mixture of public and private sector. The exemplification of this trend is FirstNet in the United States. FirstNet has been allocated 2×10 MHz of spectrum (LTE band 14) and \$7 billion funding to establish a nationwide public safety communication service. AT&T were announced during 2017 to build and manage the FirstNet network. AT&T are also investing a further \$40 billion in network expansion on top of their existing \$160 billion investment. In December 2017, it was announced that all U.S. states have explicitly opted in to the FirstNet network, rather than implement their own. Once the PPDR network is established nationwide, the 5G technology would make easy the adoption of new private networks to extend the coverage and range of services.

- ***Resource sharing***: The aforementioned system flexibility enables network-level scenarios that were difficult to implement under the sole use of 4G. In 5G, the resources could be shared between different physical deployment, between verticals using the same network slice or a different one if the technical requirements do not fit or even using a variety of network slices for different end users (e.g., different requirements for police, ambulances, firemen, etc. under the same PPDR use case or scenario) in the same vertical but using the same group of resources.

- ***Increased capabilities***: Especially in the case of PPDR, the access to enhanced network functionalities is easier (less integration period), making the technology more valuable compared with legacy communication technology (P25, TETRA, TETRAPOL). In this sense, it is easier to obtain network slices that include the required QoS management or assignment of required QCI, increase communication security and privacy, and multicast/broadcast capabilities to solve resource problems in crowded emergency areas.

■ *Involvement of different actors*: Once again the flexibility of 5G makes it easier to involve new parties that do not necessarily have all pieces of the deployment. In the case of PPDR, under 4G technology, it could be very costly and time consuming to involve different companies that provide sensors with others that provide communications or the control center of the police. Every individual party under 5G could build the service in VNFs and deploy them using same, different, or a variety of network slices without having to worry about the enabler deployment itself (orchestrator, NFVI, etc.). Thus, the time-to-market is reduced, and even small parties are easily involved.

■ *Introduce new business models and revenue streams for the sports industry equipment, applications, services*: 5G capabilities open a huge market for new sports wearables, sensors, software applications and systems, targeting well-being, training, and self-assessment. For instance, service providers can take advantage of data generated by the wearables and sensors streams, not only to further increase safety of participants but also to augment the participation in running events. One example is to use live data about the location and performance of each athlete and share it in streamed events or display it to the stadium's audience. That creates new business models for providers of such services and enhances the experience of the public.

■ *New business models by new data streams and mMTC for 5G service providers and mobile operators*: With the requirement for a flexible network infrastructure, eHealth enables new opportunities for mobile operators and 5G service providers. In particular, by taking advantage of huge amounts of data generated by wearables and other sensor streams, operators can define new business models for mMTC due to the demanding requirements that those streams pose on the network. This results in an increase of their revenue stream and enables the quicker monetization of their CAPEX/OPEX for 5G networks.

■ *New business for automotive*: The connected vehicle also opens the gate to a new world of service business for vehicle users, making 5G and reliable edge cloud computing key factors for automotive manufacturers, communication utilities, and services companies. It represents an opportunity for mobile network operators to widen their scope by offering customized solutions and E2E capacities to industrial OEMs. As it was suggested in previous sections, the "edge approach" could also foster the development of new, enhanced services for the automotive vertical.

Societal Benefits

The societal benefits created as a major effect of the AI-enabled 5G are summarized below:

- ***Environmental***: Remote access to a high-quality live video broadcast, e.g., from one's home with the means of VR/AR, will encourage some spectators to watch events like a football game or concert from their couch; thus, carbon footage is reduced due to avoiding transportation to and from a stadium.

- ***Social***: People with disabilities, who might otherwise not be able to attend live venues like a tournament, will now have equal opportunities to virtually but highly realistically attend such live events enjoying a high feeling of immersion and presence.

- ***Security***: A great impact on the society comes in terms of increased security and protection. All improvements converge in a more secure world, ranging from the network coverage being greater, the capacities being higher, the available PPDR services being more and more powerful, the overall end-to-end delay in communications being lower or the deployments being more flexible and agile. All enhanced features improve technology that at the same time helps and improves the task of first responders and finally could deliver a better, more coordinated, rapid and efficient service to the society, building 5G-ready secure and protected cities.

- ***Broader range of services and bridging the gap with patients***: The health and insurance ecosystem will be able to offer new health services that will only be possible with 5G networks and their capabilities, bridging the gap between patients and hospitals and the remaining health sector. These can leverage real-time patient information, which can be used for both remote clinical diagnosis and a more effective and faster treatment in case of emergency. At the same time, health insurance companies may adapt their services and offer higher bonuses to people with more active lifestyles and lower risk of certain diseases.

Future Perspectives

Research efforts are needed in many directions in order to promote the incorporation of deep learning and machine learning techniques in 5G systems. For example, along with advanced parallel computing, faster algorithms, and cloud computing, deep neural network acceleration and distributed deep learning systems provide an opportunity for 5G and B5G to develop intelligence in its systems towards higher throughputs and ultra-low latency [43–46].

Different categories can be considered in future perspectives of deep-neural network acceleration techniques: Methods such as layer decomposition and information distillation can be used at the architecture level, while other features (e.g., GPU, FPGA designs) can be applied at the implementation level. The complexity of deep learning can be lowered by using deep learning acceleration methods, with small losses in the accuracy of these models.

Combining these methods and techniques to create intelligence in 5G systems will have a significant effect on further exploration of the acceleration of these networks. Another way to speed up the integration of deep learning techniques is to collect and clean up data from 5G wireless communication networks, since there are not many data sets available for researchers to develop and test their models. In order to create systems that can produce data sets, efforts in this direction are extremely important.

Conclusions

Wireless 5G and AI-enabled communication/networking is a promising convergence that can enable the B5G systems to meet their performance expectations and provide the knowledge, reliability, and versatility needed to handle the scare radio resource well and provide consumers with a high quality of service for wireless networks. Further efforts are still required to achieve an efficient and functional integration in the field, reducing the sophistication of deep learning and democratizing the complexity of AI so that it can be deployed and integrated in time-sensitive networks and low-power devices, like the ones that 5G and B5G is envisaged, supporting practical scenarios and use cases of the vertical industries.

Acknowledgment

This work has been partially funded by the EU H2020/5G-PPP EVOLVED-5G Project (grant no. 101016608).

References

[1] M. E. MorochoCayamcela and W. Lim. "Artificial Intelligence in 5G Technology: A Survey." In *2018 International Conference on Information and Communication Technology Convergence (ICTC)*, Jeju (2018): 860–865. 10.1109/ICTC.2018. 8539642.
[2] X. You, C. Zhang, X. Tan, S. Jin, and H. Wu. "AI for 5G: Research Directions and Paradigms." arXiv:1807.08671
[3] R. Li, Z. Zhao, X. Zhou, G. Ding, Y. Chen, Z. Wang, and H. Zhang. "Intelligent 5G: When Cellular Networks Meet Artificial Intelligence." *IEEE Wireless Communications* 24, no. 5 (October 2017): 175–183. 10.1109/MWC.2017. 1600304WC.
[4] https://www.itu.int/en/ITU-T/focusgroups/ml5g/Pages/default.aspx, accessed 21/ 1/2021
[5] https://www.etsi.org/technologies/experiential-networked-intelligence, accessed 21/ 1/2021

[6] Q. Mao, F. Hu, and Q. Hao. "Deep Learning for Intelligent Wireless Networks: A Comprehensive Survey." *IEEE Communications Surveys & Tutorials* 20, no. 4 (Fourthquarter 2018): 2595–2621. 10.1109/COMST.2018.2846401.

[7] V. P. Kafle, Y. Fukushima, P. Martinez-Julia, and T. Miyazawa. "Consideration On Automation of 5G Network Slicing with Machine Learning." In *2018 ITU Kaleidoscope: Machine Learning for a 5G Future (ITU K)*, Santa Fe (2018): 1–8. 10.23919/ITU-WT.2018.8597639.

[8] X. Shen et al. "AI-Assisted Network-Slicing Based Next-Generation Wireless Networks." In *IEEE Open Journal of Vehicular Technology* 1 (2020): 45–66. 10. 1109/OJVT.2020.2965100.

[9] T. A. Khan, A. Mehmood, J. J. Diaz Ravera, A. Muhammad, K. Abbas, and W. Song. "Intent-Based Orchestration of Network Slices and Resource Assurance using Machine Learning." In *NOMS 2020 - 2020 IEEE/IFIP Network Operations and Management Symposium*, Budapest, Hungary (2020): 1–2. 10.1109/NOMS47738. 2020.9110408.

[10] H. Chergui and C. Verikoukis. "Big Data for 5G Intelligent Network Slicing Management." *IEEE Network* 34, no. 4 (July/August 2020): 56–61. 10.1109/ MNET.011.1900437.

[11] Y. Cui, X. Huang, D. Wu, and H. Zheng. "Machine Learning based Resource Allocation Strategy for Network Slicing in Vehicular Networks." In *2020 IEEE/ CIC International Conference on Communications in China (ICCC)*, Chongqing, China (2020): 454–459. 10.1109/ICCC49849.2020.9238991.

[12] R. K. Gupta and R. Misra. "Machine Learning-based Slice allocation Algorithms in 5G Networks." In *2019 International Conference on Advances in Computing, Communication and Control (ICAC3)*, Mumbai, India (2019): 1–4. 10.1109/ ICAC347590.2019.9036741.

[13] A. Thantharate, R. Paropkari, V. Walunj, and C. Beard. "DeepSlice: A Deep Learning Approach towards an Efficient and Reliable Network Slicing in 5G Networks." In *2019 IEEE 10th Annual Ubiquitous Computing, Electronics & Mobile Communication Conference (UEMCON)*, New York City, NY, USA (2019): 0762–0767. 10.1109/UEMCON47517.2019.8993066.

[14] D. Bega, M. Gramaglia, M. Fiore, A. Banchs, and X. Costa-Perez. "DeepCog: Cognitive Network Management in Sliced 5G Networks with Deep Learning." In *IEEE INFOCOM 2019 - IEEE Conference on Computer Communications*, Paris, France (2019): 280–288. 10.1109/INFOCOM.2019.8737488.

[15] C. Song, et al. "Machine Learning Enabling Traffic-Aware Dynamic Slicing for 5G Optical Transport Networks," In *2018 Conference on Lasers and Electro-Optics (CLEO)*, San Jose, CA (2018): 1–2

[16] Y. Abiko, T. Saito, D. Ikeda, K. Ohta, T. Mizuno, and H. Mineno. "Flexible Resource Block Allocation to Multiple Slices for Radio Access Network Slicing Using Deep Reinforcement Learning." *IEEE Access* 8 (2020): 68183–68198. 10.1109/ACCESS.2020.2986050.

[17] Y. Hua, R. Li, Z. Zhao, X. Chen, and H. Zhang. "GAN-Powered Deep Distributional Reinforcement Learning for Resource Management in Network Slicing." *IEEE Journal on Selected Areas in Communications* 38, no. 2 (Feb. 2020): 334–349. 10.1109/JSAC.2019.2959185.

[18] H. Xiang, M. Peng, Y. Sun, and S. Yan. "Mode Selection and Resource Allocation in Sliced Fog Radio Access Networks: A Reinforcement Learning Approach."

IEEE Transactions on Vehicular Technology 69, no. 4 (April 2020): 4271–4284. 10.1109/TVT.2020.2972999.

[19] H. Wang, Y. Wu, G. Min, J. Xu, P. Tang. "Data-driven Dynamic Resource Scheduling for Network Slicing: A Deep Reinforcement Learning Approach." *Information Sciences* 498 (2019): 106–116, ISSN 0020-0255, 10.1016/j.ins.2019. 05.012.

[20] M. Iannelli, M. R. Rahman, N. Choi, and L. Wang, "Applying Machine Learning to End-to-end Slice SLA Decomposition." In *2020 6th IEEE Conference on Network Softwarization (NetSoft)*, Ghent, Belgium, 2020, pp. 92–99, 10.1109/ NetSoft48620.2020.9165317.

[21] B. Khodapanah, A. Awada, I. Viering, A. N. Barreto, M. Simsek, and G. Fettweis. "Slice Management in Radio Access Network via Deep Reinforcement Learning." In *2020 IEEE 91st Vehicular Technology Conference (VTC2020-Spring)*, Antwerp, Belgium (2020): 1–6. 10.1109/VTC2020-Spring48590.2020.9128982.

[22] M. Toscano, F. Grunwald, M. Richart, J. Baliosian, E. Grampín, and A. Castro. "Machine Learning Aided Network Slicing." In *2019 21st International Conference on Transparent Optical Networks (ICTON)*, Angers, France (2019): 1–4. 10.1109/ ICTON.2019.8840141.

[23] R. Alvizu, S. Troia, G. Maier, and A. Pattavina. "Machine-Learning-Based Prediction and Optimization of Mobile Metro-Core Networks." In *2018 IEEE Photonics Society Summer Topical Meeting Series (SUM)*, Waikoloa Village, HI (2018): 155–156. 10.1109/PHOSST.2018.8456750.

[24] C. Natalino, M. R. Raza, A. Rostami, P. Öhlen, L. Wosinska, and P. Monti. "Machine Learning Aided Orchestration in Multi-tenant Networks." In *2018 IEEE Photonics Society Summer Topical Meeting Series (SUM)*, Waikoloa Village, HI (2018): 125–126. 10.1109/PHOSST.2018.8456735.

[25] L. Le, B. P. Lin, L. Tung, and D. Sinh. "SDN/NFV, Machine Learning, and Big Data Driven Network Slicing for 5G." In *2018 IEEE 5G World Forum (5GWF)*, Silicon Valley, CA (2018): 20–25. 10.1109/5GWF.2018.8516953.

[26] Michail-Alexandros Kourtis, Themis Anagnostopoulos, SławomirKukliński, MichałWierzbicki, Andreas Oikonomakis, George Xilouris, Ioannis P. Chochliouros, Na Yi, Alexandros Kostopoulos, Lechosław Tomaszewski, ThanosSarlas, HarilaosKoumaras," 5G Network Slicing Enabling Edge Services", Third International Workshop of Mobility Support in Slice-based Network Control for Heterogeneous Environments, IEEE NFV-SDN 2020 – VI IEEE Conference on Network Function Virtualization and Software Defined Networks, 9th November 2020, Madrid, Spain.

[27] H. Koumaras, D. Tsolkas, G. Gardikis, P. Merino, V. Frascolla, D. Triantafyllopoulou, M. Emmelmann, V. Koumaras, M. G. Osma, D. Munaretto, E. Atxutegi, J. S. de Puga, O. Alay, A. Brunstrom, and A.-M. C. Bosneag. "5GENESIS: The Genesis of a flexible 5G Facility." *IEEE 23rd International Workshop on Computer Aided Modeling and Design of Communication Links and Networks (CAMAD)*, Barcelona, Spain, (17-19 September 2018).

[28] V. Riccobene, M. J. McGrath, M. A. Kourtis, G. Xilouris, H. Koumaras. "Automated generation of VNF deployment rules using infrastructure affinity characterization." In *2016 IEEE NetSoft Conference and Workshops (NetSoft)*, 226–233.

[29] A. D. Zayas, G. Caso, Ö. Alay, P. Merino, A. Brunstrom, D. Tsolkas, and H. Koumaras. "A Modular Experimentation Methodology for 5G Deployments: The 5GENESIS Approach." *Sensors International Journal* 20, no. 22 (Year: 2020): 6652. 10.3390/s20226652

[30] P. S. Khodashenas, B. Blanco, M.-A. Kourtis, I. Taboada, G. Xilouris, I. Giannoulakis, E. Jimeno, I. Trajkovska, J. O. Fajardo, E. Kafetzakis, J. García, F. Liberal, A. Whitehead, M. Wilson, and H. Koumaras. "Service Mapping and Orchestration over Multi-Tenant Cloud-Enabled RAN." *IEEE Transactions on Network and Service Management* 14, no. 4 (Dec. 2017): 904–919. 10.1109/TNSM.2017.2767100.

[31] C. Gutterman, E. Grinshpun, S. Sharma, and G. Zussman. "Ran Resource Usage Prediction for a 5g slice broker," in *Proceedings of the Twentieth ACM International Symposium on Mobile Ad Hoc Networking and Computing.* (2019): 231–240, ACM.

[32] R. Ferrús, H. Koumaras, O. Sallent, G. Agapiou, T. Rasheed, M. A. Kourtis, C. Boustie, P. Gélard, and T. Ahmed. "SDN/NFV-enabled Satellite Communications Networks: Opportunities, Scenarios and Challenges", International journal Physical Communication, Elsevier, accepted for publication. 10.1016/j.phycom.2015.10.007

[33] I. Tomkos, D. Klonidis, E. Pikasis, and S. Theodoridis. "Toward the 6G Network Era: Opportunities and Challenges." *IT Professional* 22, no. 1 (1 Jan.-Feb. 2020): 34–38. 10.1109/MITP.2019.2963491.

[34] S. Yrjölä, P. Ahokangas, M. Matinmikko-Blue, R. Jurva, V. Kant, P. Karppinen, M. Kinnula, H. Koumaras, M. Rantakokko, V. Ziegler, A. Thakur, and H.-J. Zepernick. "White Paper on Business of 6G", 6G Flagship White Paper 2020, arXiv:2005.06400

[35] M.-A. Kourtis, H. Koumaras, G. Xilouris, and F. Liberal. "An NFV-based Video Quality Assessment Method over 5G Small Cell Networks." *IEEE MultiMedia* PP, no. 1 (2017): 1.

[36] X. Zhu, H. Koumaras, M. Wang, and D. Hausheer. "Network Function Virtualization and Software-Defined Networking: Advancing Multimedia Distribution." *IEEE MultiMedia* 24, no. 3 (2017): 16–18.

[37] X. Zhu, H. Koumaras, M. Wang, and D. Hausheer. "The Future of Multimedia Distribution: An Interview with Baochun Li, Diego R. Lopez, and Christian Timmerer." *IEEE MultiMedia* 24, no. 3 (2017): 48–53.

[38] F. Alvarez, D. Breitgand, D. Griffin, P. Andriani, S. Rizou, N. Zioulis, F. Moscatelli, J. Serrano, M. Keltsch, P. Trakadas, T. K. Phan, A. Weit, U. Acar, O. Prieto, F. Iadanza, G. Carrozzo, H. Koumaras, D. Zarpalas, and D. Jimenez. "An Edge-to-Cloud Virtualized Multimedia Service Platform for 5G Networks." *IEEE Transactions on Broadcasting* 65, no. 2 (2019): 369–380.

[39] N. Jawad, M. Salih, K. Ali, B. Meunier, Y. Zhang, X. Zhang, and R. Zetik, CharilaosZarakovitis, HarilaosKoumaras, Michail-Alexandros Kourtis, Lina Shi, Wojciech Mazurczyk, John Cosmas, "Smart Television Services Using NFV/SDN Network Management." *IEEE Transactions on Broadcasting* 65, no. 2 (2019): 404–413.

[40] H. Koumaras, C. Sakkas, M. A. Kourtis, C. Xilouris, V. Koumaras, G. Gardikis. "Enabling Agile Video Transcoding over SDN/NFV-enabled Networks," In *Proc.*

IEEE Telecommunications and Multimedia Conference 2016 (July 25–27 2016), Heraklion, Greece.

[41] H. Koumaras, M.-A. Kourtis, C. Sakkas, G. Xilouris, and S. Kolometsos. "In-service Video Quality Assessment based on SDN/NFV Techniques," In *Proc. 23rd IEEE International Conference on Telecommunications* (16–18 May 2016), Thessaloniki, Greece.

[42] F. Liberal, M. Ramos, J. O. Fajardo, N. Goia, A. Bizkarguenaga, I. Mesogiti, E. Theodoropoulou, H. Koumaras, L. Sun, N. Clarke, and F. Li. "User Requirements for Future Wideband Critical Communications." In *Proc of Fifth International Conference on Internet Technologies and Applications (2013) – International Workshop on Emergency Telecommunications Systems (ETS 2013)*, (10 – 13 September 2013). Wrexham, North Wales, UK.

[43] Y. Arjoune and S. Faruque. "Artificial Intelligence for 5G Wireless Systems: Opportunities, Challenges, and Future Research Direction." In *2020 10th Annual Computing and Communication Workshop and Conference (CCWC)*, Las Vegas, NV, USA, (2020): 1023–1028. 10.1109/CCWC47524.2020.9031117.

[44] R. I. Minu and G. Nagarajan. "Bridging the IoT Gap Through Edge Computing." In *Edge Computing and Computational Intelligence Paradigms for the IoT*, pp. 1–9. IGI Global, 2019.

[45] G. Nagarajan, R. I. Minu, and A. Jayanthiladevi. "Cognitive Internet of Things (C-IOT)." In *Sensing Techniques for Next Generation Cognitive Radio Networks*, pp. 299–311. IGI Global, 2019.

[46] S. V. Simpson and G. Nagarajan. "An Edge Based Trustworthy Environment Establishment for Internet of Things: An Approach for Smart Cities." Wireless Networks (2021): 1–17.

Chapter 5

An Application-Oriented Study of Security Threats and Countermeasures in Edge Computing–Assisted Internet of Things

G. Nagarajan
Sathyabama Institute of Science and Technology, Chennai, India

S.V. Simpson
Thejus Engineering College, Thrissur, Kerala, India

T. Sasikala
Sathyabama Institute of Science and Technology, Chennai, India

Contents

DOI: 10.1201/9781003145158-5

Introduction

The deployment of Internet of Things (IoT)–enabled devices at the bottom layer of the traditional network made a drastic change in our living environment. Many applications have been emerged to support the connectivity among the IoT devices. Mostly resource-limited IoT devices will be deployed due to economical considerations. Thus, all such devices require additional resource support for performing the computations. Cloud computing has been introduced for providing the storage space and the computation support. The cloud server will gather the data from the IoT devices and all such data will be processed with the help of several algorithms at the cloud layer. The cloud can respond to the service requests coming from the bottom layer of the network. Most of the applications work efficiently with a cloud server, except for the real-time applications that require quick responses. The cloud server will be placed at a remote location and the communications will be established through the networks. The cloud server can process the data quickly, but the round-trip time between the IoT devices and the cloud server will be high [1].

Figure 5.1 represents the architecture of cloud computing. The architecture of the cloud consists of storage space, controlling/managing units, and connected applications.

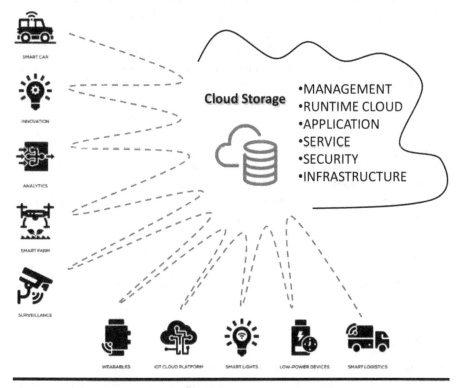

Figure 5.1 Cloud Computing Architecture.

Even a single connected IoT device will produce a large amount of data. The time required to process the generated data is called latency. In cloud computing, all the generated data have to be reached at a remotely placed cloud server. The overall latency of cloud-based data processing will be high due to the increased round-trip time between the bottom-layer IoT devices and the cloud server. Thus, the cloud server cannot offer a latency-free service to the real-time applications. Also, the bandwidth utilization will also be high due to the large volume of data. The service providing unit/server must be always available to the connected IoT devices. The applications like "voice command recognition" require immediate response from the cloud server. The cloud server works in a centralized fashion. All the connected IoT devices will be served by a single cloud server unit. Thus, the cloud server cannot ensure the availability to all the connected devices. The cloud server may experience a bottleneck effect due to the centralized architecture. All the requests have to be processed only at a cloud server. Thus, the cloud server may experience excess energy consumption. High variation in the transmission time of individual packets (called jitter) may also be experienced in cloud computing due to several reasons [2].

Edge computing has been introduced to overcome issues associated with the traditional cloud computing approach. Several edge nodes will be deployed at the edge of the network. Edge nodes can provide a cloud independent service to the connected IoT devices. All IoT devices will have at least one edge device in their range. The edge-based data processing will reduce the latency in the network [3]. Since the data need not be sent to the cloud server, the overall bandwidth utilization can be reduced. Rather than processing the request in a centralized manner, the edge nodes can accomplish the tasks in a distributive manner. The distributive approach removes the bottleneck effect and reduces the energy utilization of a single device. The edge-based processing can reduce the jitter. The edge nodes can serve the real-time applications in a more effective manner. The introduction of edge computing has initiated a new era of IoT technology. Several applications have emerged depending upon the computation efficiency of the edge nodes. The increased acceptance also increased the security threats in IoT networks [4].

This chapter is organized in the following manner: the next section categorizes the edge computing scenarios. The wide range of IoT applications and the application-specific security issues have been discussed in Section 3. The various security attacks and the available countermeasures for the edge-based IoT networks have been discussed in Section 4. Section 5 gives an overview of open research challenges in edge computing. Section 6 summarizes the chapter and discusses the future scope of edge computing.

Edge Paradigms

The three-layer architecture of edge computing is shown in Figure 5.2. The IoT network will interact with the physical world through the initial layer. The IoT

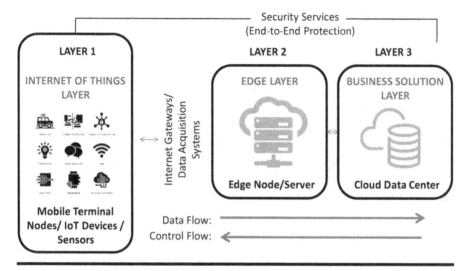

Figure 5.2 The Three-Layer Architecture of Edge Computing.

devices will be directly connected to layer 1. The sensed data will be collected by a data acquisition system. The service requests will be processed at the edge layer. A detailed report may be sent to the cloud server after processing the service requests. The cloud layer is responsible for controlling all the network-related activities inside the IoT network. The sensed data will be stored at a cloud server. Thus, the cloud server holds intelligent data-retrieving algorithms. Only the real-time data will be processed at edge nodes. Analysis on previous data will be handled by a cloud server.

The edge-based approaches can be classified into mobile cloud computing, fog computing, and mobile edge computing. All of these approaches can be differentiated based on their execution strategy.

Mobile Cloud Computing

Mobile cloud computing is the first edge-based enhancement that has been applied over the traditional cloud-based computing. The IoT devices will be served from either a cloudlet or from a cluster of cloudlets. The cloudlet is a tiny device that can be placed at the edge of the network. It can be placed either at a coffee shop or at company premises where the IoT devices require the services. A group of such cloudlets can be joined together to form a cluster. Such a cluster can establish a distributed environment for processing the service requests. All of the available resources of cloudlets in the cluster can be utilized to perform the computations. Such a cluster can also act as an edge server. Since the cloudlets are tiny in size, the cluster will have only a low resource capacity. Thus, the mobile cloud computing cannot offer a cloud independent service to the modern IoT environments [5–7].

Fog Computing

Fog computing has been introduced to provide the storage space and resource support. We cannot consider the fog nodes as a replacement for a cloud server. Fog nodes can provide only some additional support to the cloud server. The service requests that have global perspectives have to be executed only at the cloud server. The fog nodes can offer local application support. It will support local computations. Thus, the functionalities of a traditional cloud sever will remain the same in fog-based computations. The local IoT applications can make use of fog nodes to get hassle-free services [8–10].

Mobile Edge Computing

Mobile edge computing has been introduced as an optimal solution to the issues present in traditional cloud computing. The edge nodes are equally capable of performing all the computations that have been previously executed at the cloud servers. Mobile edge computing can offer truly cloud-independent services to the connected IoT devices. A detailed report may be sent to the cloud server. This will reduce the bandwidth utilization, increase the availability, remove the jitter, provide quick response, offer latency free service, and decrease the energy consumption. The security algorithms can also be integrated at cloud servers. The edge-based execution of security algorithms will enhance the efficiency of intrusion detection systems. The mobile service providers are responsible for deploying the edge nodes in the network. The deployed edge nodes can offer the services to the IoT devices present in their range [11–13].

Applications of Edge Paradigms

Edge computing supports several real-time applications, which include applications for smart city environment, industrial applications, applications for real-time road transport, healthcare applications, time-critical applications, applications for disaster management, applications for live data analytics, societal applications, etc. Each environment demands different privacy policies and security considerations. The following section discusses the security requirements and vulnerabilities of different edge-based environments. The organization of Section 3 is illustrated in Figure 5.3.

Smart City

A smart city is the most advanced step towards an Internet of Everything era. A smart city includes all the major areas of living environment. The applications in the smart city environment have heterogeneous nature. They differ in the cases of

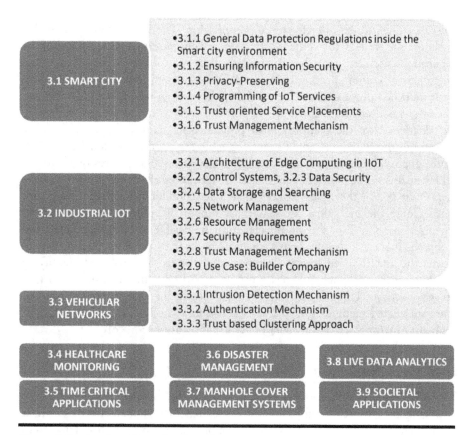

Figure 5.3 Section Organization.

security, privacy, data distribution, response time, etc. It is very important to ensure the compatibility of all the individual applications for the smooth development of smart environment. The roles of edge paradigms are highly significant in a smart city environment. Edge paradigms can better serve the applications that demand real-time support. Also, they are used to ensure the security and privacy needs of individual applications.

General Data Protection Regulations inside the Smart City Environment

The smart city environment will provide some basic services to the underlying applications. The general data protection regulations include all such mandatory requirements [14]. The smart city environment must be capable of supporting heterogeneous IoT devices, IoT brokers, and edge devices. All such devices must be discovered easily by using a device ID, sensor ID, or geo-information. Each device must be authenticated prior to the communication. The application must be able to choose the strategy for authenticating the communicating entities. Most of the applications use secure key-based authentication approaches to ensure the trustworthiness of communicating entities. All the entities in the smart city environment must be informed about the security policies of an established environment. The edge-based environment must support the application developers to manage the security. Also, the platform must provide open hardware and open-source software to the individual applications for achieving an unconditional growth. It must support different data types and the data access must be restricted to the deliberate users. The policies about data sharing must be clear and transparent. The users must get all the rights to keep their data confidentially. Rather than supporting only the individual users, it must support a group of users as well as organizations. The data-sharing policies must be flexible to both individuals and groups of users. All the personal data must be kept in the encrypted format to restrict the unauthorized access. The environment must be capable of identifying the data breach. All such findings must be shared with the data owner to take necessary actions. Upon identifying the data breach, the system must implement some automated methods to avoid such situations. The level of security must be defined to incorporate various data policies and security protocols.

Ensuring Information Security

The information security has been ensured by using the encryption approaches. The cryptographic approaches can be applied at the higher layers of a network model. It can prevent the data leakage by using public-private key mechanisms. Time complexity and operational complexity are the major drawbacks of cryptographic approaches. Also, it utilizes a large quantity of available resources for encryption, decryption, and key exchange. An intruder can attack the smart city network by utilizing the security breaches of an applied crypto system. As a solution to these problems, D. Wang et al. [15] proposed a secure approach, which can be applied at the bottom layer of the network model. The physical layer encounters several security attacks that include eavesdropping, node capturing, replay attacks, spoofing attacks, malicious code injection attacks, cryptanalysis attacks, side channel attacks, etc. In order to prevent all these attacks, the proposed method uses six security approaches. Secure wiretap coding is used to increase the predictability of data. Thus, the intruder cannot perform an eavesdropping attack. The proposed method could improve the resource efficiency by performing better resource allocation. Secure signal processing helps to increase the secrecy rate of the transmitted information. A multi-node cooperation approach is used to strengthen the signals emerging from legitimate nodes. The proposed method increases the information security by implementing physical layer key generation and authentication, but it increases the key generation overhead. The proposed method sometimes encounters security breaches due to the dynamic and heterogeneous nature of the network. In order to ensure the security in such cases, the proposed method tries to integrate the physical layer and upper layer authentication, which in turn increase the operational overhead of the smart city environment. But, the proposed method could overcome the limitations of traditional upper layer cryptographic approaches. It could work better with the energy-limited devices and low-cost networks.

Preserving Privacy

The smart city environment is a summation of several applications that help to uplift the lifestyle of the residents. Some applications in a smart city environment handle highly sensitive data. Thus, the data privacy must be ensured by creating some privacy policies. The private data can be classified into three categories: personal data, sensitive data, and identifiers. The personal data is something an individual wishes to keep confidential due to various reasons. The sensitive information needs to be kept confidential based on the worst impact that may be encountered due to a data leakage. Identifiers are the identifying elements of individual or group entities present in the smart city environment. All such private data needs to be handled based on some privacy policies. The privacy policies can be designed only by considering the nature of applications. The privacy policy assigned to a static entity cannot be reused for a dynamic entity. But, the reusability of privacy policies for similar type of applications needs to be kept in mind while designing the privacy policies. The privacy policy will be designed in two levels: IoT end device level and network level. The policy variations based on the individual needs cannot be entertained in a network level. Thus, the policies must be adaptable to all the entities in the network. Since the network is heterogeneous in nature, the policy generation will be a highly complex task. M. Gheisari et al. [16] designed a privacy policy for a smart city environment that can ensure the privacy of all the end devices. The proposed policy is a unified policy generation for all the dynamic as well as static entities. It is mandatory to achieve a common understating about privacy policies among the network entities. The policies have been designed to reuse the same when an entity switches to dynamic state from static state and backwards. It needs to consider the following while designing the privacy policy for the smart city environment, device type, device location, software architecture, context awareness, proximity, access mechanisms, access privileges, and inter-node communication pattern. Each individual IoT device will have an individual device level privacy policy. The privacy policy of a system must be compatible to the individual policies of heterogeneous end devices.

Programming of IoT Services

The programming of IoT services over cloud and edge nodes are required for performing various actions in the smart city environment. The developers can alter the programming code based on the user requirements [17]. The need for such service-level programming can be elaborated on with the help of some use cases. The anomaly detection in real-time systems can be considered as a use case. Anomaly detection will be deployed as an IoT service at an edge node. Various analyses will be carried out on data and service execution patterns to detect the anomalies present in the network. The cloud server will be notified whenever the edge node detects anomalies. The edge-based mechanism for identifying the overutilization of energy can be considered as another example for IoT service programming. An edge node will be placed at each monitoring location for finding the residual energy. The estimation of the difference with previous data will result in the amount of utilized energy over a particular time period. The large deviation from an average value indicates the overutilization. All such analysis can be done at edge nodes with the help of service-level programming.

Trust-Oriented Service Placements

All the required functionalities of IoT applications can be achieved by placing the appropriate IoT services at edge nodes. Since all the data in a smart city environment is accessible to such IoT services, the IoT services must be placed in a secure environment [18]. The service placement will be done for accomplishing the various real-time needs of end users, which include video surveillance in stadiums, user interface for displaying the results from environmental monitoring system, etc. The environmental monitoring system includes several sensing process. Crowd sensing, air pollution sensing, traffic signal monitoring, etc. can be considered as the subsystems of environmental monitoring systems. Service placements have to be done at edge nodes for all those individual subsystems. More than one IoT service placement may be required for each subsystem based on the requirements. The IoT services can be classified into: feedback-based assessments and result-based assessments. In order to get some required data, some applications may require previous results. Such feedback-based services may use some machine learning approaches to train the system. The result-based assessments depend only on the obtained values. Edge nodes are responsible for providing a secure environment to process the service requests. Some intelligent algorithms need to be incorporated at the edge nodes for maintaining the trust level.

Trust Management Mechanism

The smart city environment is always vulnerable to security attacks due to its heterogeneous nature. The trustworthiness of each entity needs to be ensured by the edge nodes. B. Wang et al. [19] implemented a reliable edge-based trust management mechanism in a smart city environment. The work has been carried out to eliminate a set of attacks, which include bad-mouthing attacks, good-mouthing attacks, ballot-stuffing attacks, and selective behavior attacks. In a bad-mouthing attack, the attacking node will contribute false trust information about a targeted legitimate node. In a good-mouthing attack, the attacker supports malicious nodes by providing good ratings and trust assurance. In some cases, malicious nodes contribute accurate trust evaluations about their neighboring nodes. Based on their good behavior, such nodes will be selected as service providers. At this juncture, the malicious nodes will provide invalid services to other nodes. This type of attack is known as a ballot-stuffing attack. The selective behavior attack is a type of ballot-stuffing attack, where the malicious nodes may selectively provide good services to some users. This approach will increase the ratings of such nodes and such malicious nodes can continue in the network for a long time. The proposed method has a trust relation-based approach to defend against all the above-mentioned attacks. It possesses a list-based mechanism to eliminate the presence of malicious nodes. Initially it analyzes the trust relationship between the end users. Afterwards, it examines the trust relationship between the edge service providers and end users. Based on the findings, it defines an edge-based trust model for identifying the presence of malicious nodes. Edge nodes will collect all the required values from the connected end devices for computing the trust value. Since all the computations have been carried out at the edge node, the operational overload for computing the trust values will not be shared with resource-limited end devices.

Industrial IOT

Industrial Internet of Things (IIoT) is the most significant research field that can directly influence the global economy. IIoT connects all the equipments in the industry through the network. The introduction of IoT to the industry could reduce the decision-making latency. Also, the introduction of edge computing could reduce the bandwidth utilization. The Industrial IoT network may be implemented for more than one industry. Each industry will have different privacy policies and private data. The cloud-based execution increases the risk of information leakage. The edge-based execution resolves this issue and provides more data privacy. The edge nodes will be placed exclusively for one industry. Thus, the chances of data sharing will be less.

Architecture of Edge Computing in IIoT

The architecture of IIoT consists of three layers: cloud application layer, edge layer, and device layer [20]. The cloud application layer controls the activities of the IIoT network. The overall application design, application management, and services will be directly performed at the cloud application layer. The cloud layer handles a big amount of data. Mostly the cloud servers will be connected to the edge nodes with wired connections. The edge layer consists of three sections: edge server, edge gateway, and edge controller. Operational control, platform management, and data processing are the responsibilities of an edge server. The edge server level operations are categorized into three categories: instruction transmission, communication management, and access authorization. In order to process the data, the edge server will do some non-sequential processes that include modeling tools, data aggregation, data analysis, heterogeneous computing, and cloud edge collaboration. The edge gateway is responsible for management, data storage, and computation. The management module performs equipment registration, communication management, and access authorization. The data storage module monitors data aggregation, cashing at edge node, and the preprocessing of data. The computation module is responsible for log management, edge intelligence enhancement, and data analysis. The edge controller unit will act as an interface between the edge layer and device layer. The edge controller unit will perform required protocol conversions. The edge layer will accept the sensed data from the device layer. Also, the edge layer will pass the control information to the device layer with the help of edge controller unit. The device layer entities will be connected to the edge layer in a wireless mode. Thus, it could support the mobility of industrial equipments. The device layer entities can be classified into four categories: industrial equipments, machines, instruments, and sensors. All such devices must be connected to at least one edge node. Thus, a sufficient number of edge nodes need to be deployed at the edge of the network to serve the device-layer entities.

Control Systems

The industrial control system utilizes the network capabilities to control the entities in the industrial environment. It requires extra computer power, storage space, and software support. Most of the control systems in industrial environment will have unique protocols. Thus, the inter-connectivity among the control systems are not always possible. The control systems will have connectivity with Internet. The managers and employees can access and control the network components from anywhere in the world. Since the protocols used in industrial control systems are more advanced than the traditional protocols, it requires an additional infrastructure support. To address these issues, M. W. Condry et al. [21] introduced a gateway centric control system for industrial IoT. The gateway centric system helps to establish the connectivity among different control systems. The gateway has been designed to act as an interface between different protocol layers of industrial control systems. The proposed method enables the possibilities of accessing the control systems even from a remotely places client machine. But, based on the nature of control devices, different types of gateways have to be deployed in the network. Thus, it became a hurdle to define uniform gateway architecture for industrial control systems. In order to design uniform architecture, the gateways have been connected to Infrastructure as a service provider in the cloud. The cloud platform could provide necessary storage space, computational support, and application programming interface. Also a cloud can act as a bridge between the user and the gateways. Thus, the developers could design three-tier control architecture for industrial IoT that includes user space, cloud, and gateways. After receiving the service requests from the users, the cloud server will check the access rights and pass the requests to the control systems through the gateways. In order to reduce the network cost, it is possible to bypass the cloud servers and sometimes the client devices will establish direct connection with the gateways.

Data Security

The operation strategies of an industry have to be kept confidential. The interactions with other industries were minimal in the traditional way of industrial communications. But, the cloud-based industrial Internet of Things increased the need and chances for inter-industrial communications. That in turn increased the chances of being vulnerable to security attacks. Most of the data handled in an industrial environment will be highly confidential. Thus, the data leakage has to be prevented effectively. W. Wang et al. [22] utilized the existing public-key encryption with keyword search mechanism to prevent the data leakage at cloud layer. In order to enhance the efficiency of the searching process the proposed framework introduced an edge-based approach. The edge-based execution reduced the latency experienced at cloud layer. The proposed cryptographic approach has been applied over the traditional cloud-based architecture. The architecture consists of data managers, cloud platform, edge platform, and IIoT devices. The data manager will generate a set of public-private key pair for each IIoT device. The generated public key will be shared with the IIoT device. The IIoT device will generate another set of public-private key pairs based on the received public key. The newly generated public key will be shared with connected edge node. The IIoT devices will encrypt the messages to generate the searchable cipher texts. The searching framework has been designed using cryptographic algorithm which utilizes the private key kept at the data manager, newly generated public key, and a search trapdoor. The involvement of a cloud server has been limited only to the setup phase. All the remaining functionalities of the framework will be directly handled by the connected edge nodes. The public-private key-based encryption provides data security to the industrial IoT network. It successfully prevents the data leakage and helps to work according to the privacy policies of different IIoT devices.

Data Storage and Searching

The industrial environment produces a bulk amount of data. It is highly important to organize the data to make it easier to retrieve. It is not possible to store the generated data in the end devices. Mostly the end devices will be resource limited devices. The generated data will be stored in the cloud servers. Some applications may require real time support. Such applications will be served by the edge nodes. Thus, it needs to have a minimum amount of storage capacity at edge devices. The edge devices will keep only the time-sensitive data and such data will be discarded when the edge node completes the computations. A copy of the raw data and the processed outcomes will be saved on cloud storage for future use. The data will be stored in the cloud with proper indexing. Most of the applications demand latency-free fast computations. Thus, the amount of time required to retrieve the data must be minimal [23].

Network Management

The industrial Internet of Things environment consists of dynamic communication controllers, gateway interfaces, and edge devices. The edge devices need sophisticated software and sensing capacity for dealing with mission-critical environments. The network designed for the industrial environment can be classified into data accusation networks, data processing network, and overall control network. The data accusation network is responsible for collecting the sensed data from the end devices. The collected data will be sent to edge servers for data processing. The data processing network will take the processed data/outcome from the edge devices and the actions will be carried out according to the outcome. The overall control network can be divided into cloud-based global controlling and the edge-based local controlling. The entire network-related control will be done directly by the cloud servers. The device-specific management will be done by the edge node. All of these networks encounter several security attacks. U. Tariq et al. [24] contributed an autonomous network management system for removing the security threats from the industrial environment. The autonomous network management offers fully automated IoT application monitoring, data-dependent device monitoring, and efficient content-filtering options. The proposed network management system has been specially designed for end point protection. It could successfully prevent data breaches, malware attacks, and denial of service attacks.

Resource Management

The increased acceptance of industrial IoT also increased the vulnerabilities of industrial environments. In order to secure the industrial platforms, several secure algorithms need to be executed in all layers of industrial Internet of Things. The cloud and edge devices are specially designed for executing the complex algorithms. But, the end device layer will always be supplied with resource limited IoT devices due to economical considerations. Such devices are not efficient enough to execute security-related algorithms. In order to avoid the risk factors present in the bottom layer, some parts of the secure algorithms require execution support from the end devices. Such tiny portions of software need to be executed at the bottom layer for collecting the security-related data directly from the end devices. Thus, the resource management at the bottom layer is a critical task in industrial environment. The improper resource allocation may create resource unavailability at the bottom layer. The complex secure algorithms placed at the upper layers of the industrial Internet of Things architecture could identify the security breaches based only on the individual contributions from the IoT devices that have been placed at the bottom layer. In order to identify the security breaches present in the industrial environment, K. A. Abuhasel et al. [25] used an enhanced version of existing Rivest-Shamir-Adelman (RSA) and hash signatures. The proper identification of security threats increased the availability of end devices. That in turn increased the efficiency of security algorithms placed at the upper layers of industrial Internet of Things architecture.

Security Requirements

The industrial Internet of Things demands some basic security requirements. The primary security goals of the network are confidentiality, integrity, and availability. The confidentiality includes data protection, data access control, privacy policy, and network isolation. The data must not have any alterations during the transmission time. In order to achieve the data integrity, the communicating entities will be authenticated by the network administrator. The service requests from the end devices must be served on time. All the required data and resources must be available to perform the tasks within the hard deadlines. Another important service requirement is authentication. The authentication of remotely placed entities cannot be performed easily. Also, the industrial Internet of Things demands a lightweight authentication algorithm to reduce the overall resource utilization. The lightweight algorithm can reduce the complexities involved with traditional authentication algorithms. Both data and the communicating entities must be authenticated before performing the tasks. Another major security-related task is key management. The network can choose either a symmetric or asymmetric key management system. In symmetric key management, a key must be shared between the clients and service providers. Rather than sharing a key through the communication medium, it is always advisable to use any key exchange algorithms that support medium independent key exchange. In the case of asymmetric key management system, the entities use public-private key pair to authenticate themselves. The same key pair can be used for data encryption. The public keys will be shared globally and the network needs to provide privacy only for private keys. Another aspect about security requirement is non-repudiation. In a trustworthy network, the sender is not allowed to deny their authorship about the message. It needs to be ensured by the network. The recipient is also not allowed to later repudiate the reception of a message [26].

Trust Management Mechanism

The attacks on industrial Internet of Things can be classified into internal and external attacks. The existing edge-based intrusion detection mechanisms can be applied for the trust management in industrial environment. Such mechanisms can successfully prevent external attacks, but the threats associated with an internal attack will remain in the network. The internal attacks will originate from the internal nodes. Since all the nodes in the network are authorized entities, the authentication mechanism fails to identify the malicious behavior of the internal nodes. It is not possible to integrate separate intelligent mechanisms to defend against all kinds of internal attacks. Thus, T. Wang et al. [27] put forward the idea of establishing a secure environment in an industrial Internet of Things environment to avoid internal attacks. The trustworthy environment establishment will increase the quality of service. The main goal is to identify the malicious service providers and malicious consumers in the network. The proposed method utilizes the capabilities of edge nodes for establishing a secure environment. In the trust evaluation phase, the method considers both old trust and new trust of both service consumers and service providers. The consumer trust and the service provider trust have been calculated independently. The final trust is a weighted sum of feedback trust and the present behavior. Based on the trust value, a local trust table will be created. The service selection will be carried out based on the values in a local trust table. The authors also contribute an efficient algorithm for service selection process. The trust-based service selection process reduces the chances of having internal attacks in an industrial Internet of Things network.

Use Case: Builder Company

In order to understand the importance of integrating an Internet of Things in an industrial environment, T. Kumar et al. [28] elaborated the impact of IoT in smart house construction. The smart house construction requires effort from various contractors and sub-contractors. The construction process needs a builder company to allocate the works to different contactors. The entire work can be subdivided and assigned to interior design contractor, raw material contractor, technology contractor, resource contactor, and log-house contractor. The authors explained the integration IoT in the works of a log-house contractor. The log-house contractor's works can be subdivided into wood harvesting, transportation, logs manufacturing, storage, and construction. The identification of trees and harvesting from a forest area will be handled by the wood-harvesting company. They need to harvest the woods secularly from the forest. They need to secure their labors form wild animal attacks and environmental threats. For this purpose, they need to use several sensors for observing the forest area and analyzing the weather conditions. The transportation of collected woods will be handled by the transportation company. The woods will be finally delivered to manufacturing company. The status update is required in each stage of the transportation. Each activity involved in this phase will be monitored by the transportation contractor through the network and the necessary update will be shared with the log-house contractor through the network. The manufacturing process requires several sensors, machines, and network support. The integration of an IoT network increases the overall performance of the manufacturing unit. A storage contractor needs to find storage spaces for manufactured wood logs and the stock details will be maintained with the help of an IoT network. The construction company is responsible for designing the final product and fitting. It requires several integrated edge-based applications to build the final product.

Vehicular Networks

Vehicular ad-hoc networks are one of the prime examples for an advanced Internet of Things network. It acts as an interface between vehicles and infrastructure. The vehicular ad-hoc network supports heterogeneous applications in different domains. In this section, the security threats and the countermeasures present in an IoT-based vehicular ad-hoc network have been discussed.

Intrusion Detection Mechanism

The vehicular network is the most critical application of Internet of Things. Most of the applications in a vehicular network are time-critical applications. Such applications need real-time responses from the service providers to perform next task. Only a small amount of delay cannot be tolerated in a vehicular network. As a solution to this problem, the edge-based service processing scenario has been adopted to the vehicular network. Thus, the network could provide services to the connected vehicles from the edge of the network. This technique reduced the latency-related risks involved in the cloud-based processing of service requests. With the help of the edge platform, the concept of a self-driving car could be taken to reality. Since the delay in service request could produce countless damage to the system, the attackers have huge interest in a vehicular network. A. Mourad et al. [29] proposed a heuristic-based intrusion detection mechanism for IoT-enabled vehicular networks. The detection method utilizes a vehicular resource-aware secure offloading algorithm to detect the presence of malicious entities. The paper proposes an edge-based solution to eliminate the threats in a vehicular network. In order to avoid the operational overload at vehicles, all the security-related commutations will be carried out at edge nodes with additional resource-level cloud support. Thus, the availability of local resources can be ensured for serving the dynamic needs.

Authentication Mechanism

All the members in the vehicular network must be authorized entities. In order to ensure the same, the vehicular network must have a good authentication framework.

Thus, an identity-based external attack cannot be performed by an intruder, but the internal compromised nodes can perform identity-based attacks by using forged legitimate identities. Z. Ali et al. [30] introduced a lightweight authentication mechanism for vehicular networks. The proposed authentication mechanism has a pre-deployment phase, registration phase, login phase, password-update phase, revocation phase, and addition phase. The initial enrolling phase is known as a pre-deployment phase. The user registration phase consists of password creation and certificate issuing processes. The login phase checks the password and username of the registered entities to grant privileged access to the network. The password update phase is a post-registration user service, where the user can change the password based on the security needs. The certificates issued to malicious nodes will be revoked permanently when their malicious behavior contributes damage to the network. Suspected malicious nodes will also be monitored and the certificates will be revoked once the edge node confirms their malicious behavior. The addition phase is a setup for including new nodes/vehicles to the network. The proposed authentication mechanism could eliminate both external as well as internal identity-based attacks.

Trust-Based Clustering Approach

All the registered vehicles in the network must have at least one edge node in their range. The vehicles will be clustered based on the connected edge node. All the inter-cluster communications will be carried out only through the connected edge nodes. K. A. Awan et al. [31] implemented a trust-based clustering mechanism for an IoT-enabled vehicular network. The trust value has been calculated based on some network parameters. It considers the node's present as well as past behavior to calculate the trust value. The clustering approach selects the most trustworthy node as the cluster head and the vehicles connected to the same edge node will be added to the same cluster as cluster members. If the vehicles have two edge nodes in their range, then one edge node will be selected based on the signal strength. The vehicles are allowed to perform intra-cluster communications without informing the connected edge nodes. The cluster head will check the malicious behavior of the cluster members and reports the same to the edge node. The edge node will send a request to the cloud server to revoke the certificate of identified malicious nodes. A stable clustering approach can enhance the service availability in a vehicular network.

Healthcare Monitoring

With the help of various sensors, IoT could make drastic changes in a healthcare monitoring system. The sensors will be deployed even at the home premises to monitor the patient health status. The sensors will monitor the heartbeat, blood pressure, temperature, etc. to predict the need of medical assistance. Upon identifying any issues, the healthcare monitoring system will pass the message to authorities to provide hospital care. The data handled in a healthcare monitoring system will be highly sensitive and such data needs to be kept confidential. The health status of a person is truly confidential. Thus, such systems need to follow some strict privacy policies. Since the healthcare monitoring system directly deals with the life of a person, the attacks on such systems need to be prevented in the early stage. G. S. Aujla et al. [32] introduced a blockchain-based secure approach for an IoT-enabled healthcare monitoring system. The system model defined by the authors includes a healthcare layer, edge layer, and cloud layer. An IoT-based healthcare layer consists of several sensors, which continuously monitor some health-related parameters. The sensed data will be passed to the edge layer. The blockchain approach has been integrated to the edge layer. The edge nodes will be placed at primary health centers. Each patient needs to register to at least one nearby edge node. The received data will be processed at the edge node and the edge layer will pass necessary instructions to the primary health center whenever a patient needs medical care. All the received as well as processed data will be passed to the cloud layer and the cloud layer will store all such data for future use. The blockchain-based approach ensures the security and privacy of the data. The healthcare system became more efficient after the introduction of an IoT network. Rather than doing self-assessments, the patients will get direct instructions from the doctors based on their present health conditions. Since all the assessments have been done based on the sensed data, the predictions about the patient's health condition will be more accurate.

Time-Critical Applications

The real-time dynamic applications in an IoT network can be considered time-critical applications. All such applications require high-end processing and large storage space. The cloud computing plays a good role in managing the large amount of data. But purely cloud-dependent data processing cannot be applied to time-critical applications. Such applications cannot bear high latency. Thus, S. Ghosh et al. [33] designed a collaborative framework of cloud-fog-edge-IoT platforms for handling time-critical applications. The proposed framework possesses a four-layer architecture. The upper cloud layer provides storage support. The roadside units are placed in a fog layer. The edge devices are placed at the user end. The tiny IoT devices come under an IoT device layer. The proposed framework provides a mobility aware routing for IoT applications. Thus, the framework can be applied to both static and mobile applications. The collaborative framework reduces the overload of each layer and enhances the overall efficiency of the network. Its proposed framework also has a predictive approach for identifying the mobility pattern. This will help to predict the upcoming mobility-related requests. Thus, the cloud layer could arrange the resources accordingly. The proper resource management will increase the service availability. The proposed framework will have a dependency on the cloud, only for data storage and analysis. All on-demand analysis will be directly executed at the edge nodes. Thus, the framework could offer a latency-free service to the time-critical applications.

Disaster Management

The edge-based IoT network can also be a part of disaster management. Since such networks could provide services from the edge of the network, the cloud-side infrastructure failure can be tolerated. Edge nodes can be used for creating a cloud-independent local network for serving at affected areas. X. Xu et al. [34] proposed an edge-based planning system for crowd evacuation at disaster areas. It is really hard to implement a centralized and well-planned evacuation system during the emergency period. The main threat to such an evocation system is the unavailability of network support. The proposed system uses the existing undamaged edge nodes for forming a controlling network. The sensors deployed at various points can be used to assess the density of the existing crowd. All possible paths to evacuate the crowd must be identified and a load-balancing approach has to be integrated at the edge node for avoiding overcrowding issues. The entire process of evacuation has been divided into collecting the position data, collecting the data about the available transfer options, evacuation planning based on existing algorithms, transfer planning, and documentation. The evacuation planning has been carried out based on the position data and the available transfer options. The evacuation planning will be done by the nearest edge nodes. The crowd will be transferred to the available transfer points based on the evacuation planning. The documentation provides the overall knowledge about global evacuation process. The proposed edge-based system supports the crowd evacuation process in all types of affected regions.

Manhole Cover Management Systems

Manhole cover accidents are common in urban areas. It happens due to manhole cover displacement, damage, and loss. G. Jia et al. [35] proposed an edge-based intelligent approach for addressing this issue. A unique frequency identification tag will be attached with a manhole cover. Along with the radio frequency identification tag, vibration sensors and tilt sensors will be deployed at the manhole cover. Any displacement to the manhole cover will be identified by the attached sensors and the same will be immediately reported to the edge node. The edge computing servers will analyze the obtained data and inform the authorities whenever manual attention is required. The same issue can be solved by utilizing the scope of image processing. Instead of deploying sensors at manhole covers, the already deployed surveillance camera can be used for cover displacement detection. Only the image comparison will be done during the detection phase. Thus, the complexity will be comparatively less. The computational overload will inversely depend on the interval size. In order to reduce the computational overload, the interval between two consecutive comparisons will be increased. But an upper limit and lower limit will be fixed for choosing the interval size. Otherwise, the misdetection rate will increase.

Live Data Analytics

The sensor-based network performs massive data collection. Almost all collected data has to be stored somewhere and a large volume of storage space has to be identified. The cloud-based storage system is capable of providing storage space for saving the sensed data. But another concern is about the data processing. The data accumulated from the sensor nodes may have heterogeneous data structure, weak data semantics, and data inaccuracy. The integration of intelligent big data analysis algorithms at cloud servers can provide the solution to the previous concerns. But most of the applications cannot tolerate the delay experienced during the cloud-based data processing. Also, the cloud servers are not efficient to provide immediate responses for the service requests coming from real-time applications. Service requests coming from real-time applications may require live data analysis. Edge computing has emerged to address the issues associated with cloud-based data processing. The edge node could provide latency-free responses to the real-time applications. Also, the edge nodes are capable of performing live data analysis with the help of cloud servers. Cloud servers help to retrieve the required data from the cloud storage. The intelligent algorithms deployed at the edge node will analyze the data for getting required results. Such intelligent algorithms will be capable of performing data mining, stochastic modeling, distributed optimization, parallel optimizations, data virtualization, batch processing, stream processing, supervised learning, unsupervised deep learning, active learning, and online learning. The edge layer provides a platform for performing live data analysis with the help of deployed algorithms [36].

Societal Applications

All applications related to society come under this category. IoT-based air quality analysis, smart agricultural economics, locating COVID-19 patients, etc. are the well-known examples of societal applications. S. Benedict [37] designed a serverless blockchain-based architecture for societal applications. The architecture consists of sensor nodes, networked devices, and actuators. Sensors are used to collect measurable properties, which include temperature, atmospheric pressure, humidity, etc. Network devices include cloud servers, edge nodes, and mobile nodes. All necessary actions in a network will be executed by actuators based on the control signals. The actuators can be classified into electrical, magnetic, pneumatic, and hydraulic actuators. The actuators will perform the actions based on the received signals either in linear fashion or in rotator fashion. All the computations required to perform in societal applications will be performed at cloud servers. In order to process the large volume of sensed data, machine learning approaches have been integrated at cloud servers. An environment-based classification of existing defense mechanisms in edge-based IoT networks have been included in Table 5.1.

Security Threats and Countermeasures

Several security threats are present in an IoT environment. The introduction of edge nodes to the IoT network also increased the network vulnerabilities. Several mechanisms are available to handle the security threats in the network. This section analyzes the existing defense mechanisms designed for removing the vulnerabilities of edge-based IoT networks. The classification of security threats in an edge-based IoT network is illustrated in Figure 5.4.

Side Channel Attack

A side channel attack is a categorization of attacks that include several classifications. Any attacks that have been performed by utilizing the information gained about network architecture can be included in this category. Based on the type of information, all such attacks can be classified further into cache-side channel attack, timing attack, power analysis attack, deep learning–based side channel attack, collision attack, etc. In a cache side channel attack, the attackers try to get the information about the keys used for cryptographic operations. The cache side channel attack does not make any disturbance to ongoing communications. In a timing attack, the attackers try to predict the cryptographic keys based on the available timing information. In a power analysis attack, the attackers make use of the available information about the power consumption of a cryptographic circuit. In a deep learning–based side channel attack, the attackers try to break the secret key of a device by observing different, but identical devices. A collision attack is the most powerful classification of a side channel attack, where the attacker nodes try to mine the cryptographic keys from the integrated encryption algorithms [38]. The attacker will analyze the vulnerabilities of the implemented encryption algorithms and try to capture the secret keys. Attacks on the S-Box of AES encryption is a classical example of a collision attack. Y. Ding et al. [39] studied the impact of a chosen plaintext collision attack on masked AES in edge computing. In a collision attack, the aim of the attacker is to find two different inputs that can produce the same hash value (collision). Based on the study, the authors have proposed a secure approach that can predict the collisions and avoid the chances of having collision attacks on masked AES. The method primarily observes the power traces that leak the masked input values of S-boxes. The proper identification and elimination of such power traces will reduce the collision attacks on an AES algorithm.

Table 5.1 Security Threats in Edge-Based IoT Environments

Sl. No.	Proposed Approach	Citation	Application Type	Contributions	Performance Metrics
1	Mechanism to provide security with respect to general data protection regulation	[14]	Smart City Environment	■ Authentication ■ Authorization and access control ■ Secure communication	■ Number of unauthorized access
2	Physical layerapproaches for enhancing information security	[15]	Smart City Environment	■ Removes the vulnerabilities present in physical layer ■ Securing resource allocation and signal processing	■ Theoretical study
3	Architecturefor privacy preserving in IoT network	[16]	Smart City Environment	■ Real-time privacy-preserving method	■ Computational cost
4	Secure programming of IoT services	[17]	Smart City Environment	■ Standard-based approach for implementing fog computing based framework	■ Throughput ■ Response time
5	Secure mechanism for Service Placement in IoT	[18]	Smart City Environment		■ Resource utilization

(Continued)

Table 5.1 (Continued) Security Threats in Edge-Based IoT Environments

Sl. No.	Proposed Approach	Citation	Application Type	Contributions	Performance Metrics
				■ Trust-oriented IoT service placement method	■ Load balance variance ■ Energy cost
6	Edge based Trust management system for smart city environment	[19]	Smart City Environment	■ Authentication mechanism ■ Machine learning based trust management mechanism	■ Service success ratio ■ Task success ratio
7	Analysis of security threats in IIoT	[20]	Industrial IoT	■ Study about architecture, advances and challenges in IIoT	■ Theoretical study
8	Method for enhancing the efficiency of control operations in IIoT	[21]	Industrial IoT	■ A direct gateway based solution for edge-based IIoT network	■ Theoretical study
9	Lightweight secure searching mechanism	[22]	Industrial IoT	■ Edge-aided searchable public-key encryption approach	■ Search cost ■ Average comm. cost ■ Decryption cost ■ Total comm. cost

(Continued)

Table 5.1 (Continued) Security Threats in Edge-Based IoT Environments

Sl. No.	Proposed Approach	Citation	Application Type	Contributions	Performance Metrics
10	Secure data storage mechanism	[23]	Industrial IoT	■ Flexible and economical edge based framework for data storage	■ Synchronization time ■ Search proportion ■ Search time
11	Autonomous securityassertion	[24]	Industrial IoT	■ Context-aware network management approach ■ Convolutional neural network based fault analysis	■ Precision ■ Accuracy ■ Completeness ■ Relevance ■ Confidentiality
12	Framework for resource management	[25]	Industrial IoT	■ Improved Rivest-Shamir-Adelman (RSA) and hash signatures	■ Latency ■ Energy consumption ■ User satisfaction index
13	Survey of industrial Internet of Things security	[26]	Industrial IoT	■ Study of IIoT security requirements ■ Study about the research works in IIoT	■ Number of publications per year ■ Popularity

(Continued)

Table 5.1 (Continued) Security Threats in Edge-Based IoT Environments

Sl. No.	Proposed Approach	Citation	Application Type	Contributions	Performance Metrics
14	Trustworthy environment establishment	[27]	Industrial IoT	■ Edge-based trust management system for IIoT ■ Trusted service selection approach	■ Precision ■ Storage size
15	Blockchain-edge framework for IIoT	[28]	Industrial IoT	■ Fog-based framework for securing the communications in cloud computing	■ Upstream bandwidth ■ Downstream bandwidth ■ Storage capabilities ■ Latency
16	Latency-free intrusion detection approach	[29]	Vehicular Network	■ Fog-enabled detection free scheme for vehicular edge computing	■ Energy ■ Time ■ Survivability
17	Lightweightauthentication mechanism	[30]	Vehicular Network	■ Lightweight scheme for symmetric key exchange ■ Man-in-the-middle attack prevention	■ Communication cost
18	Trust-based clustering mechanism	[31]	Vehicular Network	■ Centralized clustering	■ Average cluster duration

(Continued)

Table 5.1 (Continued) Security Threats in Edge-Based IoT Environments

Sl. No.	Proposed Approach	Citation	Application Type	Contributions	Performance Metrics
				mechanism for vehicular networks ■ Mechanism to determine trustworthy cluster heads	■ Average cluster head lifetime
19	A decoupled blockchain approach for healthcare monitoring	[32]	Healthcare Monitoring	■ Blockchain-based approach for preserving the privacy of patients	■ Block preparation time ■ Header generation time ■ Reduction ratio ■ Approximation error
20	Collaborative framework fortime-critical applications	[33]	Time-Critical Applications	■ Mobility aware framework for real-time applications ■ Machine learning based prediction of moving agents	■ Accuracy ■ Recall ■ F-measure

(Continued)

Table 5.1 (Continued)   Security Threats in Edge-Based IoT Environments

Sl. No.	Proposed Approach	Citation	Application Type	Contributions	Performance Metrics
21	Fast planning mechanism for disaster areas	[34]	Disaster Management	■ Crowd evacuation planning system ■ Artificial potential field with relationship attraction	■ Average evacuation time ■ Average length of evacuation route ■ Accuracy
22	Edge computing–based intelligent approach for smart cities	[35]	Manhole Cover Management Systems/ Smart City	■ Sensor-based solution for identifying the displacement of manhole cover	■ Overhead ■ Average response time
23	Collaborative edge-based framework for live data analytics	[36]	Live Data Analytics	■ A secure mechanism to coordinate the data processing between edge and cloud servers	■ Theoretical study
24	Secure framework for IoT-enabled societal applications	[37]	Societal Applications	■ Server-less blockchain-enabled architecture for IoT network	■ Query time ■ Transaction time

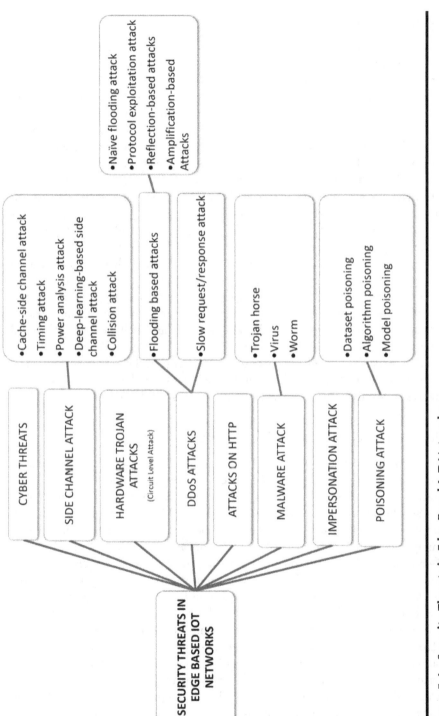

Figure 5.4 Security Threats in Edge-Based IoT Networks.

Cyber Threats

Cyber attacks can create massive damage to an IoT-based network. All domains of IoT-based computations have several reported issues of cyber attacks [40]. In 2015, three energy distribution companies in Ukraine were attacked by intruders and the attackers could stop the power supply to consumers. Similarly, several attacks have been reported on the open seas, where the network has been implemented for establishing the communications between oil tankers and floating oil rigs. In the United Kingdom, the attackers hacked the kitchen devices and formed a botnet to perform a distributed denial of service attack. A botnet is a group of network devices that can jointly perform security attacks. A botnet can steal the data, contribute delay to communications, and send spam messages. A cyber attacker can convert the smart fridges into spam-bots. These are just a few examples of cyber attacks. The attackers try to compromise more devices and all such compromised devices can be controlled by remote commands. Ransomware is the best known example for this scenario. The attackers will distribute the malicious software to all connected devices without the user's knowledge and they take control of the systems all of a sudden. The attackers may ask for cryptocurrency to release control over the hacked systems. All of these cyber attacks are becoming a major threat to IoT networks. M. Eskandari et al. [41] proposed an intelligent anomaly-based cyber attack detection system for an edge-based IoT network. As per the experimental results, the framework works better even in very cheap IoT gateways. The proposed framework blocks the unauthorized access to the network. Thus, the chances of forming botnets among the IoT devices will be reduced.

Distributed Denial of Service (DDoS) Attacks

The distributed denial of service (DDoS) attack is the most dangerous and widely performed attack in an edge-based IoT network. Both external as well as internal attacker nodes can perform a denial of service (DoS) attack. The DoS attack aims to make the service unavailable for the time being. Most of the other attacks need network permissions to perform the same. But the DoS attack can be done by simply flooding the data packets. The network cannot handle such large volumes of data and all the load-balancing approaches may fail due to flooding. The network failure will become the reason for service unavailability. This ease in the attacking strategy has become the prime reason for the global acceptance of DoS attacks among attackers. The formation of botnets and performing the denial of service attack is the typical example for distributed denial of service attack. The DDoS attacks can be classified into flooding-based attacks and slow request/response attacks. Both of these categories of attacks can be performed by both internal as well as external nodes. The slow request/response attack is the process of delaying the service requests and responses by the intermediate nodes. The flooding attacks can be further divided into naïve flooding attacks, protocol exploitation attacks, reflection-based attacks, and amplification-based attacks. The naïve flooding attack can be performed by sending a large number of communication requests to the targeted node. In a protocol exploitation attack, the attackers utilize the vulnerabilities of implemented protocols to make the resource unavailable. In a reflection-based flooding attack, the attackers will capture the genuine request packets and change the source address. The edge server will fail to differentiate the genuine and manipulated request packets. Thus, the edge server will respond to all the received request packets. This will contribute an additional delay to the network. The amplification-based attack is a variant of a reflection-based attack. In an amplification-based attack, the attacker node will force the edge server to send a large amount of response packets to the targeted node. The target node will be flooded with response packets and will become unavailable. Y. Jia et al. [42] introduced an intelligent edge-based defense mechanism for preventing the DDoS attack in an IoT network. The authors propose a machine learning approach to identify the initiation of DDoS attacks in IoT networks. They have also contributed an edge-based approach to block all such DDoS attack initiations.

Hardware Trojan Attacks

The hardware Trojan attack is a circuit-level attack. The intruder tries to inject malicious codes to the edge servers. The attacker will change the circuit level coding through the backdoor entry. The hardware Trojan attack cannot be performed without the help of developers or designers of the system. The intruder requires circuit-level design to find the available entry points [43]. Attackers cannot inject the malicious codes to a well-written circuit-level program. In some reported cases, the developers deliberately included the backdoor entry points to help the intruder. In some cases, the attack has happened due to the lack of sufficient precautionary measures. In both cases, user-level prevention could not play a great role to eliminate the injected code from the edge servers. H. Mohammed et al. [44] designed a concurrent defense mechanism to defend against different types of hardware Trojan attacks. A user cannot integrate a circuit-level algorithm without the knowledge of developers. Thus, the proposed system identifies the hardware Trojan attack by analyzing the power profiling and network traffic data. It proposes a machine learning scheme for analyzing the obtained data. The machine learning algorithm includes data pre-processing, classification, regression, clustering, and visualization.

Attacks on HTTP

The hypertext transfer protocol (HTTP) has been used in the application layer of edge-based communications. Several known as well as unknown vulnerabilities are present in HTTP. Intelligent algorithms need to be incorporated at the edge nodes to detect the anomalies present in HTTP. The anomaly detection approaches can be classified into statistical methods and machine learning methods. A statistical method detects the anomalies based on some statistical measures. Feature analysis, predefined thresholds, probabilities, standard deviations, mean, etc. can be considered for the evaluation process in the statistical method. The machine learning approach can be categorized into supervised learning, unsupervised learning, and semi-supervised learning. In a supervised learning approach, the issues can be categorized into regression problems and classification problems. The supervised learning approach requires labeled data for doing the above categorization. The clustering approach is used in unsupervised learning to detect anomalies from unlabeled data. The semi-supervised learning considers a large volume of unlabeled data and a small amount of labeled data for pattern-based anomaly detection. Y. An et al. [45] proposed a method for anomaly detection in an edge-based IoT network. The proposed approach utilizes the edge intelligence to overcome the drawbacks of HTTP in an IoT environment. It initially observes the normal conditions and extends the study to abnormal conditions. The proposed method uses machine learning–based unsupervised learning approach for detecting the anomalies present in the edge layer.

Impersonation Attacks

An impersonation attack is a type of identity-based attack in which the attacker uses the identity of a legitimate node to participate in the network communications. It can be performed by both external as well as internal nodes [46]. The node that receives the message will verify the identity of the sender. Since the communication has been initiated using the forged identity, the identity-based authentication cannot detect the intrusion. Thus, the receiver node will respond to the messages and the attacker node will receive the reply packets. In IoT applications, end users as well as the edge nodes can perform impersonation attack. The edge node is the collection point of the sensed data in an IoT network. Thus, the impersonation attack emerging from an edge node can contribute much damage to the system. Such an edge node can steal any confidential data from the network, which may directly affect the stability of the IoT networks. S. J. Lee et al. [47] proposed an impersonation attack detection method using deep auto-encoder and feature abstraction. A lightweight machine learning approach will be integrated to the edge node for identifying the identity-based attacks. It uses a three-layered unsupervised neural network learning algorithm that considers unlabeled data. The learning algorithm trains the system to identify the impersonation attacks with the help of a predefined data set.

Malware Attacks

Malware attacks can be considered a subclass of cyber attacks. The malware aims to perform unauthorized actions at targeted systems. The malware will be designed for performing some desired tasks. Also, the attacker will find some mechanism to make the malware undetectable to other network entities. An attacker can choose several methods to deliver the created malware to the targets. Malwares can be integrated to a webpage as a hyperlink that directs the user to the malware location. The malwares will be downloaded to the target system by clicking on such links. Otherwise, the attackers will append the malware with some data files. The malware will be downloaded to the target system along with such data files. In edge computing, the malware can be flooded to the system along with control messages by utilizing the vulnerabilities of network architecture. The malware present in edge computing can be classified into Trojan horse, virus, and worm. Trojan horse will appear as useful software. Attackers will design the Trojan horse as trustable software that contains malicious code in it. It is a kind of delivery mechanism adopted by the attackers. The user will trust the user interface design and try to run the software on their devices. At that time, the malicious code can take control of the targeted IoT device. A virus is also a piece of malicious software that can be propagated without any additional external force. Such self-propagating malware is called a virus. A virus will be propagated only towards a single targeted system. But the worm is a self-propagating malware that will be propagated to more than one target. The proposed malware detection approaches [48–50] analyze the possibilities of malware propagation in IoT-enabled networks and integrate architecture specific algorithms to overcome the vulnerabilities.

Poisoning Attacks

Anyone can perform an input attack over any security system. The attacker will intentionally manipulate the input data to get the desired output. Several machine learning–based secure approaches have been discussed so far in this paper that help to prevent various attacks on an edge-based IoT network. The poisoning attack is a security threat present in IoT-enabled environments, which can be performed over learning algorithms. The poisoning attack plays its major part during the training phase of learning algorithms. The attacker will contribute a malicious data set to the training algorithms. Thus, the intrusion detection system will be trained in the wrong direction, as desired by the attacker. The attacker can "poison" the AI/ML system in different ways, which include data set poisoning, algorithm poisoning, and model poisoning. In a data set poisoning attack, the attacker will inject the corrupted data set to the system. In an algorithm poisoning attack, the attacker will try to corrupt the learning algorithm used in the intrusion detection system. In a model poisoning attack, the attacker will replace the functional model with a poisoned one. All of these attacks can contribute a large level of disruption to the network. The corrupted algorithm will construct a backdoor, through which the attacker can control the entire system [51–54]. The existing security threats and the countermeasures are listed in Table 5.2.

Table 5.2 Security Attacks on Edge-Based IoT Environments

Sl. No.	Proposed Approach	Citation	Attack Type	Contributions	Performance Metrics
1	Collision power attack detection for AES algorithm	[38]	Side Channel Attack	■ Physical attack prevention ■ Detecting the collision attack on mixcolumns	■ Success rate ■ Correlation
2	Chosen-plaintext collision attack detection on masked AES	[39]	Side Channel Attack	■ Detection of collision-correlation attack on masked AES ■ Fault-tolerant approach	■ Success rate ■ Correlation
3	Web attack detection	[40]	Cyber Threats	■ Deep learning–based web attack detection	■ Accuracy ■ Recall ■ FP ■ Precision
4	Intrusion detection system for IoT edge devices	[41]	Cyber Threats	• Intelligent anomaly based intrusion detection system • Prevention of HTTP brute force attack	■ Precision ■ Recall
5	Prevention of distributed denial of service attack	[42]	DDoS Attacks	■ Edge-based DDoS detection mechanism ■ Classification of DDoS attacks	■ Accuracy ■ Precision ■ Recall ■ F1 score

(Continued)

Table 5.2 (Continued) Security Attacks on Edge-Based IoT Environments

Sl. No.	Proposed Approach	Citation	Attack Type	Contributions	Performance Metrics
6	Run-timehardware Trojan detection	[43]	Hardware Trojan Attacks	■ Machine learning–based hardware Trojan Ddetection ■ Optimizations for resource-constrained environments	■ False positives ■ False negatives ■ HT detection accuracy
7	Detection of multiple types of hardware Trojan attacks	[44]	Hardware Trojan Attacks	■ Concurrent defense mechanism ■ Classification of hardware Trojen attacks	■ Detection accuracy
8	HTTP anomalydetection framework	[45]	Attacks on HTTP	■ Distributed detection approach ■ Birch clustering algorithm	■ Precision ■ Recall ■ Accuracy ■ F-measure
9	Impersonation attack detection	[46]	Impersonation Attack	■ Fog-based approach ■ Q-learning algorithm	■ Accuracy ■ Reliability
10	Edge-based impersonation attack detection	[47]	Impersonation Attack	■ Impersonation attack detection using deep auto-encoder and feature abstraction	■ Accuracy ■ Detection rate ■ False alarm rate
11	Malware threat hunting in the edge layer	[48]	Malware Attack	■ Feature selection based multi-kernelSVM approach	■ True positive ■ Detection accuracy

(Continued)

Table 5.2 (Continued) Security Attacks on Edge-Based IoT Environments

Sl. No.	Proposed Approach	Citation	Attack Type	Contributions	Performance Metrics
12	Real-time malware detection approach	[49]	Malware Attack	■ Artificial intelligence–based real-time malware detection approach	■ Recall rates ■ Overall detection accuracy ■ False alarm ■ Malware miss ■ F1 score
13	Malware detection in industrial IoT	[50]	Malware Attack	■ Malware detection using machine learning with selective adversarial samples	■ Accuracy ■ Recall ■ G-mean ■ F1 score
14	Poisoning attack detection	[51]	Poisoning Attack	■ A poison data generation method ■ A novel generative poisoning attack detection model	■ Accuracy

Discussion

This section analyzes the existing defense mechanisms in an edge-based IoT network. The emergence of edge computing has given strength to the developers for designing several real-time applications. The attackers always aim to identify the vulnerabilities of the network. The application-level enhancements may open backdoors for the attackers. The attackers will try to make use of such unnoticed vulnerabilities of the system. This section also discusses the open research challenges in the IoT networks.

Analysis of Existing Defense Mechanisms

Several types of attacks are present in edge computing. This chapter initially discussed the environmental specific security threats present in edge computing. The attackers always choose authentication attacks, information leakage attacks, and data disclosure attacks to be performed over the smart city environment. The attackers in industrial environments will try to attack the control system. Such attacks may drastically affect the autonomous network management in industrial IoT. The healthcare monitoring systems and the time-critical applications will always encounter denial of service attacks. A delay in such systems will produce the worst outcome. The resource availability is the key goal of disaster management systems. The unavailability of network resources may badly affect the rescue operations. The impact of security attacks over the edge-based IoT network is also discussed in this chapter. The authentication and data security can be ensured in the cloud computing by integrating any crypto system to the cloud server. But several attacks like side channel attacks are present in an edge environment will directly affect the crypto systems. Thus, the developers need to understand the limitations of lightweight edge nodes while designing the security algorithms. The attackers can perform cyber attacks using the malware. Such attacks have to be prevented for stabilizing the IoT environment. Due to the large deployment of edge nodes, the centralized monitoring system cannot be deployed over the edge platform. Attackers will take it as an opportunity and count each edge node as an entry point to the system. Thus, an attacker can intrude the network by hijacking a single edge node. Such attackers may perform malicious code injection attack (hardware Trojan attack) on circuit-level algorithms to gain overall control of the network. There are several existing mechanisms to prevent all these attacks, which include machine learning approaches, anomaly detection approaches, various intrusion detection mechanisms, etc.

Open Research Challenges

The large level deployment of lightweight IoT devices increased the security challenges in the IoT environment. The end layer devices are heterogeneous in nature. Thus, the security algorithm must be capable of accommodating all types of devices. Establishing a centralized uniform environment with heterogeneous end devices became the most challenging task in an IoT network. Rather than controlling every device from a single remote location (cloud server), the IoT devices can be controlled from a nearby location with the help of edge nodes. The deployment of tiny edge devices also raised several security issues. The introduction of edge computing has increased the efficiency and popularity of the IoT networks. The increased popularity also increased the number of IoT devices in the network. Accommodating a large number of IoT devices to the network also increased the security challenges in the network.

Conclusion and Future Works

The traditional cloud computing approaches have several network-related issues. The communications may experience a large latency due to the increased round-trip time. The energy consumption of the server node will be high due to the centralized architecture. The bandwidth utilization will also be high due to the remotely placed cloud server. The edge-based data processing has increased the performance of IoT applications. Several real-time applications have emerged after the introduction of edge computing. The edge servers can offer latency-free services from the edge of the network. Thus, the bandwidth utilization and the single node energy consumption can also be reduced. Several security measures are available to defend against the security attacks in edge-based IoT networks. In order to avoid the operational overhead at the end devices, the security algorithms will be integrated to edge servers. Most of the security algorithms utilize the possibilities of machine learning algorithms. Such algorithms can provide the data security and perform intrusion detection. The identity-based attacks are the most challenging attacks in edge computing. Such attacks can be performed by both internal as well as external nodes. The external identity-based attacks can be prevented by integrating a strong authentication mechanism. But the internal nodes may steal the legitimate identity of their neighboring nodes to perform the attack. The identity-based authentication mechanisms may fail to identify the identity theft. Thus, the internal nodes can perform impersonation attacks using the identity of other legitimate nodes. Another security threat in edge computing is the chance of having cooperative attacks. All the existing defense mechanisms consider only the single node attacks. More research has to be carried out in this area to defend against identity-based internal attacks and cooperative attacks.

References

[1] C. Hsu, T. Le, C. Lu, T. Lin, and T. Chuang. "A Privacy-Preserved E2E Authenticated Key Exchange Protocol for Multi-Server Architecture in Edge Computing Networks." *IEEE Access* 8 (2020): 40791–40808.

[2] X. Li, S. Liu, F. Wu, S. Kumari, and J. J. Rodrigues. "Privacy Preserving Data Aggregation Scheme for Mobile Edge Computing Assisted IoT Applications." *IEEE Internet of Things Journal* 6, no. 3 (2018): 4755–4763.

[3] C. S. M. Babou, D. Fall, S. Kashihara, Y. Taenaka, M. H. Bhuyan, I. Niang, and Y. Kadobayashi. "Hierarchical Load Balancing and Clustering Technique for Home Edge Computing." *IEEE Access* 8 (2020): 127593–127607.

[4] T. Wang, M. Z. A. Bhuiyan, G. Wang, L. Qi, J. Wu, and T. Hayajneh. "Preserving Balance Between Privacy and Data Integrity in Edge-Assisted Internet of Things." *IEEE Internet of Things Journal* 7, no. 4 (2019): 2679–2689.

[5] A. Mathur, T. Newe, and M. Rao. "Defence Against Black Hole and Selective Forwarding Attacks for Medical WSNs in the IoT." *Sensors* 16, no. 1 (2016): 118.

[6] V. Balasubramanian and A. Karmouch. "An Infrastructure as a Service for Mobile ad-hoc Cloud." In *2017 IEEE 7th Annual Computing and Communication Workshop and Conference (CCWC)* (2017): 1–7. IEEE.

[7] A. J. Ferrer, J. M. Marques, and J. Jorba. "Ad-hoc Edge Cloud: A Framework for Dynamic Creation of Edge Computing Infrastructures." In *2019 28th International Conference on Computer Communication and Networks (ICCCN)* (2019): 1–7. IEEE.

[8] L. Tianze, W. Muqing, Z. Min, and L. Wenxing. "An Overhead-Optimizing Task Scheduling Strategy for ad-hoc Based Mobile Edge Computing." *IEEE Access* 5 (2017): 5609–5622.

[9] T. Alam and M. Benaida. "The Role of Cloud-MANET Framework in the Internet of Things (IoT)." arXiv preprint arXiv:1902.09436 (2019).

[10] H. Bangui, S. Rakrak, S. Raghay, and B. Buhnova. "Moving to the Edge-Cloud-of-Things: Recent Advances and Future Research Directions." *Electronics* 7, no. 11 (2018): 309.

[11] B. Zaghdoudi, H. K. Ayed, and I. Gnichi. "A Protocol for Setting up ad hoc Mobile Clouds Over Spontaneous MANETs: A Proof of Concept." in *2016 Cloudification of the Internet of Things (CIoT)* (2016): 1–6. IEEE.

[12] S. V. Simpson and G. Nagarajan. "SEAL—Security-Aware List-Based Routing Protocol for Mobile Ad Hoc Network." in *International Conference on Emerging Trends and Advances in Electrical Engineering and Renewable Energy* (2020): 519–530. Springer, Singapore.

[13] S. V. Simpson and G. Nagarajan. "A Table Based Attack Detection (TBAD) scheme for Internet of Things: An approach for Smart City Environment." in *2021 International Conference on Emerging Smart Computing and Informatics (ESCI)* (2021): 696–701. IEEE.

[14] C. Badii, P. Bellini, A. Difino, and P. Nesi. "Smart City iot Platform Respecting gdpr Privacy and Security Aspects." *IEEE Access* 8 (2020): 23601–23623.

[15] D. Wang, B. Bai, K. Lei, W. Zhao, Y. Yang, and Z. Han. "Enhancing Information Security via Physical Layer Approaches in Heterogeneous IoT with Multiple Access Mobile Edge Computing in Smart City." *IEEE Access* 7 (2019): 54508–54521.

[16] M. Gheisari, Q. Pham, M. Alazab, X. Zhang, C. Fernandez-Campusano, and G. Srivastava. "ECA: An Edge Computing Architecture for Privacy-Preserving in IoT-Based Smart City." *IEEE Access* 7 (2019): 155779–155786.

[17] B. Cheng, G. Solmaz, F. Cirillo, E. Kovacs, K. Terasawa, and A. Kitazawa. "FogFlow: Easy Programming of IoT Services Over Cloud and Edges for Smart Cities." *IEEE Internet of Things Journal* 5, no. 2 (2017): 696–707.

[18] X. Xu, X. Liu, Z. Xu, F. Dai, X. Zhang, and L. Qi. "Trust-Oriented IoT Service Placement for Smart Cities in Edge Computing." *IEEE Internet of Things Journal* 7, no. 5 (2019): 4084–4091.

[19] B. Wang, M. Li, X. Jin, and C. Guo. "A Reliable IoT Edge Computing Trust Management Mechanism for Smart Cities." *IEEE Access* 8 (2020): 46373–46399.

[20] T. Qiu, J. Chi, X. Zhou, Z. Ning, M. Atiquzzaman, and D. O. Wu. "Edge Computing in Industrial Internet of Things: Architecture, Advances and Challenges." *IEEE Communications Surveys & Tutorials* 22, no. 4 (2020): 2462–2488.

[21] M. W. Condry and C. B. Nelson. "Using Smart Edge IoT Devices for Safer, Rapid Response with Industry IoT Control Operations." *Proceedings of the IEEE* 104, no. 5 (2016): 938–946.

[22] W. Wang, P. Xu, D. Liu, L. T. Yang, and Z. Yan. "Lightweighted Secure Searching Over Public-Key Ciphertexts for Edge-Cloud-Assisted Industrial iot Devices." *IEEE Transactions on Industrial Informatics* 16, no. 6 (2019): 4221–4230.

[23] J. Fu, Y. Liu, H. Chao, B. K. Bhargava, and Z. Zhang. "Secure Data Storage and Searching for Industrial IoT by Integrating Fog Computing and Cloud Computing." *IEEE Transactions on Industrial Informatics* 14, no. 10 (2018): 4519–4528.

[24] U. Tariq, A. O. Aseeri, M. S. Alkatheiri, and Y. Zhuang. "Context-Aware Autonomous Security Assertion for Industrial IoT." *IEEE Access* 8 (2020): 191785–191794.

[25] K. A. Abuhasel and M. A. Khan. "A Secure Industrial Internet of Things (IIoT) Framework for Resource Management in Smart Manufacturing." *IEEE Access* 8 (2020): 117354–117364.

[26] K. Tange, M. D. Donno, X. Fafoutis, and N. Dragoni. "A Systematic Survey of Industrial Internet of Things Security: Requirements and Fog Computing Opportunities." *IEEE Communications Surveys & Tutorials* 22, no. 4 (2020): 2489–2520.

[27] T. Wang, P. Wang, S. Cai, Y. Ma, A. Liu, and M. Xie. "A Unified Trustworthy Environment Establishment Based on Edge Computing in Industrial IoT." *IEEE Transactions on Industrial Informatics* 16, no. 9 (2019): 6083–6091.

[28] T. Kumar, E. Harjula, M. Ejaz, A. Manzoor, P. Porambage, I. Ahmad, M. Liyanage, A. Braeken, and M. Ylianttila. "BlockEdge: Blockchain-Edge Framework for Industrial IoT Networks." *IEEE Access* 8 (2020): 154166–154185.

[29] A. Mourad, H. Tout, O. A. Wahab, H. Otrok, and T. Dbouk. Ad Hoc Vehicular Fog Enabling Cooperative Low-Latency Intrusion Detection. *IEEE Internet of Things Journal*, no. 2 (2020): 829–843.

[30] Z. Ali, S. A. Chaudhry, M. S. Ramzan, and F. Al-Turjman. "Securing Smart City Surveillance: A Lightweight Authentication Mechanism for Unmanned Vehicles." *IEEE Access* 8 (2020): 43711–43724.

[31] K. A. Awan, I. U. Din, A. Almogren, M. Guizani, and S. Khan. "StabTrust—A Stable and Centralized Trust-Based Clustering Mechanism for IoT Enabled Vehicular ad-hoc Networks." *IEEE Access* 8 (2020): 21159–21177.

[32] G. S. Aujla and A. Jindal. A Decoupled Blockchain Approach for Edge-Envisioned IoT-based Healthcare Monitoring. *IEEE Journal on Selected Areas in Communications*, no. 2 (2020): 491–499.

[33] S. Ghosh, A. Mukherjee, S. K. Ghosh, and R. Buyya. "Mobi-iost: Mobility-aware cloud-fog-edge-iot Collaborative Framework for Time-Critical Applications". *IEEE Transactions on Network Science and Engineering*, no. 4 (2019): 2271–2285.

[34] X. Xu, L. Zhang, S. Sotiriadis, E. Asimakopoulou, M. Li, and N. Bessis. "CLOTHO: A Large-Scale Internet of Things-Based Crowd Evacuation Planning System for Disaster Management." *IEEE Internet of Things Journal* 5, no. 5 (2018): 3559–3568.

[35] G. Jia, G. Han, H. Rao, and L. Shu. "Edge Computing-based Intelligent Manhole Cover Management System for Smart Cities." *IEEE Internet of Things Journal* 5, no. 3 (2017): 1648–1656.

[36] S. K. Sharma and X. Wang. "Live Data Analytics with Collaborative Edge and Cloud Processing in Wireless IoT Networks." *IEEE Access* 5 (2017): 4621–4635.

[37] S. Benedict. "Serverless Blockchain-Enabled Architecture for iot Societal Applications." *IEEE Transactions on Computational Social Systems* 7, no. 5 (2020): 1146–1158.

[38] Y. Niu, J. Zhang, A. Wang, and C. Chen. "An Efficient Collision Power Attack on AES Encryption in Edge Computing." *IEEE Access* 7 (2019): 18734–18748.

[39] Y. Ding, Y. Shi, A. Wang, X. Zheng, Z. Wang, and G. Zhang. "Adaptive Chosen-Plaintext Collision Attack on Masked AES in Edge Computing." *IEEE Access* 7 (2019): 63217–63229.

[40] Z. Tian, C. Luo, J. Qiu, X. Du, and M. Guizani. "A Distributed Deep Learning System for Web Attack Detection on Edge Devices." *IEEE Transactions on Industrial Informatics* 16, no. 3 (2019): 1963–1971.

[41] M. Eskandari, Z. H. Janjua, M. Vecchio, and F. Antonelli. "Passban IDS: An Intelligent Anomaly-based Intrusion Detection System for IoT Edge Devices." *IEEE Internet of Things Journal* 7, no. 8 (2020): 6882–6897.

[42] Y. Jia, F. Zhong, A. Alrawais, B. Gong, and X. Cheng. "Flowguard: An Intelligent Edge Defense Mechanism Against IoT DDoS Attacks." *IEEE Internet of Things Journal* 7, no. 10 (2020): 9552–9562.

[43] F. Khalid, S. R. Hasan, S. Zia, O. Hasan, F. Awwad, and M. Shafique. "MacLeR: Machine Learning-Based Runtime Hardware Trojan Detection in Resource-Constrained IoT Edge Devices." *IEEE Transactions on Computer-Aided Design of Integrated Circuits and Systems* 39, no. 11 (2020): 3748–3761.

[44] H. Mohammed, S. R. Hasan, and F. Awwad. "Fusion-On-Field Security and Privacy Preservation for IoT Edge Devices: Concurrent Defense Against Multiple Types of Hardware Trojan Attacks." *IEEE Access* 8 (2020): 36847–36862.

[45] Y. An, F. R. Yu, J. Li, J. Chen, and V. C. Leung. Edge intelligence (EI)-enabled HTTP anomaly detection framework for the Internet of Things (IoT). *IEEE Internet of Things Journal*, no. 5 (2020): 3554–3566.

[46] S. Tu, M. Waqas, S. U. Rehman, M. Aamir, O. U. Rehman, Z. Jianbiao, and C. Chang. "Security in Fog Computing: A Novel Technique to Tackle an Impersonation Attack." *IEEE Access* 6 (2018): 74993–75001.

[47] S. J. Lee, P. D. Yoo, A. T. Asyhari, Y. Jhi, L. Chermak, C. Y. Yeun, and K. Taha. "IMPACT: Impersonation Attack Detection via Edge Computing Using Deep Autoencoder and Feature Abstraction." *IEEE Access* 8 (2020): 65520–65529.

[48] H. Haddadpajouh, A. Mohtadi, A. Dehghantanaha, H. Karimipour, X. Lin, and K. R. Choo. A Multikernel and Metaheuristic Feature Selection Approach for IoT

Malware Threat Hunting in the Edge Layer. *IEEE Internet of Things Journal*, no. 6 (2020): 4540–4547.

[49] A. Libri, A. Bartolini, and L. Benini. "pAElla: Edge AI-Based Real-Time Malware Detection in Data Centers." *IEEE Internet of Things Journal* 7, no. 10 (2020): 9589–9599.

[50] M. E. Khoda, T. Imam, J. Kamruzzaman, I. Gondal, and A. Rahman. "Robust Malware Defense in Industrial IoT Applications Using Machine Learning with Selective Adversarial Samples." *IEEE Transactions on Industry Applications* 56, no. 4 (2019): 4415–4424.

[51] J. Zhang, B. Chen, X. Cheng, H. T. T. Binh, and S. Yu. PoisonGAN: Generative Poisoning Attacks Against Federated Learning in Edge Computing Systems. *IEEE Internet of Things Journal*, no. 5 (2020): 3310–3322.

[52] R. I. Minu and G. Nagarajan. "Bridging the IoT Gap Through Edge Computing." In *Edge Computing and Computational Intelligence Paradigms for the IoT*, pp. 1–9. IGI Global, 2019.

[53] G. Nagarajan, R. I. Minu, and A. Jayanthiladevi. "Cognitive Internet of Things (C-IOT)." In *Sensing Techniques for Next Generation Cognitive Radio Networks*, pp. 299–311. IGI Global, 2019.

[54] S. V. Simpson and G. Nagarajan. "An Edge Based Trustworthy Environment Establishment for Internet of Things: An Approach for Smart Cities." *Wireless Networks* (2021): 1–17.

Chapter 6

Edge AI for Industrial IoT Applications

S. Sivabalan and R. Minu

Department of Computing Technology, SRM Institute of Science and Technology, Chennai, India

Contents

DOI: 10.1201/9781003145158-6

General Overview

Edge AI or Tiny ML are hardware devices that perform AI locally. The hardware receives its input from the sensor data and signals provided by the system (Figure 6.1). The trained model installed in the hardware enables the edge machine to make decisions without the need for a connection.

Edge AI devices do not need to be connected to the Internet to function; they can process data and make decisions on their own. In the form of tech tools and networks, vendors offer cutting-edge AI innovations [1]. Without the need for large data sets or e-commerce, Edge AI software tools combine machine learning (ML) and edge computing technologies to transform raw data into events, observations, and forecasts. Edge computing systems allow businesses to keep the majority of their IT and operational technology close together, resulting in faster processing and better data security.

The source data is coming from Internet of Things (IoT), sensor data, images, or videos for computer vision are processed in edge nodes.

Edge Nodes

A system that serves as a point of entry into a company's or service provider's core network is known as an edge node. Just a few examples include routing switches, routers, multiplexers, integrated access devices (IADs), and a variety of metro area network (MAN) and wide area network (WAN) access devices. Edge devices also have connections to carrier and service provider networks [2]. A system that connects a

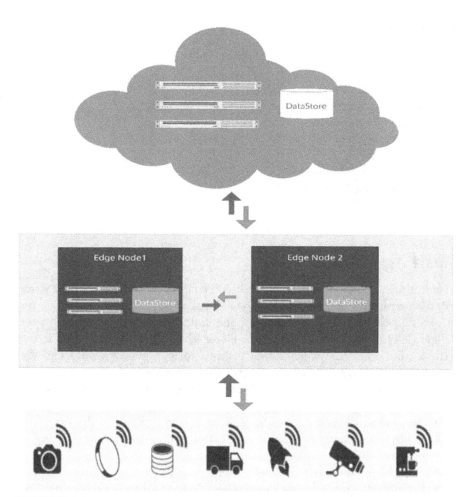

Figure 6.1 Edge AI Architecture.

local area network to a high-speed switch or backbone is known as an edge concentrator.

Features of Edge Devices:

■ Improved performance
■ Reduced operational cost
■ Reliability and resilience
■ Governance and compliance
■ Data privacy and security

Edge AI in Industries

Edge computing spans across many different industries.

1. Smart agriculture
2. Autonomous vehicles
3. Public transportation
4. Site management
5. Smart building
6. Health care and hospitals
7. The base station for 5G infrastructure
8. Energy distributions

Smart Agriculture

In agriculture, the remote operation enables the farmers [3] to control their water irrigation remotely. The traditional systems installed help to switch the motor on or off using Global System for Mobile Communications (GSM). The Internet of Things (IoT) devices help to control the motor by checking the water level in the well to avoid a dry run, which causes damages to the motor and auto start the motor when the water is filled with a level after some hours.

The Edge Artificial Intelligence (AI) can make decisions in the following cases:

■ To control the motor when the water level is low to avoid a dry run.
■ If there is a power fluctuation, the motor will remain turned off until it becomes stable.
■ Stop the motor if there is rain/lightning.
■ Controls the gate valve by checking the change field has enough water and give water to the next field.
■ Edge AI controls climate, light, nutrients, airflow, and humidity in a greenhouse.

Agribots

Autopilot tractors and robotic machinery can operate by communicating with nearby sensors in order to get the necessary environmental data [4]. The most effective routes for covering the required area can be calculated using computer vision and preloaded field data taking into consideration the task, the number of cars currently in the field, the size of the devices, etc.

In addition, in the event of an unexpected barrier or if an animal or a human is on the way, they may re-route automatically. As a result, smart equipment can do a wide range of tasks, such as irrigating and weeding areas where necessary or even harvesting crops autonomously.

Farm Automation

Like farming, IoT edge computing can be used for a greenhouse or even whole farms. In other words, the closed ecosystem is able to handle the collected data, e.g., watering plants, feeding cattle, managing the temperature, light, moisture, etc. without the need of a remote server (Figure 6.2) [6]. As with agribots, edge computing enables farm or greenhouse operators to operate independently of the connection with the main server and to decide locally on the basis of local sensor data. This could increase reliability of processes and reduce waste, which would make agriculture more sustainable.

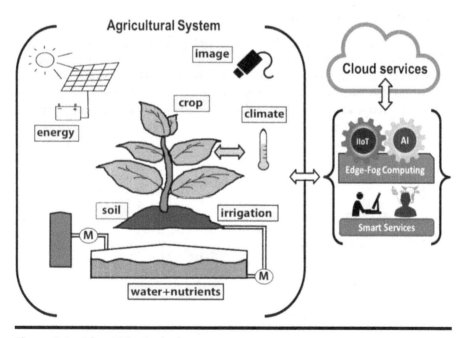

Figure 6.2   Edge AI in Agriculture.

Credits: Francisco Javier Ferrández-Pastor, Juan Manuel García-Chamizo, Mario Nieto-Hidalgo and José Mora-Martínez.

Source: Precision Agriculture Design Method Using a Distributed Computing Architecture on Internet of Things Context.

Disaster Protection

IoT systems can make informed decisions about potential environmental dangers or natural disasters through advanced computing. In other words, remote sensors can collect and analyze weather or environment change data to prevent potential disasters and immediately notify the general control center if there are certain signs of hazard. In the event of a wildfire [7], for example, farmers can take timely measures to protect their crops, at least in part.

Autonomous Vehicles

A self-driving car, or autonomous vehicle, is one that can sense its environment and operate without the assistance of a person. A human passenger is not required to take control of the vehicle at any stage, nor is he or she required to be present in the vehicle at all. A self-driving car can go anywhere a regular car can go and perform all the tasks that a human driver can.

AI in Self-Driving Cars

In self-driving cars, cameras, LIDAR (for laser or light radar use), sonar sensors, and other sensing devices are all present. According to several self-driving car manufacturers, the data from the sensors would flow up into the cloud that the automaker has set up for their self-driving cars (Figure 6.3) [8]. Automakers can now accumulate a large amount of driving data and analyze it using machine learning.

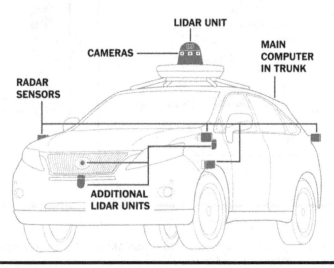

Figure 6.3 Autonomous Vehicle Components.

Source: https://softwareengineeringdaily.com/2018/12/27/self-driving-deep-learning-with-lex-fridman-holiday-repeat/

■ Conditional Automation: The vehicle has environmental detection capabilities. Human intervention is required. Performs well in environments like auto parking and a single lane without any traffic.

■ High Automation: The vehicle could perform all the driving tasks under a controlled environment. Human intervention is an option.

■ Full Automation: The vehicle needs zero human intervention and achieve high accuracy in decision making and vehicle control.

Edge AI Steps

1. Autonomous cars create and preserve [9] a map of their surroundings using a number of sensors in the vehicle.
2. Radar sensors monitor the movement of the vehicles in the area.
3. Video cameras track traffic lights, and often read road signs, control other vehicles, and search for pedestrians (Figure 6.4).
4. By bouncing light signals off the car's surroundings, Lidar (light detection and ranging) sensors measure distances, monitor road edges, and discern lane markers.

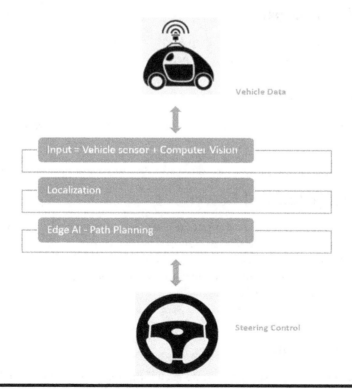

Figure 6.4 Autonomous Vehicle Data Process.

5. Ultrasonic sensors in the wheels detect curbs and other vehicles while parking.
6. The Edge AI in the car then analyzes all of the sensory data, plans a course, and sends commands to the car's actuators, which monitor acceleration, braking, and steering.
7. The AI follows traffic laws and navigates obstacles using hard-coded rules, obstacle avoidance algorithms, predictive modeling, and object recognition.

Edge Computing Needs and Challenges

- Edge computing systems that are scalable
- Data acquisition interfaces and digital twins for OT/IT integration
- Consolidation of hazardous workloads
- Vertical certifications are required in each industry
- Deployments in difficult environments
- Connectivity that is unreliable and costly
- Edge management from afar
- Physical security

Edge AI in Industries

Today, we use cloud computing and an API to train and serve an ML model. Edge AI, then, performs ML tasks close to the user.

Drawbacks of Edge AI

Edge AI has less computational power than cloud computing and results in much more machine variation.

Less Computational Power

The processing power of edge computing is not yet comparable to that of a cloud computing system. As a result, an edge computer can only perform a limited number of AI tasks. The cloud will continue [10] to build and support large models, but edge devices will infer smaller models on-device. Edge computers can also perform small transfer learning tasks.

Machine Variations

When we depend on edge machines, we get a lot more variety in device styles. As a result, failure is more common. Orchestrators can assist in the transition of jobs to other clusters in the event of a failure, ensuring system resiliency. In the long term, though, there will be more failures.

Edge AI and Blockchain for Privacy-Critical and Data-Sensitive Applications

General Overview

A blockchain is an ever-growing list of cryptographically connected documents known as blocks. Each block contains a timestamp, a cryptographic hash of the previous block, and transaction details (generally represented as a Merkle tree). The timestamp proves that the transaction data existed at the time the block was written, which is required to get into the hash. By containing the hash of the previous block, each subsequent block strengthens the ones before it, resulting in a chain. As a result, blockchains are impervious to data manipulation because the data in any given block, once documented, cannot be altered retroactively without affecting all subsequent blocks.

Data Privacy

Application end users and businesses are becoming more aware of the value of protecting personal data and online privacy. This is a particularly pressing concern in the Internet of Things, where a slew of security concerns has been identified by the research community. In recent years, a wide variety of IoT platforms and applications have embraced blockchain technology to mitigate multiple privacy risks and allow secure transactions without the need for a trusted third party (Figure 6.5). On the other hand, current IoT blockchain integrations have concentrated on securing compatibility without changing the interaction topology.

Data Security

Every day banks handle enormous amounts of data. Banks, for example, manage thousands of ATMs and personal transaction records at different points.

The case is usually sorted only after a customer reports a fraud that increases the risk of loss. The difference with the edge calculation is the receipt and analysis of video feedback from the complaint requiring little or no human action at once. Edge computing also ensures ATMs are guaranteed against fraudsters who try to deal with them. The screen data will not react. In further attempts, the machine

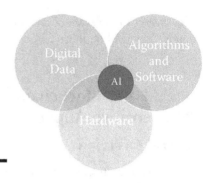

Figure 6.5 Edge AI with Data.

will likely be shut down. In addition, edge computing can protect customers' personal data with their information.

Business Continuity

Edge computing and other emerging technologies contribute to increased security and business continuity. Edge computing facilitates data processing by bringing data closer to the source. As a result, systems are more quickly scaled. Edge computing also helps banks stay afloat in the event of unforeseen events like network outages.

Edge computing ensures that when a bank loses connectivity, the financial institution stays operational with minimal downtime. Computer vision will be available in branches, allowing them to lessen their dependence on on-site assets and human staff. Since moving data to and from a data center is not a [11] long process, banks can process data much faster with edge computing.

Next-Generation Analytics

Banks may also use edge computing to gain a deeper understanding of their customers, allowing them to better respond to their evolving needs and desires. Edge computing is important in the production of customized products and targeted promotions.

It's also useful for selling similar products to branch clients, thanks to near-field communication systems, mobile devices, and location services. Anonymized data is used to do this.

Banks can now easily have enhanced experiences thanks to new technologies like APIs and edge computing. These technologies help banks meet the needs of their customers and gain a competitive advantage.

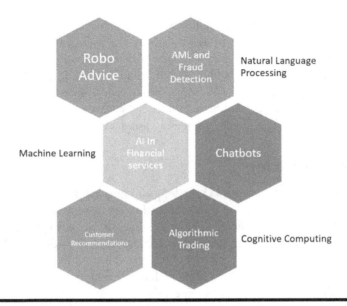

Figure 6.6   Edge AI in Financial Services.

Increased Innovation

Businesses are constantly using IoT software to connect with customers, and banks are no exception. More powerful data processing is needed by kiosks, ATMs, bank applications, and other technologies (Figure 6.6).

Edge computing bridges the gap, allowing more IoT applications to operate with lower data limits. Innovation becomes more feasible as a bank's protection and speed improves, as well as its IoT implementation options grow.

If these benefits are combined with the potential cost savings of edge computing, banks will benefit greatly. They could, for example, speed up the implementation of solutions that would otherwise be delayed.

Customer Experience

One of the most significant benefits of edge computing for banks is the ability to have individualized customer experiences. Due to speed and latency problems, digital tellers and facial recognition were historically difficult to introduce. Because of edge computing, these advancements are now possible. A near-the-edge infrastructure might recognize a customer's face and submit data to branch staff. Customers can then offer instant loan offers tailored to their specific needs, as well as a highly personalized customer experience. Face recognition technology, near-field communications, and other technological advancements have made generic products obsolete.

Advanced technology has undoubtedly had a significant effect on the financial industry growth. For example, the user experience was transformed in a varying way by AI and application programming interfaces (APIs). For example, edge computing is here to stay, so that banks should be aware of it. For the future digital industry, the advantages of edge computing will benefit banks. To sum up, companies need to adopt emerging technologies to thrive in today's digital economy. The organization can only offer 5G, IoT, and edge computing in a few of its technical options.

Influencing Factors

A variety of factors influence edge computing and Edge AI. Personalization features are available only after user authorization within the app, as users become more aware of where their data is stored. This will enable companies to provide more AI-powered personalized features while also enabling users to understand how their data is collected.

Multiple layers of encryption and more dynamic encryption methods are being pushed as distributed networks become more prevalent and data stored in the cloud becomes more sensitive with an increasing number of AI-enabled products, such as speakers, on the market.

The most obvious reason for tasks being done on the edge is latency. Since our systems are more distributed at both the network and device levels, there are more latency problems when transmitting data across networks and devices (Figure 6.7). On increasingly distributed systems, multiple load balancing endpoints are needed to improve the application end-to-end resiliency. To boost device resiliency, this introduces the idea of a Cloudlet, which resides on the edge or near the mobile device.

Edge AI–Enabled IoT Devices

In a matter of years, billions of connected devices will be installed worldwide in our homes, cities, vehicles, and industries. Limited resource devices interact with users and the environment. Many of these devices are intended for decoding senses and sensor actions, making accurate predictions and choosing machine learning

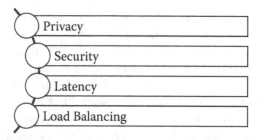

Figure 6.7   Edge AI Influencing Factors.

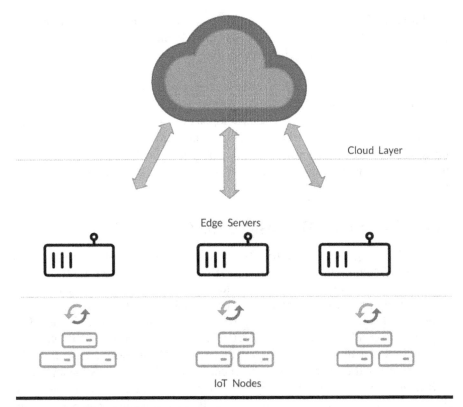

Figure 6.8 Edge IoT Devices.

models. The bottleneck is the network's high connectivity level. The need is to integrate information into terminal devices by using an algorithm.

The Internet of Things (IoT) is based on the Internet connected by billions of real physical objects and mobile devices. With the development of connected devices, the idea of edge computing has gained prominence and is widely accepted (Figure 6.8). Edge computing offers more proximity to the grid edge to solve scalability and latency problems, analyses, storage, and control.

However, edge calculation has difficulties with various IoT configurations. These different applications generate a great deal of big data that can be processed efficiently. Existing architectures face several challenges and the biggest task is to process big data.

Benefits of Edge AI in IoT Devices

Edge computing enables AI technologies to operate offline in situations with small or low bandwidth demands, typically served by SaaS. This feature is especially helpful for IoT edge AI. In an IoT development project you have to compromise performance and network latency. Calculation is much faster and gives you a greater degree of control, but it can also lead to reactivity problems that affect your customer experience.

When the user cannot reach your device with a powerful network signal, things start to collapse. Cloud computing also opens up data to more security risks than local computing. With Edge AI, companies are able to operate local on-edge devices to counteract performance and latency issues through their machine learning models. Feedback on the mission-critical applications can be provided in real time by AI systems. As the data is not transmitted through the cloud, it is safer.

Edge Computing Downsides for IoT

In the field of edge computing, IoT still has a large vacuum. Many providers work in this field on optimum protocols and processes. However, when we construct the open website, the infrastructure we take for granted lags behind in years.

Developing limited AI products not only requires AI/ML but also hardware, software, networking, and safety. This becomes easier to achieve with the wider implementation of projects like LF EDGE over time. These standards allow the development of additional tools in open-source areas. These instruments can then be used to build high-performance systems of enterprises. The most effective way to get started with Edge AI in the IoT is to consider the entire spectrum of devices – IoT devices or "things" aren't the only new hardware to be concerned about. Components that can be used in networked environments include micro-datacenters and IoT gateways in the region. The amount of latency your device can handle, as well as the size of the data operations you need to run, decide your edge infrastructure requirements.

The journey from testing to deployment of AI on the edge is just beginning. Over the next few years, expect a lot of exciting developments in this area (Figure 6.9).

Edge AI–Enabled IoT Devices

A traditional database and a blockchain structure data in very different ways. A blockchain is a distributed ledger that divides data into blocks, each containing a collection of information. When a block's storage capacity is exhausted, it is chained onto the previous block, forming a "blockchain" of data. After the newly inserted block, all new knowledge is integrated into a new block, which is then added to the chain until it is complete.

Edge Computing Interest

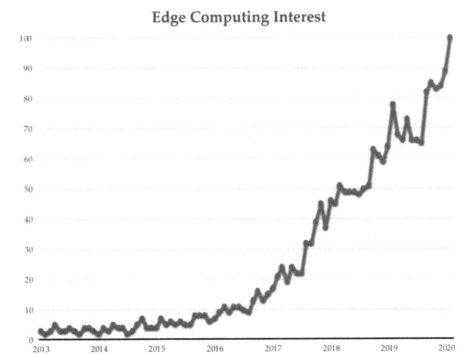

Figure 6.9   Edge Computing Interest.

Source: https://www.osolabs.com/blog/edge-computing-is-coming/

Security: In a variety of ways, blockchain technology handles security and trust issues. To begin, new blocks are usually organized in a sequential and chronological order. That is, they are widely utilized on the "top" layer of the blockchain. You'll note that each block on the Bitcoin blockchain has its own "height" when you look at it. The block's height had reached 656,197 blocks as of November 2020.

Here's why it's so important in terms of safety. Assume a hacker tries to change the blockchain in order to steal Bitcoin from the rest of the world. Someone else's copy would no longer fit if they made a change to their single copy. As more people compare their versions, they'll notice how dissimilar this one is, and the hacker's chain will be regarded as bogus.

Changing the contents of a block after it has been appended to the end of the blockchain is exceedingly difficult unless the majority agrees. This is because each block has its own hash, as well as the hash of the preceding block and the time stamp described earlier. Hash codes are formed by converting digital data into a string of numbers and letters using a math formula. If the information is altered in any manner, the hash code changes.

Blockchain as an Infrastructure

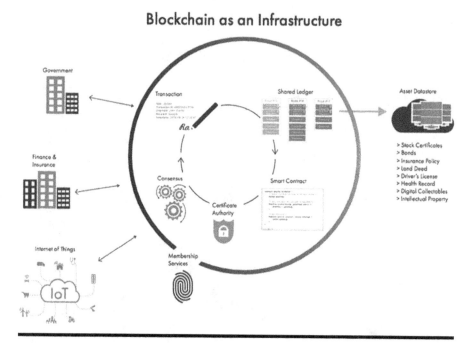

Figure 6.10 Blockchain Infrastructure.

To succeed, the hacker would have to take control of and change 51% of the blockchain copies at the same moment, ensuring that their new copy becomes the majority copy and so the agreed-upon chain (Figure 6.10). Because the time stamps and hash codes would be different now, an assault like this would cost a lot of money and time because all of the blocks would have to be re-created.

The expense of executing such a feat would definitely be insurmountable, given the scale of Bitcoin's network and how quickly it is growing. Not only would this be outrageously expensive, but it would also be meaningless. Such substantial enhancements to the blockchain would be detected by members of the network, and such behavior would not go undetected. Members of the network would then fork off to a new, unaffected iteration of the chain. The attacker's version of Bitcoin would lose value, rendering the attack futile because the bad guy would be in possession of a worthless asset. If a bad person attacked Bitcoin's most recent fork, the same thing would happen (Figure 6.11). It's set up in this way such that joining the network pays off much better than breaking in.

The attacker's version of Bitcoin would lose value, rendering the attack futile because the bad guy would be in possession of a worthless asset. If a bad person attacked Bitcoin's most recent fork, the same thing would happen. It's set up in this way such that joining the network pays off much better than breaking in.

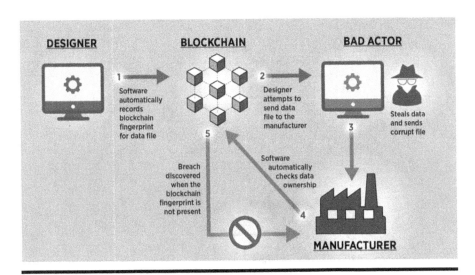

Figure 6.11   Blockchain Security.

Source: https://www.nist.gov/image/blockchainmanufacturingfinalpng

Case Study: Edge Deduction

This case study demonstrates how to detect edges in an image. We will gain a grasp of computer vision and self-driving automobiles by writing an edge detection algorithm. To understand objects in an image, edge detection is widely utilized. It also aids the machines in making more accurate forecasts. Writing an edge detection program is a fantastic approach to learn how computers perceive the world around them. This will help us gain a better understanding of computer vision (Figure 6.12).

In prior articles, I discussed face detection, face recognition, and text recognition, which are all computer vision principles. Today, we'll use Python to work on edge detection.

Libraries:

Install the libraries required for the application
pip install numpy matplotlib opencv-python

Edge detection is a type of image processing that uses mathematical approaches to locate edges in a digital image. Internally, edge detection works by applying a filter/kernel to a digital image and detecting discontinuities in image regions such as sharp changes in pixel brightness/intensity values. (Figure 6.13).

The Canny edge detector is an edge detection operator that uses a multi-stage algorithm to detect a wide range of edges in images. The Canny edge detection model is another name for this OpenCV detection approach.

In [18]:

```
import cv2
import numpy as np
import matplotlib.pyplot as plt
image = cv2.imread('D:\Flower.jpg',0)
Calc_Edge = cv2.Canny(image, 100,200)
images = [image , edges_detected]
location = [121, 122]
for loc, edge_image in zip(location, images):
    plt.subplot(loc)
    plt.imshow(edge_image, cmap='gray')
    cv2.imwrite('d:\edge_flower.png', Calc_Edge)
    plt.savefig('Out_Edge.png')
    plt.show()
```

Figure 6.12   Edge Deduction Using Python Program.

Figure 6.13   Edge-Deducted Image.

Applications:

1. License plate detection
2. Detecting hidden information in medical images
3. Fingerprint matching
4. Object deduction

Above are the applications of edge deduction and the program done in hardware devices to detect the objects and act as an Edge AI.

Ethereum Blockchain with Edge AI

The Internet of Things (IoT), which develops many business models that deliver multiple ubiquitous and intelligent services, is becoming one of the most valuable assets in today's data-driven digital economy. These data contain sensitive personal data and can reveal the identity of the stakeholders involved (Figure 6.14). If there is no proper mechanism for privacy preservation; for instance, a malicious actor who has access to personal information can use your identity in order to obtain a financial benefit or other benefits on behalf of the other person.

The concerns of IoT's distributed architecture, large volume, and lack of resources for processing power, storage capacity, bandwidth, etc. do not provide a safe application privacy platform. In addition, conventional IoT network apps are designed to perform data management functions centrally, i.e., collection of data, data storage, processing, data sharing, and data destruction, without taking into consideration the distributed nature of IoT devices.

Edge Computing Downsides for IoT

Edge gates are smart gateways on both sides and work with local networks only. SBCs have the computer capability to perform AI algorithms for resource-contracted devils, like Raspberry Pi boards or Intel UP boards. Edge gateways are available. The capability to participate directly in the blockchain network is not met by multiple drives and sensors in the sensor layer. Therefore, sensor nodes are connected to the edge portal that acts as their intermediary.

These edge portals are running sidechains to store hacks of your previous data and validation documents for transactions. In the data processing, encryption, and storage blocks, complete flows of data batch generation, processing at edge gates, and storage on the cloud layer.

Sensor nodes are linked to only one edge node, which minimizes data from vulnerable channels. If an opponent can only affect that node if a node is affected. The encrypted link increases data security, ensures that the data is accessed properly

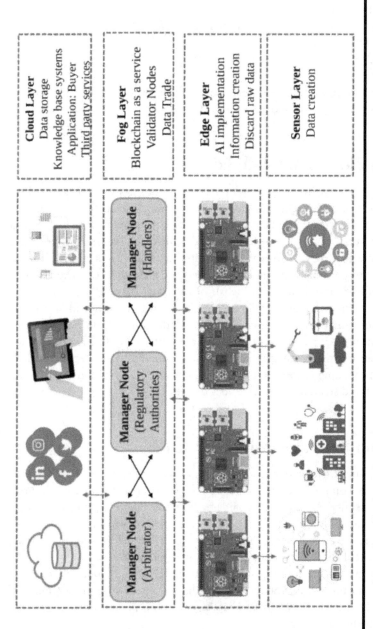

Figure 6.14 Architecture of EdgeBoT, a Distributed P2P Data Trade and Fair Access Network Model Based on the Ethereum Platform.

Source: Edge Computing to Secure IoT Data Ownership and Trade with the Ethereum Blockchain https:// www.ncbi.nlm.nih.gov/pmc/articles/PMC7412471/

and properly held, and adds sensor nodes to the EdgeBoT backbone network. On the other hand, the fog layer manager nodes are fully independent; they are able to communicate in a network without external monitoring with any other manager node. These nodes can also be used as a customized access control model.

Data Trade through Ethereum

The EdgeBoT backbone is Ethereum, where all transactions within the network are recorded with a time stamp system and cryptographic hazards to avoid retroactive alterations. All requirements for a particular user, such as limited access time to a network, can be defined, ensured, and recorded through the use of smart contracts.

In the initialization of the transaction block in Figure 6.15, the complete sequence of the transaction is shown in EdgeBoT. Whenever an external buyer wants to acquire data, he or she joins the network and requests a given data batch using publicly available batch headers. The transaction price and conditions are met by a

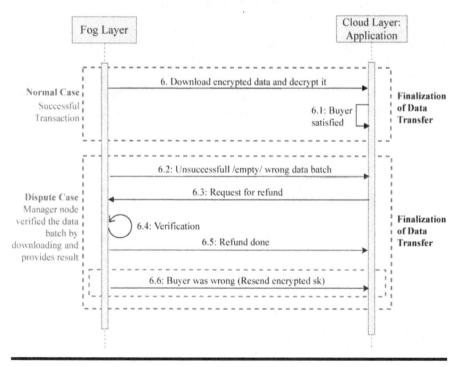

Figure 6.15 Transaction Request Flow.

Source: Edge Computing to Secure IoT Data Ownership and Trade with the Ethereum Blockchain https://www.ncbi.nlm.nih.gov/pmc/articles/PMC7412471/

manager node at the layer of fog. If the buyer accepts the conditions, the manager node validates the transaction by encoding it using the public key of the buyer along with the data batch address, sending the unique secret encryption key (driven by CKD).

The buyer downloads the cloud-layer (storage) encrypted data batch and decrypts it with the public key. Possible scenarios are shown in Figure 6.3 after the required data have been received. In a normal case, the data received is met by the buyer. In a dispute, the buyer cannot download or decrypt the data received or is dissatisfied with the received information. The buyer may request a refund in this case. In this case, once the refund application is received, the request is verified by a manager node through the download of the data load. Reimbursement will be processed if the buyer is legitimate (Figure 6.15). Should the buyer be incorrect, the manager node will again return the encryption that completes the request for the transaction.

Case Study: Blockchain for Transaction

An increasing list of linked records (i.e., blocks) is referred to as a blockchain. The Bitcoin system based on blockchains was the first successful application of this system, and was founded on the same principles shortly after its popularity. However, this system is not limited to the storage of financial data. Instead, the type of data stored does not matter and is separate from the blockchain network.

Below is the standard JSON format for each block to store the data.

```
{
    "author": "author_name",
    "timestamp": "transaction_time",
    "data": "transaction_data"
}
```

Python Program:

```
defadd_block(self, block, proof):
    previous_hash = self.last_block.hash
    if previous_hash != block.previous_hash:
        returnFalse
    ifnot self.is_valid_proof(block, proof):
        returnFalse
```

```
block.hash = proof
self.chain.append(block)
returnTrue
```

We add a few methods for building a chain together. We will first store data for each transaction in unfirmed transactions. Once the valid proof that the new block meets the challenge criteria is confirmed, we can add it to the chain. This system is often referred to as mining in the computer process.

Expected Output:

{"length": 1, "chain": [{"index": 0, "transactions": [], "timestamp": 1576665446.403836, "previous_hash": "0", "nonce": 0, "hash": "e2a1ec32fcf89d0388f3d0d8abcd914f941d056c080df1c765a3f6035626fc94"}]}

Conclusion

More companies and developers recognize the importance of more effective immediate service while increasing their profit margin through the deployment of edge technology. This opens up a new world for AI-based services, user convenience, and company satisfaction.

Long-standing companies such as Microsoft and Apple have spent millions to develop their Edge AI systems. Therefore, the only way to remain competitive is by participating and leading in these technologies. In contrast, a growing request for IoT systems will enable the adoption of 5G and edge computing networks. Data is still being processed in the cloud, but edge can operate and process user-generated data, which belongs only to users.

References

[1] X. Lin, J. Li, J. Wu, H. Liang, and W. Yang. "Making Knowledge Tradable in edge-AI Enabled IoT: A Consortium Blockchain-based Efficient and Incentive Approach." *IEEE Transactions on Industrial Informatics* 15, no. 12 (2019): 6367–6378.
[2] A. Nawaz, T. N. Gia, J. P. Queralta, and T. Westerlund. "Edge AI and Blockchain for Privacy-Critical and Data-Sensitive Applications." In *2019 Twelfth International Conference on Mobile Computing and Ubiquitous Network (ICMU)* (2019): 1–2. IEEE.

[3] F. J. Ferrández-Pastor, J. M. García-Chamizo, M. Nieto-Hidalgo, and J. Mora-Martínez. "Precision Agriculture Design Method Using a Distributed Computing Architecture on Internet of Things Context." *Sensors* 18, no. 6 (2018): 1731.

[4] T. Rausch and S. Dustdar. "Edge Intelligence: The Convergence of Humans, Things, and ai." In *2019 IEEE International Conference on Cloud Engineering (IC2E)* (2019): 86–96. IEEE.

[5] M. Satyanarayanan, P. Simoens, Y. Xiao, P. Pillai, Z. Chen, K. Ha, W. Hu, and B. Amos. "Edge Analytics in the Internet of Things." *IEEE Pervasive Computing* 14, no. 2 (2015): 24–31.

[6] S. Deng, H. Zhao, W. Fang, J. Yin, S. Dustdar, and A. Y. Zomaya. "Edge Intelligence: The Confluence of Edge Computing and Artificial Intelligence." *IEEE Internet of Things Journal* 7, no. 8 (2020): 7457–7469.

[7] S. Liu, L. Liu, J. Tang, B. Yu, Y. Wang, and W. Shi. "Edge Computing for Autonomous Driving: Opportunities and Challenges." *Proceedings of the IEEE* 107, no. 8 (2019): 1697–1716.

[8] B. Chen, J. Wan, A. Celesti, D. Li, H. Abbas, and Q. Zhang. "Edge Computing in IoT-based Manufacturing." *IEEE Communications Magazine* 56, no. 9 (2018): 103–109.

[9] R.I. Minu and G. Nagarajan. "Bridging the IoT Gap Through Edge Computing." In *Edge Computing and Computational Intelligence Paradigms for the IoT*, pp. 1–9. IGI Global, 2019.

[10] G. Nagarajan, R. I. Minu, and A. Jayanthiladevi. "Cognitive Internet of Things (C-IOT)." In *Sensing Techniques for Next Generation Cognitive Radio Networks*, pp. 299–311. IGI Global, 2019, US.

[11] S. V. Simpson and G. Nagarajan. "An Edge based Trustworthy Environment Establishment for Internet of Things: an Approach for Smart Cities." *Wireless Networks* (2021): 1–17.

Chapter 7

Edge AI: From the Perspective of Predictive Maintenance

S. Sharanya
Department of Computer Science and Engineering, SRM Institute of Science and Technology, Chennai, India

R. Venkataraman
School of Computing, SRM Institute of Science and Technology, Chennai, India

G. Murali
Department of Mechatronics, SRM Institute of Science and Technology, Chennai, India

Contents

DOI: 10.1201/9781003145158-7

Industry 4.0: Country's Vision to Become a Superpower

Industry 4.0, popularly known as the Fourth Industrial Revolution, has transformed the perception of the country's manufacturing landscape [1]. The primary goal of Industry 4.0 is to establish automation through connectivity, smartness, and flexibility. The convergence of a multitude of technologies like artificial intelligence, cloud computing, quantum computing, additive manufacturing, virtual and augmented reality, Edge AI, Internet of Things, etc. has escalated the induction of smartness in manufacturing industries. The Industrial Revolution in different years is visualized as an evolution rather than a revolution. The important milestones in each industrial revolution are given in Figure 7.1.

The current industry landscape is the amalgamation of various technologies that coexist with each other to attain profitability with optimized resources. The exhaustive list of cutting-edge technologies in Industry 4.0 are given below:

- *Cloud Computing:* Smart manufacturing integrated with the cloud can transform the way in which the processes are happening in industries by

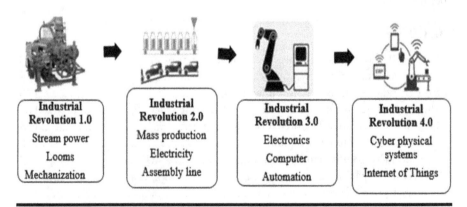

Figure 7.1 Evolution of Industry 4.0.

enhancing the operations and improving scalability, making the business better [2].

■ *Internet of Things (IoT) and Industrial IoT (IIoT):* These technologies are cohesive with machine learning, deep learning, sensor networks, big data analytics, M2M communication, and AI to bring advancements in automation. These technologies are intertwined to form a smart, connected, and collaborative industrial ecosystem [3].

■ *Artificial Intelligence:* Business intelligence and analytics have become a vital part of any field because of the advent of AI. Second-generation AI has transformed intelligent manufacturing into smart manufacturing by augmenting a wide spectra of other technologies [4].

■ *Big Data Analytics:* This uncovers the hidden trends and patterns in the voluminous data generated by smart sensors to discover the performance bottlenecks in operations. Big data analytics has emerged as indispensable technology for supporting supply chain management, optimized production costs, condition monitoring, predictive maintenance, fault diagnosis, and smart resource management [5].

■ *Cyber Physical Systems (CPS):* Realization of smart manufacturing without the element of CPS is not possible. This is a complex, multidimensional system that incorporates a virtual cyber environment with the automated and vibrant physical world [6].

■ *Smart Sensors:* The fundamental data collecting unit is a sensor and fabricating smart sensors are more viable options in the context of smart manufacturing [7]. They are the backbone of any network of smart devices with specific communication standards like Zigbee, IEEE 802.15.1, and IEEE 802.15.4.

■ *Additive Manufacturing:* This technique is used to create complex geometries, miniature prototypes, models, end-use parts, versatile printing methods, etc. [8] with minimal material wastage. The famed 3-D printing technology is an application of additive manufacturing.

■ *Smart Material:* They are otherwise termed intelligent or responsive materials that change their inherent properties in accordance with the external environment. They are called smart because of their capability to revert to their original state after discarding the external stimulus [9].

■ *Augmented Reality and Simulation:* This technology centers on constructing realistic visually appealing models that demonstrate the smart behavior of synthetic materials. This is viewed as an extension of virtual reality. The components involved in augmented reality are generally computer-generated inputs and make these virtual elements coexist with real-world entities [10].

■ *Digital Twin:* This is conceptualizing the digital replica into a realistic component by deploying smart sensors [11]. This computer-generated virtual replica of the original product is modeled by integrating AI and data analytics to give projections.

■ *Edge and Fog Computing:* These computing paradigms extend the computation, networking, and storage capabilities of cloud computing. Edge and fog offer the same processing power of the cloud but at very reduced latency, bandwidth, and real-time response, along with data processing techniques at greatly reduced traffic at the factory site [12].

■ *Blockchain:* Blockchain is a dynamically growing distributed record that is interlinked with one another with inherent security measures. These entities can be deployed in supply chain management to manage the resources [13].

■ *Predictive Analytics:* This focus is on integrating the predictive power in building intelligent systems with self-aware and self-maintainable traits in processing and machines. Predictive analytics can find its application in almost all fields in Industry 4.0 (Figure 7.2).

The mentioned technologies have brought Industry 4.0 into existence. These technologies culminate human intelligence into the factory floors by acting on the key components, the data.

Smart Manufacturing

Smart manufacturing restructures the entire manufacturing sector, which is not only confined to production units but also in the manufacturing, management, and supply chain, to build a smart ecosystem by integrating the power of diverse technologies. The two main pillars of smart manufacturing are data analytics and automation. The industrial world is diligently working to adopt protocols and standardizations to foster the interoperability between the extent of diverse technologies. The transformation of classical manufacturing into smart manufacturing is attributed by the presence of the following activities:

■ Increasing degree of automation

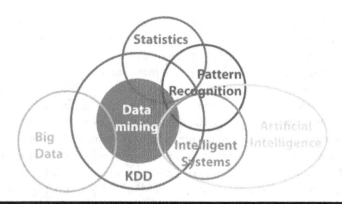

Figure 7.2 Predictive Analytics and Its Allied Technologies.

- Exploring trends and patterns through data analytics
- Interfacing the physical and virtual (digital) environment
- Introducing new technologies like additive manufacturing
- Incorporating operational and information technology
- Evolving smart solutions to address the challenges due to change in human, social, and economic conditions Figure 7.3

Smart manufacturing exhibits a very extensive horizon to explore the scope of driving the intelligence into the devices and manufacturing processes. The various entities of manufacturing that can be used in smart manufacturing include:

- *Objects:* numbering end-use parts, product numbers, specification, etc.
- *Equipment:* data from sensors, operation profiles, machines and their allied components, etc.
- *Process:* surveillance, condition monitoring, total quality management, performance assessments, etc.
- *People:* GPS, location trackers, attendance systems, etc.
- *Environment:* electricity consumption, Internet usage, cloud usage, utilization of other amenities and resources.

Integrating intelligence in all of the mentioned elements of the industry will slowly metamorphosize into a smart industry. The notion of smart manufacturing creates ample opportunities for augmenting AI-based technologies in the industrial ecosystem. Some of the noteworthy ones are listed as follows:

- Condition monitoring
- Fault diagnosis

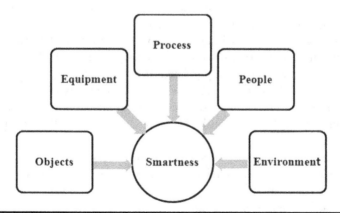

Figure 7.3   Elements in Smart Manufacturing.

- Inspection of surface integration
- Predictive maintenance
- Defect prognosis
- Performance monitoring
- Consumer behavior prediction
- Multi-channel sales prediction
- Fraud detection
- Customer relationship management
- Demand planning
- Automating supply chain management
- Budget forecasting
- Material distribution and tracking

Recent days have seen a great surge in the publications, products, and business solutions in both research and development (R&D) and commercial sectors. Amalgamation of versatile technologies to build robust infrastructure, frameworks, and conceptualizations are the immediate needs of Industry 4.0.

Pursuit of Edge AI in Smart Manufacturing

The recent developments highlight that accentuating the power of data analytics will contribute to the improvement of overall efficacy of industries. As Edge AI drills down the decision-making capability with greatly reduced connection, optimal bandwidth consumption, resource management, load balancing, and data processing bottlenecks, it is a natural one-source solution to implement smart manufacturing solutions in micro, small, and medium enterprises (MSME) [14]. The traits of Edge AI can help in building an industrial ecosystem that is highly interconnected with an intelligence-integrated assembly line apart from augmenting the decisive power. The power of Edge AI is vividly portrayed in Figure 7.4.

Edge AI is a computing enclosure that is proximal to the end devices located in the manufacturing industries, to add intelligence to the localized infrastructures. The edge devices will be accommodated with processing power and analytic capabilities to handle a specific task. This technology facilitates horizontal integration of heterogeneous components to bring the notion of smart manufacturing into effect. Edge AI can be implemented in three different ways:

- As local devices designed to a very specific purpose
- As pre-engineered localized data centers with remarkable processing, analytic, and storage capabilities
- Only as high-end storage centers

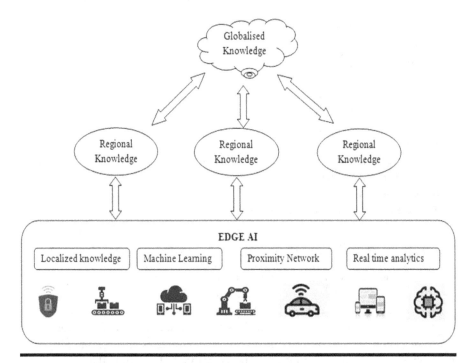

Figure 7.4   Edge AI in Smart Industries.

Edge AI can be leveraged in applications with any level of granularity and scalability. This integration of two equally competent technologies, namely Edge and AI, envision excellent scope in the near future in all dimensions of smart manufacturing. This chapter focuses on deploying Edge AI in dynamic predictive maintenance, a proactive failure prediction strategy that forwarns the faults and failures of equipment and devices by analyzing the vital parameters and ensures smooth functioning.

Predictive Maintenance: The Future Era of Maintenance

Predictive maintenance (PdM) is a proactive maintenance technique that predicts the time to schedule the maintenance activity of any system or equipment before it enters into failure mode of operation. This competitive strategy is not limited to be applied to all the industry verticals but also in other sectors like health care, processing industries, food, oil and gas industries, etc. The PdM can be adopted as an integrated strategy or as a stand-alone technique. The global market of PdM is expected to contribute an increase of 37.9% in the Compound Annual Growth Rate (CAGR) in the year 2025 [15]. Hence, all the industries are now shifting their focus to deploy PdM solutions at their site so as to achieve the following benefits:

- Reducing equipment downtime
- Analyzing failure causes
- Mitigating repair costs
- Decreasing maintenance costs
- Planning maintenance scheduling
- Avoiding unexpected downtime
- Temporal repairing
- Consistent performance
- Balancing the limited availability of skilled labor for maintenance activities
- Fostering non-intrusive testing
- Reducing operational costs
- Increasing useful production time

Genesis of Predictive Maintenance and Its Future

Predictive maintenance is seen as a gamechanger in smart manufacturing. Though the cost for initial deployment and training is high, the benefits of predictive maintenance overlook these barriers. Implementation of predictive maintenance is built over condition monitoring, which is the continuous process of monitoring the vital parameters of any system or equipment to assess its efficacy [16]. The parameters are monitored through sensors without disrupting the equipment's normal operational flow. Some of the common parameters that are monitored in the industries are noise, vibrations, fluid flow, fluid level, temperature, oil level, corrosion, electricity, etc. The decline in cost of sensing technologies has expanded the horizons of condition monitoring to remarkable extent.

Industrial or plant maintenance is a broad field that aims to build the reliability of the systems so as to increase the productivity time. This is a vital activity that attempts to mitigate the effect of faults and failures by employing time to time functionality checks, equipment servicing, replacing defective components, and fixing repairs. In addition to all of these, proper maintenance activity is a crucial trust factor for any organization or industry. The roots of maintenance activity are very deep, sourced from reactive maintenance to advanced prescriptive maintenance. The evolution of maintenance strategies are visualized in Figure 7.5.

Reactive Maintenance

Reactive maintenance is adopted after the occurrence of a failure of fault in the equipment. This is a very cost-effective way to restore the equipment to its normal state and to resume its functioning. The major limitation of this approach is that it could not be accepted as a long-term sustainable activity.

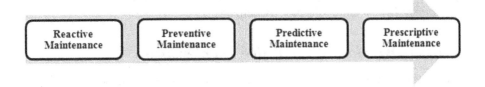

Figure 7.5 Evolution of Maintenance Strategies.

Preventive Maintenance

The main objective of preventive maintenance is to decrease the chances of any equipment to enter into its fault or failure profile. This is a proactive strategy that fixes the defect even before it occurs. Preventive maintenance increases the life span of the equipment and retards its degradation rate. The two kinds of preventative maintenance are as follows:

   i. *Time-based preventive maintenance:* Maintenance activity of the equipment is carried out after a fixed time limit. This is widely used in equipment with wearable parts and also in devices whose Mean Time Between Failure (MTBF) is pre-determined. Maintenance activities are scheduled after the fixed time interval.
  ii. *Risk-based preventive maintenance:* Maintenance activities of the equipment are done by assessing the risks associated with the equipment. The equipment that has a high risk of failure is closely monitored and frequent maintenance is done to minimize the effect of risks.

Predictive Maintenance

Predictive maintenance is done by assessing the deviations of the critical variables that characterize the system under study. This increases the reliability measure of the system and also decreases the time and effort required to carry out the maintenance activities. This is a proactive maintenance strategy that fixes the failures by scheduling maintenance activity when the early signs of deviations are noted in the critical variables that are monitored [17].

Prescriptive Maintenance

Prescriptive maintenance is the next-generation maintenance scheme, which provides adaptive recommendations about the maintenance tasks to be performed based on the AI techniques [18]. It helps the maintenance engineers to carry out maintenance by offering solutions to the predicted fault. It is indispensable for the prescriptive maintenance system to thoroughly understand the operations of the equipment before rendering the recommendations.

A Brief Overview of Predictive Maintenance

The amalgamation of big data analytics, AI, IoT, predictive analytics, and Edge AI has led to enormous developments in industrial predictive maintenance. This maintenance strategy is adopted for the equipment whose malfunctioning will cause a greater degree of damage in terms of performance, productivity, loss to life, and property. By implementing predictive maintenance policies, the industries confirm the stable equipment operation with the support of intelligent manufacturing [19]. The three main phases in the implementation of predictive maintenance in industries are illustrated in Figure 7.6.

The initial but important step in implementing the predictive maintenance is identifying the key process variable or critical variable that characterizes the equipment under consideration. The next phase is to perform condition monitoring of the isolated critical variables to detect any early signs of faults and failures. The pivotal symptom of fault is the deviation of the critical variables from their normal operational profile. If a deviation is observed, then the reliability mission of predictive maintenance must be initiated to avoid any devastations. Thus, scheduling predictive maintenance interrupts the normal production tasks. But the impact of predictive maintenance should not be underrated, since it is crucial to ensure the safety and reliability of the systems.

Figure 7.7 shows a more granulated view of the predictive maintenance activities. The data acquired from the sensors are analyzed to isolate the critical variables or indicator variables that characterize the system's operational profile.

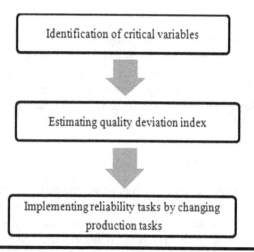

Figure 7.6 Phases of Predictive Maintenance.

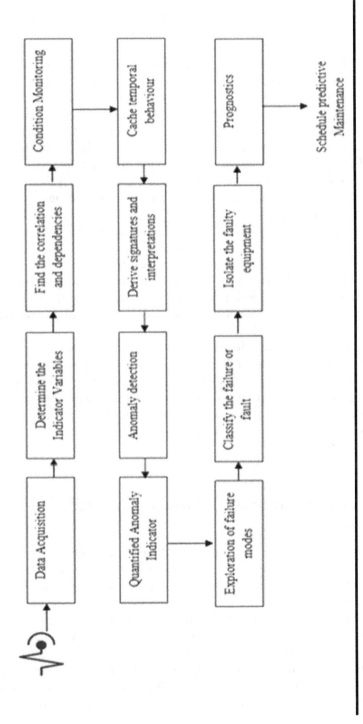

Figure 7.7 Pipeline of Activities in Predictive Maintenance.

These indicator variables are decided on by the domain experts and maintenance engineers. These variables are distinct for each system.

The next step is to find the correlation and interdependencies between the variables. This will give insight to the maintenance team about multiple and co-existing faults and failures that may occur in the system. These variables are continuously monitored around the clock without much physical invasion in the system's functionalities. This process of surveillance of the physical parameters of the equipment or system is known as condition monitoring (CM).

The results of CM are temporarily cached to assess the health state of the system. The significant operational profiles, normal and fault signatures, and early symptoms of deviation of the signals are studied. The deviant operational profile is extracted and it constitutes the indication of the occurrence of fault. This step is called anomaly detection.

Expressing the fault in quantitative terms is very important for gaining a deeper understanding about the severity of the fault. So a quantified anomaly indicator is a direct implication of the fault magnitude. The next step is to explore all possible failure modes in which the system is expected to operate. Determine the failure mode in which the current deviant signature is associated. Classify the severity of the failure and isolate the equipment that has failed among a multitude of components.

The real learning phase is done in the last step, where the deviant conditions, its potential failure modes, and preventive maintenance activities to be planned are given as input into any AI algorithms, which can determine the faults and its associated predictive maintenance activity in early signs of sensor deviation. Thus, the predictive maintenance is accomplished through a series of tasks to predict the occurrence of faults and plan the maintenance activities to avoid unexpected equipment downtime.

Niche of Edge and Fog Computing in Predictive Maintenance

The distributed computing has empowered the industries and other ventures to segment their computing activities to multiple locations. This trend has become much more prevalent after the advent of cloud computing and its allied technologies like fog and edge computing. Amalgamation of AI techniques in the domain of edge to localize the decision making on hardware device has witnessed an overwhelming response from the industries. Most of the production and manufacturing industries are reluctant to invest in constructing a complete network so that commuting information between various devices becomes easy. Edge AI is a lucrative technology, which could be deployed even on devices capable of housing microprocessors and sensors. Imparting AI to localized devices to make domain-specific decisions could entirely change the perception of the maintenance sector.

Limitations of Implementing Cloud-Based Predictive Maintenance

Aggregating the benefits of a cloud platform is not a totally new venture. Cloud-based maintenance frameworks coexist with the AI techniques that offer support to maintenance activities in industries. But these technologies come with their inherent complexities. Some of them are discussed below:

■ Transferring abundant information onto the cloud platform raises the issue of data privacy and security. The sensitivity of data being transferred at multiple locations should not be diluted. Any compromise in the security measures at the site of processing or at the storage site are serious threats to the entire industry.
■ Building decent communication infrastructure is essential for AI-based cloud platforms. The communication bottlenecks like limited bandwidth, poor connectivity, and ensuring availability at data centers demands the deployment of high-end technologies, which is expensive. Also, maintenance of these infrastructures adds additional costs to the industries.
■ The advent of IoT has opened the doors of small- and medium-scale industries to adopt AI-based solutions. So less expensive fog or edge technologies will be natural and affordable solutions to them to implement predictive maintenance.

Types of Edge AI in Industries

Imparting AI into edge devices can be done in a variety of ways. A few of the notable ones are discussed here:

■ *Distributed systems:* The data-intensive AI algorithms require enormous amounts of processing power to handle industrial big data. Decentralizing the processing capabilities to the edge devices invites IoT and blockchain-based solutions.
■ *Sophisticated algorithms:* Continuous research in the fields of AI, ML, and DL has resulted in the development of less intensive data processing algorithms without compromising their efficacy. These algorithms could be administered in edge devices to accomplish the domain-specific tasks.
■ *AI co-processors:* External processors which inculcate the computing power of graphical processing units (GPUs) can brace the edge devices to present AI-based solutions.

Stature of Edge AI in Predictive Maintenance

Edge AI is generally deployed in end devices that have low computing capability. The general notion of predictive maintenance when implemented on edge devices is given in Figure 7.8. The components or equipment to be monitored should be housed with smart sensors, which are continuously condition monitored. The streaming sensor data from these devices are processed at the gateway. The predictive analytic solution powered by AI techniques is encased at the edge devices, localized to the site of equipment location. The results of the gateway can be communicated even to remote locations. Thus, Edge AI empowers the edge devices with decision making and prediction capabilities, thereby avoiding traffic of data, installation of complex networking infrastructure, and equipping high-powered GPUs.

The general architecture of Edge AI in predictive maintenance is discussed previously. But the literature has witnessed many other indigenous frameworks and infrastructures in employing edge and cloud-based AI solutions in imparting predictive maintenance. Some of the notable works are discussed here.

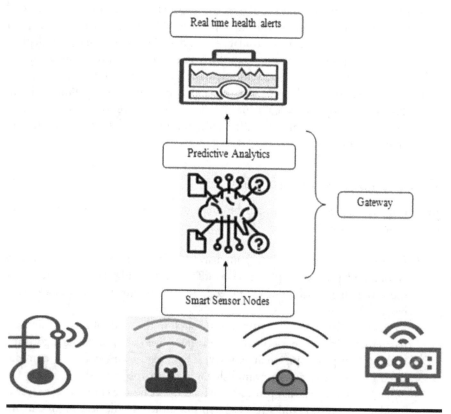

Figure 7.8 Notion of Edge AI in Predictive Maintenance.

Edge PLC (Programmable Logic Controller)–based fault diagnosis of a complete industrial setup of a chemical model simulation comprises a condenser, reactor, gas liquid separator, reactor, and product desorption tower is done by P. Liu et al [20]. The feature selection is done through random forest and the optimal number of edge devices to diagnose the faults is determined using a set coverage algorithm.

Edge AI is also useful in diagnosing faults in rotating machinery. An edge computing node monitors the vibration and current of the motor, from which four features were extracted [21]. These signals are fused to form an indicator at the edge node, which characterizes the health state of the machine. A. H. Sodhro et al. proposed an Edge AI–based reliability model for IoT-based devices [22]. Vibration-based battery level detection is carried out using an Edge AI framework. Imparting intelligence to edge devices is also done through deep learning methods. LSTM-based real-time fault detection can be done by analyzing the temperature, pressure, and vibration signals of machineries [23]. The classification of the health state is done by training the LSTM model and the fault monitoring module creates visualizations like dashboards (as shown in Figure 7.9) to give more insights about the nature of the faults to the maintenance engineers.

(a)   (b)

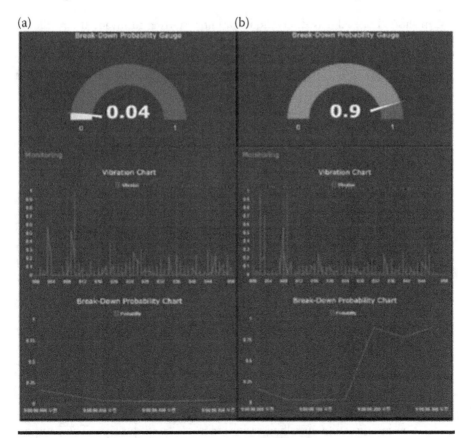

Figure 7.9   Dashboard: a) Normal Condition; b) Faulty Condition.

Edge AI is used in traction control of trains to provide online fault diagnosis in a shorter time [24]. This train data analysis platform does not demand any prior knowledge or mathematical models to predict the faults dynamically. State space models with Kalman's filter are used to estimate the safety level of the train. Predictive maintenance in hydraulic systems from real-time multivariate temporal data designed by Syafrudin et al. [25] uses genetic algorithms to isolate the features. LSTM-based autoencoders are employed for predicting the faults from real time data. This method proved to be very effective in handling noisy real-time data. Abnormal events in the assembly line of production units can also be determined by Edge AI–based devices. The proposed method uses ambient light, air quality, gyroscopes, accelerometers, temperature, and humidity to predict the assembly line faults. This methodology is implemented in a Korean automobile industry and was found to have greater efficiency than other state-of-the-art techniques.

Edge AI–based maintenance systems are prevalent in distributed power systems [26–29]. Wavelet transform of real-time temporal signals is used to extract the features and more visualizations are done in agile and other business processing software.

In short, Edge AI–based techniques are now starting to invade the predictive maintenance industry. The requirements such as minimal bandwidth, low battery power, lack of long-distance transmission, enhanced security, and privacy has made Edge AI techniques a more lucrative option in implementing predictive maintenance.

Edge AI Framework for Predictive Maintenance in Industries

The detailed literature in the field of predictive maintenance shows that there is ample scope for designing more robust frameworks that can integrate the multivariate data from heterogeneous sensors. The proposed framework provisions the incorporation of data emanating from various types of sensors from the system under study. These data are then amalgamated at the edge server through weighted variances that act as a single metric that could characterize the health state of the signal. The learning algorithms are augmented in the edge devices that also act as communication gateways. These algorithms either classify the health state of the machinery or predict the remaining useful life of the machinery based on the demands of the industry. Figure 7.10 shows the Edge AI–based framework for predictive maintenance in industries. A more detailed view of the proposed framework is presented below:

  i. *Heterogeneous Smart Sensors:* The machinery under study should be condition monitored by installing various sensors at multiple sites. These sensors

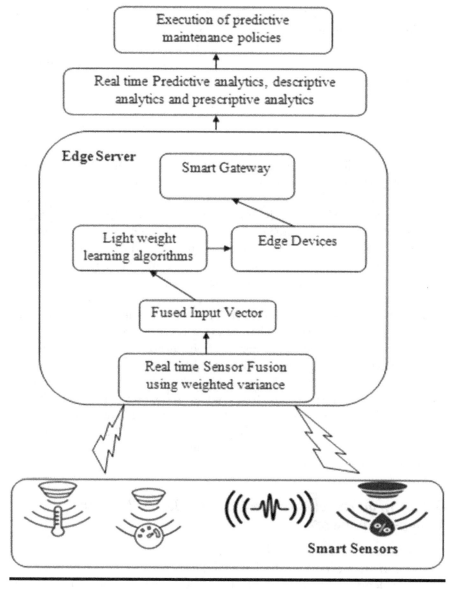

Figure 7.10 Framework of Edge AI for Predictive Maintenance in Industries.

capture the respective signals like temperature, vibration, humidity, pressure, flow rate, and other physical parameters. Installing digital sensors mitigates the need for complex signal processing. To measure the data from these sensors, it is streamed through a wireless connection to the customized edge server.

ii. *Edge Server:* The edge server houses most of the activities needed to implement predictive maintenance exploring the Edge AI. The real-time heterogeneous sensor data from the smart sensors will be collected and combined to form the fused input vector. This fusion is achieved through the method of weighted variances given by equation 7.1.

$$F\_IV = \frac{S_1 V_1 + S_2 V_2 + \ldots + S_n V_n}{V_1^{-1} + V_2^{-1} + \ldots V_n^{-1}} \tag{7.1}$$

F_IV is a distinct measure that characterizes the deviation in the signal properties measured by the sensors. This input vector is handled by light-weight machine learning algorithms that are incorporated on edge devices. Apart from predicting the health state, the edge server also acts as a gateway that interfaces between the devices and the high-end analytical platforms.

iii. *Analytical Platforms:* The AI-based predictions from the edge server are processed by analytical platforms. Small- and medium-scale industries can sustain descriptive and predictive maintenance. Large-scale industries can opt for a higher level of analytics, namely prescriptive maintenance.

iv. *Repository of Maintenance Policies:* The results of the analytical platforms may be in the form of dashboards, graphs, text, or any other mode. These are matched with the repository of maintenance policies to schedule the activities by anticipating the failure modes.

Thus, the proposed predictive analytic framework housing Edge AI at the edge server is a robust model that wades off the processing and communication overhead between the devices and predictive analytics platform. The edge server is the core component that establishes a meaningful link between the sensor data and the maintenance engineers.

Design Requirements of the Edge AI–Based Predictive Analytic Framework

The proposed framework is highly flexible and scalable to suit any type of manufacturing or production industry. Their robustness provides a scope for extending it to other domains as well. However, the choice of design constraints and specifications contribute to the sustainability of the framework in the real-time industrial deployment. The issues in the design requirements are addressed here:

i. *Choice of Sensors:* Though the sensors and their deployment have become widely prevalent in any type of industry, there is still a reluctance among most of the industries to adopt a smarter mode of operation. Also, the availability of a wide variety of sensors from low cost hand-held to smart sensors is causing a trade-off between cost, compatibility, and performance.

ii. *Lightweight Learning Algorithms:* There are numerous ML and DL algorithms extensively used in predictive maintenance. The right choice of algorithm plays a crucial role in the success of the proposed predictive maintenance framework. The criteria for selecting the most suitable algorithm is an exhaustive list. But the nature of sensor data, amount of data, equipment which is condition monitored, featured engineering process, integration of sensor data, and accuracy measure of the algorithms are some of the prominent factors to be considered.

Another very pivotal factor that deserves special mention is the computational complexity of the algorithm and the computational capacity of the edge server on which it is implemented. Since edge devices are low-powered devices, they have limited processing power. Hence, the computationally expensive algorithms like deep neural networks will be a poor choice to be incorporated on edge servers.

iii. *Other Bottlenecks:* The edge server integrates the functionality of the AI module as well as interfacing and communication module. A striking balance of processing and computation power is expected to be instilled on the server.

Challenges in the Edge AI–Based Predictive Analytic Framework

The proposed framework is suitable for deployment in real-time industries without heavy investments on the infrastructure. However, there are a handful of challenges that could evolve as potential areas of futuristic research and are given here:

■ *Validation of sensors:* As the sensors are installed in industrial environments that can have dynamic and movable parts, their accuracy must be validated frequently. Hence, an efficient and non-invasive sensor validation scheme will make the proposed framework a more comprehensive one.

■ *Wireless/wired network:* The sensor values reach the edge server through a transmitting network, which may be a wireless or wired connection. The network QOS parameters play a vital role in acquiring accurate predictions at the right time.

■ *Security:* Network security, data security, and physical security of devices have to be considered. Proper security protocols must be implemented in order to prevent any security breach, which may dilute the efficacy of the framework.

- *Limited computing power:* As the edge devices are low powered, intensive computations cannot be carried out in these devices. The prowess of cloud platforms cannot be simulated in the edge environment. Executing larger modules will cause the edge devices to exhibit poor performance.
- *Loss of data:* The data emanating from the sensor devices are handled only in the edge server. Hence, there are chances for losing important source data and even intermediate results, if a server crash is experienced.
- *Protocols and standards:* The edge devices communicate with other components based on standard communication protocols. Customization of edge devices with AI components must not hinder or deteriorate the normal functioning of edge devices.
- *Top management decisions:* The policy decisions made by the stakeholders of the industries also affect the deployment of predictive maintenance. Since the strategy of implementing predictive maintenance incurs initial costs, they promise to offer reliable services in the long run.
- *Memory management:* It is true that edge computing demands extra memory capacity, so the existing infrastructures must be upgraded. Hardware and software compatibility must be ensured. Also, augmenting the power of AI in the edge devices adds additional processing overhead. Hence, the processing capability like integrating graphical processing units (GPUs) and high-end CPUs will incur additional costs.
- *Fault tolerance:* In addition to executing AI algorithms, the edge server does multiple operations like data processing, analyzing, communication with other devices, etc.; they are heavily overloaded. Hence, fault tolerance should be a fundamental design criteria for the edge server.

Conclusion and Future Work

Predictive maintenance has become the buzzword of small- and medium-scale industries. The genesis of Edge AI and smart sensors has made it feasible for the industries to deploy lightweight predictive maintenance solutions to extend the lifetime of the industrial equipment. The proposed framework suggests an Edge AI–based server that collects and integrates multivariate sensor data. It also makes predictions about the health state of the equipment from the deviant values. The higher-level analytics are done in an isolated module that directly communicates with the predictive maintenance policies furnished by the industry. This framework is robust and it recommends the usage of lightweight ML algorithms for mitigating the computation overhead on the edge server. This work opens the doors for culminating add-on features like dashboards, charts, or even natural language processing–based recommendations. The predictive analytic framework could be transited to more advanced prescriptive analytics frameworks in the near future, without loss of generality.

References

[1] A. Rojko. "Industry 4.0 Concept: Background and Overview." *International Journal of Interactive Mobile Technologies* 11, no. 5 (2017): 77–90.

[2] A. German, F. L. S. Dalenogare, and N. FabiánAyala. "Industry 4.0 Technologies: Implementation Patterns in Manufacturing Companies." *International Journal of Production Economics* 210 (2010): 15–26.

[3] J. Cheng, W. Chen, F. Tao, and Chun-Liang. "Industrial IoT in 5G Environment Towards Smart Manufacturing." *Journal of Industrial Information Integration* 10 (2018): 10–19.

[4] X. Yao, J. Zhou, J. Zhang, and C. R. Boër. "From Intelligent Manufacturing to Smart Manufacturing for Industry 4.0 Driven by Next Generation Artificial Intelligence and Further On." In *5th International Conference on Enterprise Systems (ES)* (2017): 311–318, Beijing. 10.1109/ES.2017.58.

[5] A. Sharma and H. Pandey. "Big Data and Analytics in Industry 4.0." in A. Nayyar and A. Kumar (eds.), *A Roadmap to Industry 4.0: Smart Production, Sharp Business and Sustainable Development. Advances in Science, Technology & Innovation (IEREK Interdisciplinary Series for Sustainable Development).* Springer, 2020. 10.1007/978-3-030-14544-6.

[6] L. Yang. "Industry 4.0: A Survey on Technologies, Applications and Open Research Issues." *Journal of Industrial Information Integration* 6 (2017): 1–10.

[7] H. S. Kang, J. Y. Lee, S. Choi, H. Kim, J. H. Park, J. Y. Son, B. H. Kim, and S. D. Noh. "Smart Manufacturing: Past Research, Present Findings, and Future Directions." *International Journal of Precision Engineering and Manufacturing-Green Technology* 3, no. 1 (2016): 111–128.

[8] A. Paolin, S. Kollmannsberger, and E. Rank. "Additive Manufacturing in Construction: A Review on Processes, Applications, and Digital Planning Methods." *Additive Manufacturing* 30 (2019): 100894.

[9] F. Guo and Z. Guo. "Inspired Smart Materials with External Stimuli Responsive Wettability: A Review." *RSC Advances* 43 (2016). 10.1039/C6RA04079A.

[10] E. Ragan, C. Wilkes, D. A. Bowman, and T. Hollerer. "Simulation of Augmented Reality Systems in Purely Virtual Environments." *IEEE Virtual Reality Conference* (2009): 287–288, Lafayette, LA. 10.1109/VR.2009.4811058.

[11] W. Kritzinger, M. Karner, G. Traar, J. Henjes, Wilfried. "Digital Twin in Manufacturing: A Categorical Literature Review and Classification." *International Federation of Automated Control* 51, no. 11 (2018): 1016–1022.

[12] Q. Qi and F. Tao. "A Smart Manufacturing Service System Based on Edge Computing, Fog Computing, and Cloud Computing," *IEEE Access* 7 (2019): 86769–86777. 10.1109/ACCESS.2019.2923610.

[13] N. Mohamed and J. Al-Jaroodi. "Applying Blockchain in Industry 4.0 Applications," *IEEE 9th Annual Computing and Communication Workshop and Conference (CCWC)* (2019): 0852–0858, Las Vegas, NV, USA. 10.1109/CCWC.2019.8666558.

[14] X. Li, J. Wan, H. Dai, M. Imran, M. Xia, and A. Celesti. "A Hybrid Computing Solution and Resource Scheduling Strategy for Edge Computing in Smart Manufacturing." *IEEE Transactions on Industrial Informatics* 15, no. 7 (2019): 4225–4234. 10.1109/TII.2019.2899679.

[15] Predictive Maintenance Market Size, Share & Trends Analysis Report By Solution (Integrated, Standalone), By Service, By Deployment, By Enterprise Size, By End Use, By Region, And Segment Forecasts, 2019.

[16] J. Liu, R. Seraoui, V. Vitelli, and E. Zio. "Nuclear Power Plant Components Condition Monitoring by Probabilistic Support Vector Machine." *Annals of Nuclear Energy, Elsevier Masson* 56 (2013): 23–33.

[17] T. P. Carvalho, F. A. A. M. N. Soares, R. Vita, R. D. P. Francisco, J. P. Basto, and S. G. S. Alcalá. "A Systematic Literature Review of Machine Learning Methods Applied to Predictive Maintenance." *Computers & Industrial Engineering* 137 (2019).

[18] H. G., Marques, Alesandro. "Prescriptive Maintenance: Building Alternative Plans for Smart Operations," (2019): 231–236, 10.3384/ecp19162027.

[19] H. D. Faria, J. G. S. Costa, and J. L. M. Olivas. "A Review of Monitoring Methods for Predictive Maintenance of Electric Power Transformers Based on Dissolved Gas Analysis." *Renewable and Sustainable Energy Reviews*, 46 (2015): 201–209.

[20] P. Liu, Y. Zhang, H. Wu, and T. Fu. "Optimization of Edge-PLC-Based Fault Diagnosis With Random Forest in Industrial Internet of Things." *IEEE Internet of Things Journal* 7, no. 10 (2020): 9664–9674.

[21] G. Qian, S. Lu, D. Pan, H. Tang, Y. Liu, and Q. Wang. "Edge Computing: A Promising Framework for Real-Time Fault Diagnosis and Dynamic Control of Rotating Machines Using Multi-Sensor Data." *IEEE Sensors Journal* 19, no. 11 (2019): 4211–4220.

[22] A. H. Sodhro, S. Pirbhulal, and V. H. C. de Albuquerque. "Artificial Intelligence-Driven Mechanism for Edge Computing-Based Industrial Applications." *IEEE Transactions on Industrial Informatics* 15, no. 7 (2019): 4235–4243.

[23] D. Park, S. Kim, Y. An, and J. Jung. "LiReD: A Light-Weight Real-Time Fault Detection System for Edge Computing Using LSTM Recurrent Neural Networks." *Sensors*, 18 (2018): 2110.

[24] H. Chen, B. Jiang, W. Chen, and Z. Li, "Edge Computing-Aided Framework of Fault Detection for Traction Control Systems in High-Speed Trains." *IEEE Transactions on Vehicular Technology*, 69 no. 2 (2020): 1309–1318.

[25] M. F. Syafrudin, N. Alfian, and G. Rhee. "An Affordable Fast Early Warning System for Edge Computing in Assembly Line." *Applied Science* 9, no. 1 (2018): 84.

[26] W. Huo, F. Liu, L. Wang, Y. Jin, and L. Wang. "Research on Distributed Power Distribution Fault Detection Based on Edge Computing." *IEEE Access* 8 (2020): 24643–24652.

[27] R. I. Minu and G. Nagarajan. "Bridging the IoT Gap Through Edge Computing." In *Edge Computing and Computational Intelligence Paradigms for the IoT*, pp. 1–9. IGI Global, 2019.

[28] G. Nagarajan, R. I. Minu, and A. Jayanthiladevi. "Cognitive Internet of Things (C-IOT)." In *Sensing Techniques for Next Generation Cognitive Radio Networks*, pp. 299–311. IGI Global, 2019.

[29] S. V. Simpson and G. Nagarajan. "An Edge Based Trustworthy Environment Establishment for Internet of Things: An Approach for Smart Cities." *Wireless Networks* (2021): 1–17.

Chapter 8

Unlocking the Potential of (AI-Powered) Blockchain Technology in Environment Sustainability and Social Good

R. Sivarethinamohan and P. Jovin
Associate Professor, CHRIST University, Bangalore, India

S. Sujatha
Professor, K. Ramakrishnan College of Technology, Tamil Nadu, India

Contents

DOI: 10.1201/9781003145158-8

Introduction

The world is currently observing dangerous swings as the novel coronavirus continues to affect almost all sectors of the economy. The spread of infection and the mortality rate reported by the World Health Organization (WHO) and the United Nations Environment Program (UNEP) about the pandemic predicts an increasing threat towards human and animal well-being, ecosystem integrity, and economic development of all countries. The outbreak which has already caused unconceivable devastation will have profound economic and social consequences in every corner of the earth. Nature is in a crunch, as it is threatened by toxic pollution, global heating, and biodiversity habitat loss [1]. The tropics are encountering deforestation, wildlife poaching, land grabbing, illegal mining, climatic changes, and so on. Environment sustainability is facing increased compression during the pandemic, but addressing those can heal the global threats on biodiversity that will result in environmental sustainability [2].

With the help of emerging blockchain technology and AI, a decentralized ledger of all dealings across a peer-to-peer network participants can ratify transactions without the need for a central authority. Blockchain has significance in more than digital finance alone. It can act as a disruptive technology in managing the world's most pressurizing environmental issues if blockchain lives up to its potential and if concentrated on the right problem. Blockchain has real capabilities to enable a shift to cleaner and more resource conserving decentralized solutions, to unravel natural capital and empower communities. For instance, with a distributed intelligent approach to global water management, blockchain data securitization protocols converge with AI algorithms trained by remote sensor water data that are used to distribute water. Integration of these technologies is helpful in efficient water abundance and scarcity pattern identification for equitable multi-sale water resource management under climate change conditions.

Most governments are presently suffering from the lack of a defined mechanism to detect environment risks [3]. To alleviate this challenge, this study proposes an innovative approach to deal with environmental sustainability with the help of blockchain technology and AI. This chapter suggests a blockchain-based framework that explores the possibility of decentralized storage leads of blockchain to build a new system to verify and detect unknown environmental threats. Moreover, the proposed move will enable experts to forecast environmental threats through an innovative design of the P2P network. The proposed approach aims to produce an effective structure which will support governments, environmental activists, green leaders, and citizens to decide regarding working together to detect global environmental threats and strive toward environmental sustainability.

Operational definitions:

i. Dictionary meaning of **environment** relates to the natural world and the impact of human activity on its condition.

ii. **Sustainability** is most often defined as meeting the needs of the present without compromising the ability of future generations to meet theirs

iii. **Environmental sustainability** is concerned with whether environmental resources will be protected and maintained for future generations.

iv. **Social good** is something that benefits the largest number of people in the largest possible way, such as clean air, health care, and literacy.

COVID-19 Tracking Blockchain Powered by AI Platform and Global Environmental Sustainability

The way humans live is destructive in nature. The way we acquire natural resources resembles our selfish nature, as almost every action of humans is detrimental to the health of biodiversity. We are killing the land, air, sea, animals, trees, and everything that has life. We are literally poisoning nature in the way we acquire the resources as a result of which we encounter many natural disasters like deforestation, climate change, air, water and soil pollution, species extinction and biodiversity loss, and plastics in the ocean which acts as threat to sea species [4]. With the hope of a better earth, both for humanity and the planet earth [5], sustainable development goals were introduced and adopted by United Nations member states in order to achieve environmental sustainability with some specific goals in the list. The repercussion of unhealthy practices towards animals have led to the novel coronavirus (COVID-19) which is said to be zoonotic, which means it was transferred from animals and we can see it spreading at a fast pace around the globe [6]. It is not just a health issue but also affects the environment in varied ways. There is a perception that nature was better during the pandemic. Instead, many tropic regions are facing increased stress from deforestation, illegal mining, wildlife poaching, and along with this, the spread of the deadly virus has forced people to wear masks, use gloves, and apply sanitizer on an everyday basis, which has resulted in generation of massive medical wastes which in turn can harm biodiversity. Recycling has become a major issue during the pandemic. Recycling initiatives were stopped in a few countries around the globe as people were concerned about the risk of coronavirus at recycling centers. Today, we make sure of some astonishing things by extracting value from data using blockchain, artificial intelligence (AI), and the cloud. Even though blockchain does not prevent the emergence of new viruses itself, it can create the first line of rapid protection through a network of connected devices that alert about disease outbreaks [7]. Therefore, the application of blockchain-enabled platforms prevents these pandemics by enabling early detection of epidemics, fast-tracking drug trials, and impact management of outbreaks and treatment [8]. For instance, by creating digital assets on the blockchain like AarogyaSetu, Apthamitra (in Karnataka), etc. and using its state-of-the-art multi-admin module layer, BelYo knows how to simplify the tracking of all the COVID-19 patients in India from symptoms to vaccination certificate in a decentralized manner, without compromising the privacy of the data. BelYo employs the BelfricsBTBelrium blockchain platform to convert COVID-19-related clinical and vaccination data of citizens presently from the physical form into digital assets which are retrieved by any contact tracing apps like AarogyaSetu via APIs. Individuals can scan and retrieve data through a QR code. BelYo can also issue certificates for COVID-19 clinical records and immunization certificates on blockchain [9].

Blockchain Powered by AI and Its Application in Environmental Sustainability and Social Good

The World Economic Forum identified blockchain as a mechanism to repair the world's most challenging environmental issues. It is one of the promising technologies currently gaining a lot of attention in environment protection. Blockchain is a decentralized ledger that records transactions in a chronological order on a real-time basis and allows any two parties to transact between each other without the need for trusted outsiders.

Further, blockchain and artificial intelligence (AI) are two of the hottest technology trends right now. In many ways, blockchain and AI are like oil and water. Even though the two technologies have highly different developing parties and applications, both AI and blockchain involve technical complexity and there seems to be a sense of agreement among experts that these technologies will have serious implications in the next five to ten years. The dual use of the two technologies might alter the tech and environment paradigm significantly enough for environmentalists to take more notice of developments in this space. For instance, farmers are using AgroPad to monitor the health of their soil and water, an exploratory prototype, which enables real-time, on location, chemical analysis of a soil or water sample using AI. IBM's Smarter Building program applies analytics to existing building system operational data and sends out automatic alerts when systems are operating outside of optimal conditions.

Clusters of transformative technologies such as artificial intelligence (AI), robotics, additive manufacturing (or 3D printing), Internet of Things (IoT), drones, and autonomous vehicles, biotechnologies, virtual and augmented reality, and blockchain, along with technologies and capabilities offer profound implications for innovative approaches to managing environmental footprints. 4IR solutions within advanced materials also play a significant role in enabling low and zero emissions vehicles (electric vehicles, fuel cells, and hydrogen) to compete with and ultimately replace the carbon-intensive internal combustion engine. Geospatial data monitoring platforms such as the Global Forest Watch, Global Fishing Watch, and Eyes on the Sea apply advanced sensors and satellite imagery, combined with big data analytics, to support anyone with a smartphone to track and monitor activity within important environmental systems.

The Earth Bank of Code as an undertaking aimed at mapping the DNA of the Amazon Basin (creating an "Amazon Bank of Codes"). The Amazon Bank of Codes as an open, global digital platform registers and maps the genetic sequences of Amazon register biological and biomimetic intellectual property assets on the blockchain as a regulatory platform. The Nagoya Protocol governs access to genetic resources. So the blockchain has the possibility of becoming a most powerful technological application which can be applied in environment protection. It has the capability of addressing a wide range of global environmental challenges. This session studies the applicability of blockchain in protecting and sustaining the global environment on various levels such as life on land, life below the earth, and climate changes. The deployment of blockchain technology is needed in areas such as climate change, biodiversity conservation, healthy water bodies etc [10].

Application of Blockchain Technology in Climate Change

The United Nations Climate Change (UNFCCC) recognizes the potential and supports the integration of blockchain in addressing adverse climatic conditions. Climate change is the issue of how weather patterns tend to change over time. Climate change ultimately takes place due to natural and human influences [11]. Since the Industrial Revolution in 1750, humans have immensely contributed to climatic change through emission of greenhouse gases and aerosols, and through variations in land usage, resulting in a rise of global temperatures. An increase in temperature would lead to floods, increase in sea levels, storms, droughts, glaciers, etc. All climatic repercussions will lead to financial crises across many sectors in the economy. This is where blockchain can act as a powerful technology in combating these disasters and challenges to the best extent possible. It can improve on the carbon emission trading by improving on the carbon asset, by facilitating clean energy trading, by effectively tracking on the greenhouse gases. It could help in developing crowdfunding and P2P network financial transactions, which can help

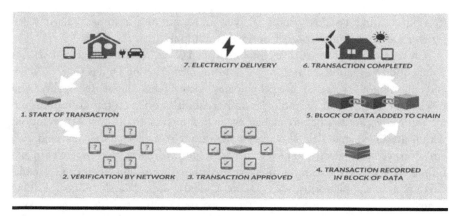

Figure 8.1 Overview of Blockchain Utilities.

climate change projects where financing as projects can be monitored and transparency ensured. The distributed nature of blockchain will improve sustainability in aid of collective action addressing climate change. The decentralized nature of blockchain networks would avert a monopolistic system. The transparent nature of blockchain will ensure transparency intransactions. Figure 8.1 describes how blockchain technology develops peer-to-peer trade of clean energy for certified and facilitated transactions among consumers.

With the help of blockchain technology, we can fight against the climate change in some of the following ways:

a. **Carbon markets or carbon emission trading:** Blockchain enables a mechanism for trading and accounting of mitigation outcomes. Further, it improves the system of carbon asset transactions. For instance, IBM and Energy Blockchain Lab are presently working together to advance a blockchain platform for trading carbon assets in China. Recording carbon assets on a public blockchain also promises transparency and confirms that transactions are usable and settled spontaneously.

b. **Clean energy trading:** The technology allows for the development of platforms for peer-to-peer renewable energy trade. Clients could buy, sell, or exchange renewable energy with each other, with the help of tokens or tradable digital assets, signifying a certain quantity of energy production.

c. **Climate finance:** Blockchain technology assists to develop crowdfunding and peer-to-peer financial transactions in support of climate action. In other words, it facilitates and enables climate-smart investments through traceability of financial flows.

d. **Improved tracking and reporting of greenhouse gas (GHG) emissions reduction and avoidance of double counting:** The technology provides further transparency regarding GHG emissions and track and report emission reductions, in so doing addressing possible double counting issues. It monitors the progress made in implementing the nationally determined contributions under the Paris Agreement, as well as in company targets.

Blockchain and Biodiversity Protection

Humans are not the only beings on the planet. Mother earth also belongs to several other species equally. Our human nature is so demanding that nature becomes helpless at times in providing what we need and become extinct. Everything in the ecosystem is connected and needs to "co-exist". We never have an idea on how many living species can become extinct before the system becomes extinct. Plants and animals add value to our lives and to the ecosystem as a whole by helping us in the way of quality atmosphere, free from tissue damage or infection [12], soil health, medicinal nature providing health to the human body, and thereby beautiful crown to mother earth. It is so evident that biodiversity conservation is one of the world's most challenging issues, which requires great attention [13]. Biodiversity conservation is the action of saving and managing in order to obtain the resources for sustainability. Biodiversity comprises three components: protecting the species, sustainable utilization of the ecosystem, and to uphold a life-saving system and needed ecological processes. Therefore, we need to function as a part of a system co-co-living. We need find better blockchain techniques to reduce the disastrous loss of species and come out with a structure to protect and maintain them [14].

How Are Biodiversity and Ecosystems Protected?

Figure 8.2 describes in what manner biodiversity and ecosystems are protected. General public and organizations produce greenhouse gas emissions from burning gasoline when they drive, burning oil or gas for home heating, or using electricity generated from coal, natural gas, and oil. The main greenhouse gases are water vapor, carbon dioxide, methane, ozone, nitrous oxide, and chlorofluorocarbon carbon is a raw material for photosynthesis, in the form of carbon dioxide. Photosynthesis captures energy from sunlight to convert carbon dioxide into carbohydrates. Photosynthesis separates carbon dioxide and water known as CO_2 and H_2O, respectively, into their individual molecules and combines them into new products. Once the process is done, the plant releases oxygen, or O_2, into the surrounding air. Quite a lot of start-ups tackle the issue with blockchain, either by tokenizing carbon credits or creating carbon credit-backed cryptocurrencies. Micro Green Bond Platform enables the general public and organizations to invest in environmental asset projects and directly fund the restoration of key ecosystems. A level of transparency and efficiency of the environmental asset markets is possible

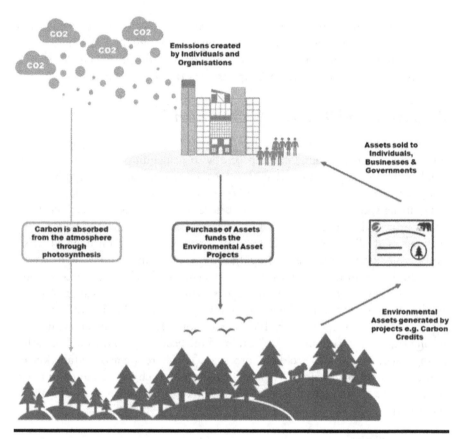

Figure 8.2 Means Wherein Biodiversity and Ecosystems Are Protected.

with blockchain because they record the underlying environmental project's data and track asset ownership.

Some of the applications of blockchain technology in biodiversity conservation are listed below:

a. Using **cryptocurrency to invest** in restoring habitat and conserving species from its annihilation.
b. Tracking and tracing geographic areas and species in danger of extinction.
c. **Incentivizing small farmers to protect the environment** as they are the custodians of major natural resources in rural areas. The technology enables farmers to trace their yield right from its harvesting to the finished product in the hands of the consumer.
d. **Tracking the of natural resources and recording** the same in a decentralized ledger for further action toward resource conservation.

e. **Natural asset and capital exchange on a decentralized platform** which aims to create a marketplace that brings in verified producers of natural assets with the real consumers of such assets.

f. **Digital structure for tracking species and controlling disease** which can start from species like COVID-19, considered a zoonotic disease, while government, medical practitioners, and related parties can be part of the loop to check the progress on a real-time basis with the help of blockchain technology [15].

g. **Credit incentive initiative for effective waste management** – Incentivizing the waste collector and waste management system with cryptocurrency as credit to purchase goods and services.

h. **Real-time monitoring of the supply chain** – Supply chain management can be quite complex for some products, which involves different locations, multiple invoices, and different parties in moving goods from the warehouse to delivering it to consumers and making and receiving payments. To this complex process, blockchain can offer an effective solution by tracking and verifying all the stages on a real-time basis.

Blockchain and Marine/Ocean Conservation

Water bodies cover 70% of the planet and are the greatest treasure of the world's most precious natural resource. Oceans manage weather conditions, provide clean air, feed millions, and provide living for countless numbers of creatures on the planet. Yet the selfish nature of humans has resulted in the marine ecosystem drowning the trash, acidification, noise pollution, overfishing, offshore drilling, and by industrial poisonous liquid waste [16]. Here, smart water management or intelligent water management in the management of water resources is managing the quantity, quality, efficiency of irrigation water use, monitoring the security of natural resource infrastructure, handling risks related to natural disasters related to water, as well as drought. Real-time monitor water source infrastructure through the dam operational and improvement safety project program as well as various uses and strategies optimize the use of water resources.

Oceans have become a place for much of the pollution that humans produce. We as human beings must follow the principle of "live and co-live", which is the ultimate motto behind sustainable development goals. Autonomous garbage collection trucks, powered by AI, are assisting us to get rid of the trash from oceans. Machine learning also aids to assess the harmful changing conditions that affect the ocean, such as illegal fishing, discharging industrial effluents into water bodies, and illegal solid waste disposal by the local people. IoT and AI-powered blockchain support and improve the water quality by monitoring pollution levels in real time to determine if any illegal activities are hampering the water quality. Here are some of the practices on how blockchain can pitch in and solve dangerous threats in the form of marine pollution and ensure a sustainable ocean.

Blockchain Applications towards a Sustainable Ocean

a. **Tracking the origin of fish:** Blockchain can help in tracking fishes by regarding their origin, where it was fished, and how it was processed. This information is stored in a system that is impossible to tamper with

b. **Monitoring illegal fishing activities:** Illegal fishing in the form of overfishing or unreported/unregulated fishing is a dangerous threat to sea creatures. Blockchain tracks unregulated fishing, making it impossible for these fishers to enter the market. It can also record the boat that caught the fish

c. **Incentivized ocean plastic recycling initiatives:** Researchers say that 80% of the plastic is from land and that needs to be stopped first. The next step would be toward removing and recycling these plastics with the help of a waste collector, whose primary job will be to collect waste and get incentives for it. Blockchain would provide a secure system to track, store, and record the value of plastic that got the plastic center

d. **Transparent ledger for quicker, secure, and more efficient shipping:** To shipping industries that find it challenging, blockchain can help in providing an environment friendly solution due to high cost and high pollution [17]

e. **Raising funds for conserving marine creature:** Blockchain helps in raising funds with its secured system where a philanthropist or giver can be assured he has given money to the right place while the fundraising center can also be assured of funds not being diverted from the sources due to the transparency feature of blockchain

Blockchain-Enabled Technological Projects

Here are some of the blockchain-enabled technological projects that can help in environmental sustainability and social good.

a. **Trading energy** – It's a blockchain-enabled technology where energy is derived from the renewable sources and traded. Producers of renewable energy attract investment by giving investors token assets. The technology brings in manufacturers and producers to trade energy on a bidding basis. Companies like "we power" have this kind of infrastructure wherein the system works by auction where the producers of energy auction their energy and buyers start bidding for specific price and quantity. After getting the bid, the authorized person gets a purchase power agreement which fixes the cost and the quantity of energy to be received and also startups like "Power Ledger", which is blockchain enabled, uses a software to purchase and sell electricity on a real-time basis. For example, users will share the surplus energy derived from their solar panels to people who are in need and users can come with their own price to trade at affordable rates. All these transactions are recorded in the blockchain, which assures transparency and security of the transaction between the user and third party safely and efficiently.

b. **Trash bank** – One of the biggest threats to oceans is trash that enters the sea from the land or from ships. Trash bank acts as a center for collection of plastic and recycling. It also works toward fighting pollution and poverty by making profits from recycling for stressed communities in the world. These banks help waste collectors whose primary job is to collect waste, to collect plastics from the land and the ocean, and get it to these banks and receive token credit, a kind of reward using cryptocurrencies. These tokens can be further used to buy goods and services. Blockchain records this information, which banks receive on a daily basis.

c. **Tracking mechanism for waste disposal** – Issuing cryptocurrencies as a reward for responsible and accepted behavior will increase loyalty among individuals. The decentralized ledger blockchain can track on both individuals and business-level disposal mechanisms. It can also offer constructive feedback in places where improvements are expected.

d. **Non-profit reporting on a real-time basis** – Blockchain with its transparent nature can help philanthropists concerned about their money going to the right place. Donors can monitor their flow to charities on a real-time basis with the blockchain.

Techniques and Practices to Protect the Environment and Social Good through the AI-Powered Blockchain Models

The following blockchains have a positive effect on the environment and the needs of man to be met without threatening the ability of the future (Figure 8.3).

i. **Environmental Treaties:**
   Blockchain tracks the real impact and compliance of environmental treaties and decreases fraud and manipulation as the technology ensures tracking important environmental data transparently to reveal whether commitments were met. The tracked data remains forever. All legal documents stored on the blockchain are expurgated permanently for fraud and manipulation during any future action.

ii. **Carbon Tax:**
   Blockchain calculates tax for products based on the carbon footprint and creates a reputation system for companies based on emissions. Carbon tax provides little incentive for consumers to buy products with a low carbon footprint, and little incentive for companies to sell such products. Blockchain tracks the carbon footprint of each product and determines the

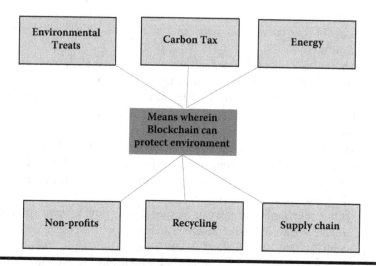

Figure 8.3   Means Wherein Blockchain Can Protect Environment.

amount of carbon tax to be charged at the point of sale. If a product with a large carbon footprint is more expensive, it will automatically make buyers opt for environmentally friendly products.

iii. **Energy:**

Blockchain, for instance a peer-to-peer blockchain-based energy system, escalates efficiency with P2P electrical grids and increases access to power in areas with poverty or battered by natural disaster. It transmits electricity over long distances, reducing the need for energy storage. The figure shows a few models that save energy and protect the environment (Figure 8.4).

iv. **Non-profits:**

Blockchain tracks where donations are going and decreases inefficiency and bureaucracy in charities. It safeguards money intended as a reward for conservation, or a payment to a specific cause. It delivers the money without a bank account to the correct parties in response to meeting specific environmental targets (Figure 8.5).

v. **Recycling:**

Blockchain ensures recycling by giving tokenized rewards and tracks to evaluate the efficacy of recycling programs. Mostly, there are two foremost methods to recycle plastic: (1) mechanical recycling ("chop and wash"), where the plastic is washed, ground into powders and melted, and (2) chemical recycling, where the plastic is broken down into basic components. For recycling to work, the public must be talented to cost effectively collect and sort plastic, and industries must be ready to agree to the material for processing. Collection is costly, for the reason that plastic bottles are light yet bulky, making it hard to efficiently collect noteworthy amounts of matching plastic. Blockchain through recycling programs could inspire

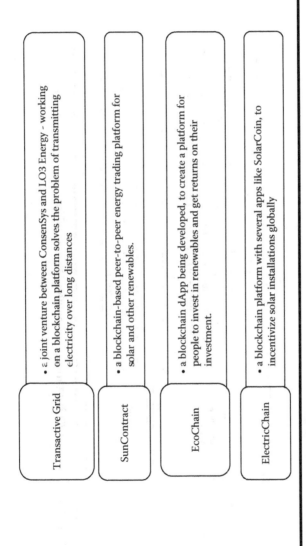

Transactive Grid
- a joint venture between ConsenSys and LO3 Energy - working on a blockchain platform solves the problem of transmitting electricity over long distances

SunContract
- a blockchain-based peer-to-peer energy trading platform for solar and other renewables.

EcoChain
- a blockchain dApp being developed, to create a platform for people to invest in renewables and get returns on their investment.

ElectricChain
- a blockchain platform with several apps like SolarCoin, to incentivize solar installations globally

Figure 8.4 Blockchain-Based Energy System.

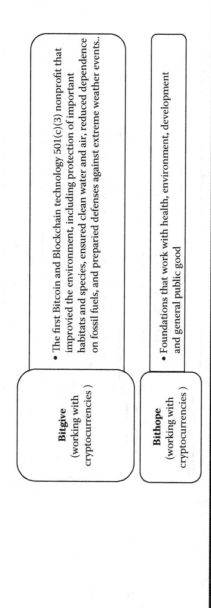

Figure 8.5   Non-Profits Without Going through a Complex Web of Middlemen or a Centralized Authority.

participation by providing financial rewards in the form of a cryptographic token in exchange for depositing recyclables like plastic containers, cans, or bottles (Figure 8.6).

vi. **Supply chain:**
Blockchain obviously tracks products from origin to store shelf and decreases the carbon footprint and unsustainable carry-out. Organizations can digitize physical assets and generate a decentralized immutable record of all transactions, and track assets from production to delivery or use by client.

Challenges Facing the Blockchain Model in Environment Safety and Social Good

By 2022, at least one innovative business built on blockchain technology will be worth $10 billion. By 2026, the business value added by blockchain will grow to just over $360 billion, then by 2030 grow to more than $3.1 trillion. However, to create a more efficient and prosperous world, users are facing numerous challenges to adopting blockchain technology [18]. Let us discuss the potential challenges Figure 8.7.

i. **Deployment challenge** – Blockchain has great potential to address some of the world's greatest environmental threats. Blockchain is still in its teething stage. When it comes to its deployment, stakeholders become reluctant to accept the reliability, security, and the transparency of the technology. Overcoming this reluctant nature of people will be a challenge.

ii. **Security** – Blockchain is known for its untampered nature due to its strong cryptographic structure. But all the information technology is prone to cyber-security threats. As we know, the main feature of blockchain is to make the ledger available to the public through its peer-to-peer network, it requires data to be sent to a multitude of people. Most of the business entities resist exposing their company data which will remain secured in a centralized system.

iii. **Technological risks** – The decentralized nature of blockchain requires validation from all peers for every transaction. As the blockchain grows, there will be challenges in processing a transaction with limited capacity leading to heavy time consumption when huge fees will be charged on the transaction where users bid with each other to get a complete transaction immediately. In order to reach its scalability, the number of peer nodes should be reduced so that it can save time from multiple nodes validating it without losing trust.

iv. **Regulatory challenges** – The blockchain's decentralized ledger does not have a specific place to do transactions. It takes place across the globe,

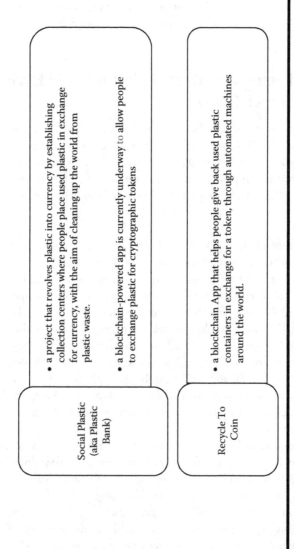

Figure 8.6 Recycling Program on the Blockchain.

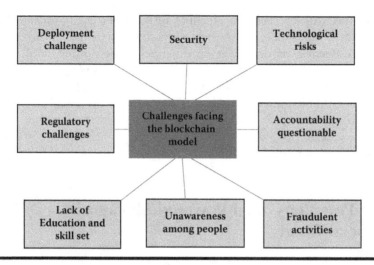

Figure 8.7   Challenges Facing the Blockchain Model That Helps Environment Protection.

which means peers across countries in the form of nodes will create confusion when something goes wrong. The jurisdiction under which the blockchain will come and during litigation deciding on which law and court will take up the matter will be quite critical. If blockchain needs to be successful, it should be given a legal structure to operate on for which we need the blockchain to be recognized by the law and smart contracts should become valid and enforced.

v. **Accountability questionable** – When it comes to accountability in blockchain, it becomes questionable as to which participant in the node will be accountable for running it and how it will function. The legal system should provide clarity on the accountability and responsibility structures.

vi. **Lack of education and skill set** – As we know, the blockchain is a booming technological innovation. Identifying a qualified person to operate and manage a blockchain will be highly challenging. On the other hand, demand for human resources is rising. Finding the right set of people with required skills to operate would incur huge costs. As blockchain becomes a benchmark, universities and other skill training institutes should come up with courses, programs, and training on blockchain and train passionate youngsters who want to work on this technological innovation.

vii. **Unawareness among people** – A major portion of the population is still unaware of what a blockchain is and its capabilities. Some are just aware of its implication in financial industries and some only know that bitcoin is associated with it. Many fail to understand its implication on a wider perspective, especially its potential on environmental sustainability. It needs to gain wider acceptance from the audience for it to be successful [8].

viii. **Fraudulent activities** – The decentralized features of the blockchain can act as a gateway for those who want to enter with criminal intention, as the decentralized network would not know your true identity. This allows bitcoin to be utilized as currency illegally in the open market. Fraudsters now utilize these cryptocurrencies to buy restricted unlawful equipment. The best way to overcome this is to stop the criminal association and start legal deployment of blockchain technology.

Future Potentials of AI-Powered Blockchain and Social Good

Blockchain is used in almost all sectors. It has great potential in dealing with major environmental threats the world currently faces. It can act as a catalyst toward promoting environmental sustainability. Here are some ways on how a blockchain can be deployed in the environmental sector [19].

- **Environmental financing opportunities** – With the help of blockchain-enabled technology, it is possible to crowdfund environmental projects or ventures with both stakeholders and investors. These environmental investment initiatives can pool in a huge number of investors to invest in the blockchain automation system. This will remove the need for a centralized system and make it the access capital for organizations that intend to address environmental challenges. With the help of decentralized structure of blockchain technology, it can reduce transaction cost and increase efficiency. It is a leap forward for financial investment opportunities where individuals can join hands to create value for SDGs.

- **Advance environmental reporting and monitoring** – Organizations' credentials and their image are directly related to their responsible environmental practices and work to ensure sustainability. Sustainable environmental practices are the need of the hour and companies are facing stress from the government, green leaders, and stakeholders to create a sustainable model. Blockchain technology companies can have a better reporting system in place where stakeholders can see a realistic picture of the company's performance and credit can be given to stakeholders as incentives for verifying reports and data, to increase their transparency and authenticity.

- **Rewarding circular economies** – The potential of blockchain to incentivize individuals, businesses, and governments for their sustainable action toward wasted, disposed, and invaluable resources after use by recycling, reusing, and re-creating resources. For example, companies like Plastic Bank provide cryptocurrencies for waste collectors to collect trash from the ocean. Such cryptocurrencies can be used to purchase goods and services. A similar idea can be to reward markets for goods and services when they conserve natural resources.

■ **Geo management platform** – Blockchain has the ability to monitor and manage the earth's vast resources like life on land and in water currently facing stress from human activities. It collects data of genetic biodiversity of the habitat and manages it to inform conservation practices [20]. In the context of the sea, a global ocean data platform is being created for data access. This helps to develop strategies based on the health of the ocean. It monitors the oceans' resources, and administers fishing rights. Geomanagement or a geospatial ledger is still in its infancy, but this could help monitor and manage and protect the seas from global environmental threats [21].

■ **Automatic disaster relief** – Preparing for disasters and managing them when they occur can be helped by the blockchain, which can play a greater role in managing the disaster effectively by connecting community needs with suppliers who can provide goods and services at affordable rates. To enable this solution, smart-contract technology will select which deal is the best based on the need and delivery options of the community along with quantity, cost, location, and timing.

■ **Blockchain identity** – In the future, every individual and their assets will have a blockchain identity with blockchain technology acting as the sole verification for individuals and their possessions. This will provide a secured system, efficiency, decentralized verification, lower security breaches, store information safe on ledgers, and create new identities not controlled by any centralized system.

■ **Upsurges the standard of living** – Blockchain ensures transparency. When dealing with transactions, details of all assets including land, money, and belongings will be stored in a decentralized ledger that cannot be tampered with. Movement of these assets in the ledger is traced and verified by a huge network of nodes and so making alterations and laundering will be practically impossible. By using blockchain technology, there will be no need for banking institutions or the government to permit individuals to have a bank account. Blockchain can help people access crypto cash through the use of smartphones, thereby contributing toward financial inclusion and providing everyone access to financial services.

Conclusion

Blockchain, as an innovative and widely accepted technology, can be a major gamechanger with its ability of trust, transparency, decentralized ledger, and unchanged nature. It can offer varied solutions to many environmental challenges such climate change, pollution, overuse of natural resources, deforestation, trash in the oceans, overfishing, carbon emission, etc. that the world currently faces and helps promote global environmental sustainability. The technology has a great relevance in maintaining the best and safe environmental practices by fostering collaborations between consumers, producers, and all stakeholders by helping people and businesses to adopt sustainable practices in their approach. Blockchain can be used to reinforce privileges, use natural assets or resources, validate claims of reduced environmental control, and reward environmentally sustainable actions. To harness the potential of blockchain technology to the environment, governments of economically backward countries must invest in digital infrastructure and get their citizens involved in training on these innovations and thereby be future ready. Innovators can work on catering blockchain solutions to some environmental problems that the blockchain can solve. To conclude, AI-enabled blockchain is a technological boon for future environmental sustainability.

References

[1] I. S. Martins, L. M. Navarro, H. M. Pereira, and I. M. Rosa. Alternative Pathways to a Sustainable Future Lead to Contrasting Biodiversity Responses. *Global Ecology and Conservation* (2020): 22, e01028.

[2] M. Le Sève, N. Mason, and D. Nassiry. "Delivering Blockchain's Potential for Environmental Sustainability." *Oversees Development Institute* (2018): 1–13.

[3] M. A. Zambrano-Monserrate, M. A. Ruano, and L. Sanchez-Alcalde. "Indirect Effects of COVID-19 on the Environment." *Science of the Total Environment* 728 (2020). 10.1016/j.scitotenv.2020.138813

[4] S. Morand. "Emerging Diseases, Livestock Expansion and Biodiversity Loss are Positively Related at Global Scale." *Biological Conservation* 248, no. April (2020): 108707. 10.1016/j.biocon.2020.108707

[5] Word Economic Forum. "Building Block(chain)s for a Better Planet - Fourth Industrial Revolution for the Earth Series." *Weforum.Org* (2018). *September*. http://www3.weforum.org/docs/WEF_Building-Blockchains.pdf%0Ahttps://es.weforum.org/reports/building-block-chain-for-a-better-planet

[6] K. D. Kanniah, N. A. F. Kamarul Zaman, D. G. Kaskaoutis, and M. T. Latif. "COVID-19's Impact on the Atmospheric Environment in the Southeast Asia region." *Science of the Total Environment 736*, no. 2 (2020): 139658. 10.1016/j.scitotenv.2020.139658

[7] S. Saadat, D. Rawtani, and C. M. Hussain. "Environmental Perspective of COVID-19." *Science of the Total Environment* 728 (2020): 138870. 10.1016/j.scitotenv.2020.138870

[8] P. Lal, A. Kumar, S. Kumar, S. Kumari, P. Saikia, A. Dayanandan, D. Adhikari, and M. L. Khan. "The Dark Cloud With a Silver Lining: Assessing the Impact of the SARS COVID-19 Pandemic on the Global Environment." *Science of the Total Environment* 732 (2020): 139297. 10.1016/j.scitotenv.2020.139297

[9] S. Lokhandwala and P. Gautam. "Indirect Impact of COVID-19 on environment: A brief study in Indian Context. *Environmental Research 188*, no. April (2020). 109807. 10.1016/j.envres.2020.109807

[10] F. Casino, T. K. Dasaklis, and C. Patsakis. "A Systematic Literature Review of Blockchain-Based Applications: Current Status, Classification and Open Issues." *Telematics and Informatics* 36, November 2018 (2019): 55–81. 10.1016/j.tele. 2018.11.006

[11] B. Brath, T. Friesen, Y. Guérard, C. Jacques-Brissette, C. Lindman, K. Lockridge, S., Mulgund, and B. Walke. "Research Paper: Climate Change and Resource Sustainability – An Overview for Actuaries. August." (2015). https://www.cia-ica. ca/docs/default-source/2015/215068e.pdf

[12] S. H. Burstein. "ur l P re. damages and Other Lipid Mediators." (2020): 106408. 10.1016/j.prostaglandins.2020.106408

[13] K. Norris, A. Terry, J. P. Hansford, and S. T. Turvey. "Biodiversity Conservation and the Earth System: Mind the Gap." *Trends in Ecology and Evolution xx*, no. xx (2020): 1–8. 10.1016/j.tree.2020.06.010

[14] P. Raven and M. Wackernagel. "Maintaining Biodiversity will Define our Long-Term Success." *Plant Diversity* xxxx (2020). 10.1016/j.pld.2020.06.002

[15] M. H. Shakil, Z. H. Munim, M. Tasnia, and S. Sarowar. "COVID-19 and the Environment: A Critical Review and Research Agenda." *Science of the Total Environment* 745 (2020): 141022. 10.1016/j.scitotenv.2020.141022

[16] I. M. D. Rosa, A. Purvis, R. Alkemade, R. Chaplin-Kramer, S. Ferrier, C. A. Guerra, G.,Hurtt, H. J. Kim, P. Leadley, I. S. Martins, A. Popp, A. M. Schipper, D. van Vuuren, and H. M. Pereira. "Challenges in Producing Policy-Relevant Global Scenarios of Biodiversity and Ecosystem Services." *Global Ecology and Conservation* 22 (2020). 10.1016/j.gecco.2019.e00886

[17] B. P. J. Andree "Incidence of COVID-19 and Connections with Air Pollution Exposure: Evidence from the Netherlands." 1, no. April (2020). 10.1101/2020.04 .27.20081562

[18] B. Karanjia, S. G. Shankar Lakshman. "Blockchain Technology in India: Opportunities and Challenges." *Deloitte* 17 (2017). https://www2.deloitte.com/ content/dam/Deloitte/in/Documents/strategy/in-strategy-innovation-blockchain-technology-india-opportunities-challenges-noexp.pdf

[19] M. Kouhizadeh and J. Sarkis. "Blockchain Practices, Potentials, and Perspectives in Greening Supply Chains." *Sustainability (Switzerland)* 10, no. 10 (2018). 10. 3390/su10103652

[20] P. R. Whitehorn, L. M. Navarro, M. Schröter, M. Fernandez, X. Rotllan-Puig, and A. Marques. "Mainstreaming Biodiversity: A Review of National Strategies." *Biological Conservation* 235, no. February (2019): 157–163. 10.1016/j.biocon. 2019.04.016

[21] I. Chakraborty and P. Maity "COVID-19 Outbreak: Migration, Effects on Society, Global Environment and Prevention." *Science of the Total Environment* 728 (2020): 138882. 10.1016/j.scitotenv.2020.138882

Chapter 9

UAV-Based Smart Wing Inspection System

S. Karthikeyan, A. Dulvi, R. Raghavi, and S. Sai Suresh

Department of Aerospace Engineering, B. S. Abdur Rahman Crescent Institute of Science and Technology, Chennai, India

Contents

DOI: 10.1201/9781003145158-9

Introduction

Monitoring maintenance of various aircraft parts and components such as wings and fuselage are an expensive yet essential task in maintaining safe operations. One of the most important aspects of the maintenance of an aircraft is the inspection process. It is the first step in maintenance, which is essential for increasing the life of the aircraft and its proper functioning. If the inspector misses any defect, it could lead to the failure of the aircraft and can prove fatal to the passengers and crew.

Traditional methods, such as NDT inspection, which requires human intervention, are very time consuming, increases work labor, additional expenses, and several other factors [1]. This chapter focuses on the use of an unmanned aerial vehicle (UAV), integrated with edge artificial intelligence to perform the inspection of a wing of an aircraft. This will be able to reduce the inspection time, workload, manpower, and expenses with more accuracy. The manufacture and use of UAVs have grown exponentially over the last decade in almost every field. This is because they are easy to handle and control, their maneuverability is very handy, they can hover and fly at very low speeds at low altitudes, and they can be automated.

UAVs have been used by NASA to prevent wildfires or detect them in their early stages. To track the spread pattern of malaria in Africa, UAVs had been deployed. The military uses drones for attack and reconnaissance purposes. The United States used UAVs armed with Hellfire missiles named MQ-1 Predator. This is the main platform for hitting ground targets. UAVs also play a role in photography, filming, crop surveys, search and rescue, border patrol missions, delivering medical supplies to otherwise inaccessible areas, inspection, maintenance, and the list goes on.

In this modern era of technological advancements, Edge AI is taking over in almost every field. Edge AI allows data creation, decision making, and action. It has been applied in many modern devices such as Amazon Echo, Fire TV Stick, Google Home with voice recognition systems, self-driving vehicles with autopilot, video games, smartphones with face and finger recognition system, robots, drones/ UAVs, smartwatches, smart speakers, cameras, tracking devices, wearable health monitoring devices, etc. The most recent and famous application of Edge AI is in self-driving cars manufactured by Tesla.

Unmanned aerial vehicles integrated with Edge AI, automation, infrared thermography, and image processing techniques will prove to be a gamechanger in the inspection process. The objective of this chapter is to inspect theoretically the internal and external defects of a wing using these methods.

Aircraft Wing Structure

The wing of an aircraft plays a vital role in terms of providing a lift to the aircraft. There are different ways the wing design, size, and shape are used by many manufacturing industries. The wing is attached to the various position of the fuselage such as top, bottom, and middle. The wing structure has a specific characteristic that carries fuel for the aircraft. Ribs, stringer, wing spar, and wingtip are the components of the wing structure. Among this, wing spar and ribs provide strength and rigidity to the wing structure. Protruding positions of the wing structure are flaps, spoilers, and ailerons. The first aircraft wing structure was made of wood covered with fabric in order to make the aircraft lighter and aluminum is used as a major material for manufacturing the wing structure. Modern aircraft such as Boeing 787 and A350XWB use composites such as carbon fiber reinforced material for manufacturing [2].

The wing structure has two aerodynamic forces: pressure force in general acting normal to the object surface and shear acting tangential to the object surface. The result of these forces creates life and drag to the aircraft. The wing's internal structure comprises spars and stringers that run along the spans of the wing, bulkhead, formers, and ribs cover the leading and trailing edge of wing. They are three types of wing construction such as monospar, multispar, and boxbeam. The monospar wing constitutes one longitudinal member; the ribs and bulkheads are provided based on the shape of the airfoil. If there are two or more longitudinal members, that is known as a multispar. Most commercial aircraft use box beam types of wing construction as they contain two key longitudinal members connected to the bulkheads to give extra strength to the wing structure. Cross-section of the wing's ribs is in the form of a truss structure [3]. The skin of the wing act as an outer covering of the wing structure. The skin of the aircraft is mainly made up of wood, fabric, and aluminum. Honeycomb structure wing panels are commonly used in modern aircraft. Engines are being mounted on the wing structure, which provides beneficial wing bending relief in flight Figure 9.1.

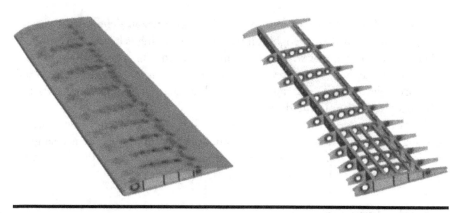

Figure 9.1 Wing Ribs and Spars.

Types of Aircraft Wing Structures

In order to increase the performance of the aircraft, various wing configurations are made such as sweptback wing, delta wing, tapered leading and trailing edges, straight leading and trailing edges, straight leading edge and tapered trailing edge, tapered leading edge, and straight trailing edge [4,5].

UAV and Its Specifications

In recent years, unmanned aerial vehicles have been used in various fields such as military, industrial sector, commercial (payload delivery), research, and agriculture. In many sectors, human beings are replaced by an unmanned aerial vehicle. Multi-rotors and the small aerial vehicle have significant attention in civil and military purposes [6].

A UAV is recognized as an aircraft that operates in threatening situations that are difficult to access. The aircraft doesn't need a crew to fly. UAVs usually collect or gather information in terms of images and photogrammetric products, which in turn allows the users to attain information in an uncomplicated way. A UAV has the ability to measure accurately on different traits.

Due to the evolution of modern technologies, there is a need for a UAV to unveil its capabilities, such as to elicit information by capturing images, detecting, clustering, and acknowledging the targets. For these types of complex operations, a set of algorithms is implemented. Some research has been made in the field of inspection and monitoring of various infrastructures such as photovoltaic systems and transmission cable lines. Utilization of a UAV can reduce the risk of hazards, costs, and time induced for inspection [1].

The UAVs have two types of wings: fixed wing and rotary wing. A fixed-wing UAV has the ability to fly for a longer duration compared to a rotary-wing UAV due to its simple structure because it can fly at high speeds. These require runways for takeoff. Rotary UAVs are skilled at hovering and land vertically; due to its complex structure, it can a fly for short duration at a low speed. A rotary UAV does not need a runway for takeoff [7].

Specifications

- RGB camera: 16 MP
- IR camera: 400–700 nanometer
- Dimensions: length* wingspan * height = 2.1 m * 3.0 m * 0.6 m
- Maximum takeoff weight: 13 kg
- Maximum payload: 3 kg
- Take-off and landing distance: 20 to 40 m
- Take-off speed: 55 km/h
- Landing speed: 60 km/h
- Stall speed: 50 km/h
- Maximum ascent speed: 12 m/s
- Maximum speed: 150 km/h
- Cruising speed: 100–110 km/h
- Maximum service ceiling: 5000 m
- Endurance: 2 hours
- Maximum wind speed resistance: strong breeze (10.8–13.8 m/s)
- Automatic flying mode: GPS navigation measure radius (in intervisible): 30 km
- Off-shell-type ground control station

This specification is taken from the DB3 UAV Remote Sensing System for a particular UAV.

Edge AI

Edge AI is installing human intelligence into machines through programming to think like humans and imitate their actions. AI has recently advanced the process of deep learning (DL), algorithms, big data, and computing power. AI is most achieved and given a wider breakthrough in different sectors like speech recognition, analyzing visual data, a wide spectrum of the field, and processing the natural language (e.g., Robo reader, the commercial flight uses an AI autopilot). Applications of AI are video surveillance, smart home appliances, digital assistants, e-payments, and text editors; using this technology changes our lifestyle and can be used for human safety purposes.

A combination of edge computing and AI gives a new world without any communication load called edge artificial intelligence (AI) or edge intelligence (EI). EI is a developing technology over five to ten years, and a lot of production and research has gone on. The wireless system is made up of ultra-dense edge nodes, contains edge servers placed at the base stations, and wireless access points; edge devices are smartphones, smart vehicles, and drones. What is important is reducing the amount of data transferred to the cloud; as a result, removing the network traffic load, privacy, and latency concerns. Some computation-intensive that inference tasks based on AI this can edge devices, and edge service, but heavy communication expensive cost. Edge AI needs larger storage sizes and intensive computations. Instead of completely relying on the cloud, Edge AI makes a wider range of edge resources to gain a deep understanding of AI. Edge AI gives more importance to industries and academia. These industries are more interested in Edge AI (Google, Microsoft, Intel, and IBM). Some of the projects were launched, and they have lots of projects and research in an ongoing process. Applications of Edge AI are image analytics, audio analytics, inertial sensor/environmental sensor analytics, agriculture purposes, and industrial Internet of Things (IIOT) [8] Figure 9.2.

Causes for Wing Failure

During various flight conditions, an aircraft wing structure undergoes stress and damage due to the environment, payloads, etc. This can cause the wing to fail with

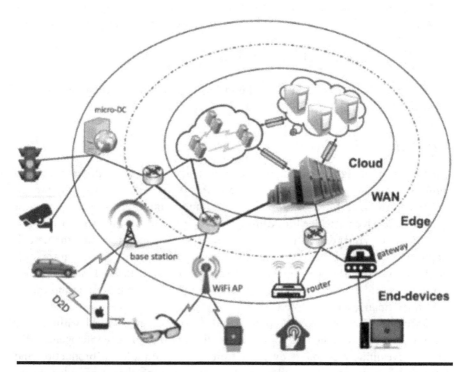

Figure 9.2   Edge AI Process.

a catastrophic consequence to life and aircraft. In order to avoid this inspection, analysis and maintenance of the wing are vital.

Failure is commonly caused due to design errors such as misalignment of rivets and holes, fatigue cracks, and turbulence. Environmental causes are corrosion, stress caused by a difference in temperature such as ice formation, and lightning strikes.

Various Modes of Wing Failure

The following various modes of failures mostly occurred in the wing's structure.

Fatigue Cracks

Fatigue cracks occur due to alternating or cyclic mechanical stresses. They generally initiate at stress concentration points on the surface. Changing the cross-section and surface defects causes cracks. Beach marks are formed when the magnitude or direction of loading changes. Decreasing the cross-section by increasing stress finally leads to residual fracture. The stresses can be caused by bolts, studs, screws, environment, turbulence, etc. [9].

Corrosion

When metals react with the environment, it causes chemical degradation called corrosion. When a part of the metal component corrodes, the whole component fails when the remaining material is not able to withstand the applied loads. Corrosion leads to other failures such as fatigue [9].

Lightning Strikes

Lightning strikes usually occur at an altitude of 500–15,000 ft, and pits, burn marks, discolored material or small circular holes indicate lightning damage. Some damages due to lightning include melt through, resistive heating, missing structure at the aircraft empennage, and wing tips. Bonding straps can also get damaged by lightning. Composite structures without or inadequate protection or proper design can get damaged in the form of fiber damage, burnt point, and removal of composite layer.

Ice Formation

Ice forms on the surface of an aircraft either in flight or on the ground. On the ground, when the outside temperature is 0 degrees Celsius or below, precipitation falls on the aircraft and freezes. It forms on the top of the using and tail. That ice is de-iced with a de-icing fluid like propylene glycol. Water droplets make up the cloud. During winter, the temperature at the clouds is less than 0 degrees Celcius (approximately up to −40 degrees Celcius). If the droplet doesn't have a surface to freeze on, they maintain their liquid form. When an aircraft flies through these clouds, the droplets get a surface and freeze on the leading edges of the wings, nose, and tail.

The ice deforms the aerodynamic shape of the wing and tail, thereby increasing drag, reducing lift, and causing the plane to stall [10].

Design and Manufacturing Errors

Design and manufacturing errors include the presence of holes on the surface, rough surface, improper rigging of control surface, etc.; fitting the rivets, screws, nuts, and bolts too tight can lead to cracks and other damage [9].

Hydrogen Embrittlement

When metals are acted upon with high tensile or residual stresses of more than 1100 Mpa react with hydrogen, this causes hydrogen embrittlement. It usually occurs during processes such as pickling and electroplating [9].

NDT Inspection Methods

Ultrasonic Testing (UT)

Discontinuities and defects, their size, location, and orientation in composite structures can be detected using ultrasonic waves. Misalignment in composite fibers can be efficiently detected as the sound beam propagates along the axis direction of the fibers. Discrete reflection and transmission loss are two major concerns that arise due to deboned fibers and delamination. Porosity scatters the waves and causes transmission loss. The structural differences are isolated by time and frequency domain signal processing methods. The multiple waves reflect from the surface of CFRP composites. The deviation in the wave structures helps in detection and localization of the defects. The phased array sensors, augmented with time reversal methods, disclose the misalignment between the probe and composite structure, thus increasing the coverage area. This technique is used in Airbus operations.

The mismatch between the air and solid materials makes the inspection of a honeycomb structure a laborious task. Immersion testing is performed over the honeycomb structures to combat this challenge. The process of immersion testing is done by immersing the transducer along with the object in a water tank. The sound waves from the transducer will be coupled with the object. Any deviation from the normal operational profile is an indication of the presence of defect. Though this method effectively detects the surface level cracks, it inherently demands a drying process, as the honeycomb panels may absorb water. This technique breaks the normal operational pipeline of activities, as the test object needs to be dismantled from the structure. In addition to this, this activity is time consuming.

Ultrasonic testing (UT) is a more popular method to detect surface level cracks, but the process is comparatively slow and it may take a few hours to test large composite panels. The limited resolution property of UT makes tracking the interaction of multi-defect types a difficult task. In addition to this, the UT is not capable of detecting latent defects. So, scanning acoustic microscopy is used to detect micro level and hidden faults. In this technique, high-range ultrasonic frequencies in the range of 30 MHZ–2 GHZ are subjected to the microstructure of the composite material. This frequency range is sensitive to interfacial debonding and progression of microscopic crack damage. Hence, larger wave scattering and multiple reflections will be caused by the damaged surface, thus making the detection of discontinuities in non-homogeneous tiresome. Lower frequency ranges are generally deployed to reduce the attenuation of waveforms, but this comes with the cost of reduced penetration depth. All of these factors do not recommend the application of UT in diagnosing deeper defects [11] Figure 9.3.

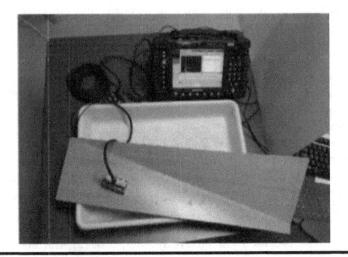

Figure 9.3   Ultrasonic Testing.

Infrared Thermography (IRT)

The IRT technique uses thermal energy to detect the presence of faults or defects in material. Thermal energy is diffused into the object under testing. A variation in the emissivity coefficients can be observed, in case the waves reach a material defect like matrix cracking, porosity, and inclusions. The severity of the damage can be assessed by the resulting thermal gradient. The thermal output is captured by infrared cameras, which generate a temperature map of the structure under investigation. Thus, the defects in the base material can be successfully isolated by monitoring their thermal properties.

The IRT technique is bifurcated into active and passive IRT. Passive IRT is applicable for structures that exhibit thermal contrast with their surroundings. This is commonly used in the detection of water ingress in honeycomb sandwich panels. In the active IRT method, the structure is exposed to different heat sources to generate a difference in the temperature in the area under study. Based on the heat sources, the active IRT is further categorized into optically stimulated, ultrasonic, metal-based, and eddy current stimulated thermography. Optically stimulated thermography deserves a special mention, since it is widely used in aerospace structures. Lock-in and pulsed/transient thermography are two widely used methods of optically stimulated thermography.

The lock-in thermography effectively controls the energy deposit on the structure's surface. The analysis of signal to noise ratio (SNR) of deeper defects shows that both methods result in the same findings. The lock-in thermography finds its applications in characterizing delamination in CFRPs, detection of subsurface defects in CFRPs, investigation of fatigue behaviors, and detection of disbands in titanium alloy honeycomb sandwich structures. However, this method needs a separate experiment for different depths of defect [12,13].

Pulsed thermography is more suitable for detection of shallow defects, but this method suffers from a multitude of problems like environmental reflection, nonuniform heating, surface geometry, etc. This demands more complex signal and image processing techniques like gapped heat conduction-based three-dimensional normalization, smoothing algorithm, partial least-squares regression, and coefficient clustering analysis.

In spite of all these factors, IRT is a superior method to detect defects like fiber breakage, delamination, and matrix micro-cracks. The impact energy, which is in turn dissipated as heat, is spent in the formation of such defects. An infrared camera is employed to capture real-time information about the development of delamination.

However, IRT is suitable for detection of near-surface damage with low aspect ratios. Their effectiveness is not witnessed in deeper damages in the range of ten microns to a few millimeters. It is evident that varying the orientation angles between the subsequent layers will decline the observable temperature contrast.

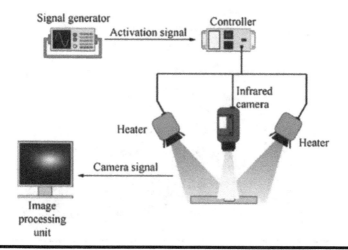

Figure 9.4 Infrared Thermography.

Due to this effect, detection of defects in multi-angles and cross-ply becomes tougher [11] Figure 9.4.

Acoustic Emission (AE)

AE waves propagate in all directions into the surface material. In composite materials, fiber-matrix debonding, fiber breakage, delamination, matrix cracking, fiber pull-out, and fiber misalignment generate acoustic emission. These sources release higher AE energy in a short time period (transient/burst-type AE signal) and therefore can be more easily characterized. AE measurements have been effectively used to indicate impact damages.

There is a need for more sophisticated techniques for signal processing to distinguish defective structures from healthy ones, and to separate different defects from each other. This is because it had been reported that matrix cracking and fiber debonding emitted AE signals of relatively similar amplitude, although fiber failure generated much lower AE amplitudes. A particular test cannot be perfectly reproduced, because each AE event is a unique stress and cannot be reproduced or stopped. The AE signals received by the AE sensor will be slightly different from the signals emitted by the composite; they will incur significant changes across the transmission path [11] Figure 9.5.

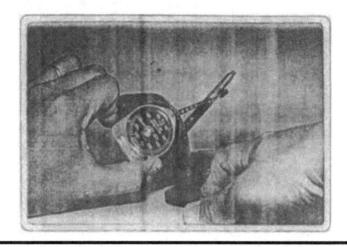

Figure 9.5   Acoustic Emission.

Eddy Current Testing (ECT)

Conductive composite materials like carbon fiber reinforced polymer (CFRP) and metal-matrix composites can be inspected using eddy currents. In CFRPs, measurement of ECT resp ones to the carbon fibers specially. Hence, damage, and other damages that affect the fibers can be detected using eddy currents.

For visualizing resin reach regions, delamination, fiber orientation, fiber fraction fluctuations, and impact damage in CFRP composites, a high-frequency eddy current technique (HF-ECT) was developed. It works better for less conductive materials. However, when high frequencies (e.g., ≥50 MHz) are applied, only the near-surface defects can be characterized as the penetration depth becomes limited to the top few piles below the surface. To get deeper below the surface of the structure, such as a sandwich structure, lower frequencies are used.

Eddy current holography is an advanced method developed to inspect composite structures for defects like surface and near-surface cracks, delamination, and corrosion. It was reported that delamination due to impact energies exceeding 0.75 J in quasi-isotopically carbon-epoxy composites were visualized using this method.

Some disadvantages of ECT are: (1) it is difficult to interpret the measured signals; (2) the penetration depth is limited to surface and subsurface defects; (3)

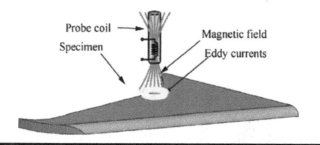

Figure 9.6 Eddy Current Testing.

this method is suitable mostly for composites with conductive fiber (e.g., carbon fiber) [11] Figure 9.6.

Laser Shearography (LS)

The principle of laser shearography is based on processing the interferometry images achieved using two laser beams with an identical wavelength that becomes nearly collinear. A charge-coupled device (CCD) video sensor is used to image the heat subject. Because of the inherent surface roughness of the test subject, the interference is produced by the reflection of a coherent light beam. When the object is externally loaded or deformed, the speckle pattern will be slightly altered. While loading, there is a need to induce some deformation or the surface of the sample changes the deformation state.

The integrity of the object is then evaluated by speckle photography in two sequential ways (before and after deformation). Subtracting the two-speckle pattern produces a fringe pattern depicting the displacement derivative with respect to the direction of shearing. Quantitative evaluation methods using spatial carrier frequency or temporal phase shifting can be used for further improvement in image quality.

Suitable external loading increments must be applied to the test subject during the inspection. For that reason, some suitable loading methods are required for the inspection. As the depth of the defect or its diameter is increased, the changes observed in the derivative of the displacement pattern decrease. Successful application of digital shearography for features of defects (except for delamination) are extremely difficult for the aerospace industry composites but still depend on illumination, etc. [11] Figure 9.7.

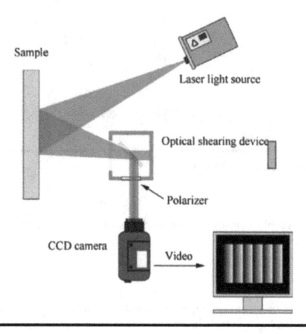

Figure 9.7 Laser Shearography.

Deep Learning and Deep Neural Networks

Machine learning and deep learning are two core areas in implementation of artificial intelligent concepts. Deep learning is gaining more significance because of its property of automatic feature learning. The deep neural networks are seen as a genesis of artificial neural networks (ANNs), which have greater predictive power with enhanced accuracy.

The deep learning model consists of a series of layers to constitute a deep neural network (DNN). A DNN is a collection of neurons that can generate based on the data nonlinear output from the input of the neuron. The input of the neuron gets the data and generates them to the middle layer and the input. The total weighted input and total weighted output are used for the specific activation function and the output generated to the output layer. They are three popular structures of DNNs: convolution neural network (CNN), multilayer perception (MLP), and recurrent neural network (RNN). MLPs are the most basic DNN model, which is a collection of series of complete connected layers. A CNN model can express the represented high-level input data, making it the most famous computer vision task. Regarding the UAV indoor navigation tasks, CNN has advanced recently successful applications like changing the direction through map image to high-level

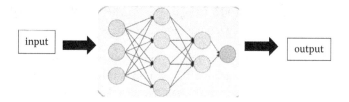

Figure 9.8   Multi-Layer Perceptron: A Forerunner for DNN.

behavior directives (for example turn left, turn right, rotate left, and rotate right). RNN models are most widely used for the tasks of natural language processing like machine translation, answering questions, and language modeling. Deep learning expresses the latest artificial intelligence technology as well as a highly resource-demanding capability that naturally suits edge computing [14].

Deep learning techniques are extensively used in almost all scientific researches areas. One of the interesting domains is motion control. Motion control is solving various robotic control problems and analytic manners, and allowing robots to perform complex movements. Even so, standard control theory only solves some of the problems for an approximate robot model and for a particular case, and is not able to easily fit to change in the robot model like propeller gets damage in the UAV, rain. A DNN provides developing benefits to infer complex behaviors from incomplete observation data.

Deep learning is used as a method in wing failure analysis. The processed image captured from the UAV is compared with a pre-processed image that is stored in the cloud system. Based on this comparison, the data is clustered as defects or non-defects [8] Figures 9.8 and 9.9.

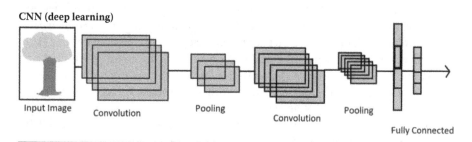

Figure 9.9   Layers in Convolutional Neural Network.

Architectural Design of Edge AI–Based Wing Inspection System

They are two human-based input providers: ground control station and radio control receiver. A UAV ground control station acts as a one of the input providers where the pilot sits in front of a number of screens (map screen and aircraft instrumentation) and it also consists of conventional aircraft joystick through which the pilot operates the UAV. The other input provider is a radio controller that transmits the pulse position modulation signals to the RC transmitter mounted on the UAV; this also requires human operation. An autopilot sensor is mounted on the UAV that gains the input that enhances the UAV to follow the trajectory or reference path. A GPS sensor places a major role in autonomous control of a UAV as it creates a grid layout that localizes the target and provides the absolute position measurement. In case of any emergency situation, a UAV manually operates the RC receiver.

With the help of autopilot and GPS sensors, the UAV flight flies through the trajectory path and localizes the wing structure where the UAV captured the images using the RGB and IR camera. The wing structure is made of composites such as carbon fiber reinforced polymer (CFRP), as it has a high heat emissivity and retains heat much longer than other materials. The detection of visual defects such as cracks, dents, scratches, misalignment rivets, etc. is done by using a RGB camera. An infrared camera gives the data of the defects that are not visible with a human eye or RGB camera. An external heater is fixed facing the wing to create a temperature difference between the different regions within the wing structure (active IRT). When the heat waves propagate from the IR heater through the wing specimen and reach the defects such as cracks, delaminations, etc., the thermal properties of the defected area differ with the non-defected area; by this, the infrared camera detects the heat variations between these areas. Commonly, red, orange, yellow, and white colors indicate the warmer parts, while blue and purple indicate cooler parts. Green usually indicates areas at room temperature [15].

The image processed from the cameras is computed with the help of Edge AI. Edge AI is the cloud computing system where the data is being collected by means of the Internet of Things (IoT) such as wireless gadgets through base stations [16]. Edge AI can generate data through deep learning on the cloud to develop deductive and predictive models. The deep learning approach is a faster R-CNN that compares and clusters the obtained data with pre-processed data storage in the cloud system. Based on the clustering, artificial intelligence providers determine whether it is internal or external defects. If the defects are obtained, the Figure 9.10 process comes to an end [8,14]. If not, UAVs move to a different area and the process starts from the beginning. By using MATLAB® or Python software, it takes less code and builds a deep learning without needing to be a specialist in the techniques. For external defects, edge detection tool MATLAB software is used where the RGB images are converted into gray-scale images that discontinuous in the wing structure is been highlighted with the red particle filler [7].

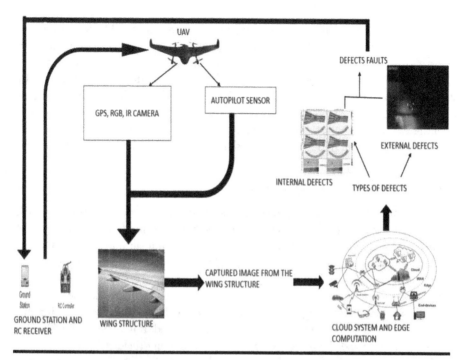

Figure 9.10 Architectural Design of Edge AI–Based Wing Inspection System.

Motivation – A Need for Edge AI

Edge AI is the amalgamation of AI and edge computing. Edge AI aims to explore the innumerable associations and relationships in the data that is generated by the edge devices in a more proximal and localized fashion. Implementation of AI artifacts in low-dimensional devices to accomplish mission-specific task is the real success of Edge AI.

Edge Networking Data Generating Using AI

The surge in the number of IoT, mobile, and wireless devices in the surroundings facilitated the rapid streaming of heterogeneous data. AI, ML, and DL techniques are used to explore this voluminous data to unleash the latent knowledge for enabling high-quality decision making. These algorithms have proven their prowess in detecting underlying trends and patterns to excavate useful knowledge from them. For instance, environmental data like air quality index (AQI), temperature, humidity, and pressure are analyzed through machine learning algorithms to gain deeper insights about these factors and also to arrive at accurate meteorological predictions.

Deep learning is gaining more popularity. The improvement of deep learning is inborn; the role of data by the effect of algorithms and hardware has been mostly overlooked. Using a deep neural network (DNN) improves the deep learning algorithm with more layers of neurons. For learning more parameters in a DNN, we need to increase the training for the required data. In this way, we are learning the importance of the data for the AI. Before, this data was created and stored in megascale data centers. Nowadays, IoT has been rapidly developed and become famous. A report was given by the production at the edge side. Processing the data by AI algorithms at the cloud data center consumes more bandwidth resources, thus creating great pressure. To combat this challenge, a new notion called edge computing came into existence to achieve the data processing process with minimal latency by shifting the computations to the edge side [8].

Implementation Algorithm

The input provided to a UAV flight comprises autopilot, GPS, and camera RGB or IR. In general, an autopilot system is termed a *micro-electromechanical system,* which is used in the automatic guidance of UAV without the help of human intervention. The autopilot system of a UAV flight enhances the flight to follow the trajectory reference path. The GPS system in the UAV flight provides the grid layout for the target localization. The camera (RGB or IR) captures the image over wing structures, and the processed image is been inspected using an edge detection tool (MATLAB software). Using this software, if defects are obtained, the process comes to an end. If not, the UAV will move to a different area and the process starts from the beginning (Figure 9.11).

Using input provided to the UAV flight, the inspection over a wing structure is undertaken. The image processed using the camera is being compared using the deep learning analysis. Using the deep learning process, the processed image is being clustered based on defects and non-defects. If the defects are obtained, the process comes to an end. If not, UAVs move to a different area and the process starts from the beginning [17–21] (Figure 9.12).

Software Requirement

In deep learning, one of the popular structures of the neural network is the convolutional neural network (CNN). This convolutional neural network is commonly used in terms of visualizing and analyzing the capture. A convolutional neural network is used in image recognition. An edge detection tool MATLAB software is used for image and video processing and deep learning [3,6,7,12–14,16].

Hardware Selection

Hardware is considered a physical part that requires a set of instructions to perform a task. Hardware setup mainly compromises an unmanned aerial vehicle (fixed wing), ground control station (GCS), base station, and wing panel for inspection. Typical of the UAV autopilot system, it comprises a GPS sensor and RC flight controller. A red, green, and blue (RGB) and infrared thermography (IR) camera is used for the identification of defects [1,4,5,8–11,15].

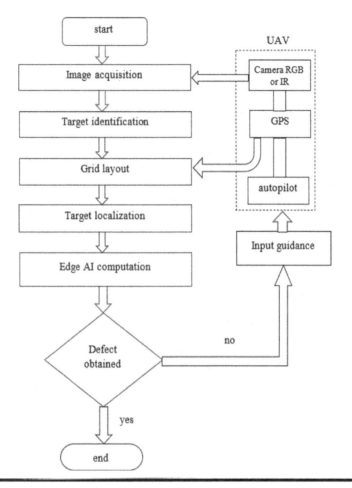

Figure 9.11   Implementation Algorithm.

Scope for Future Development

Recently a smart leading-edge device was developed for a smooth leading surface to understand a structure/system solution, application for transport aircraft it is capable of being deflection into a regular high left. This smart leading-edge device has the potential to reduce airframe noise and drag.

In recent times, there are lots of development in cyber technology (e.g., automated dependent surveillance-broadcast and Internet protocol networking) that proposes the framework to protect traffic data communication from the aircraft.

In recent times, technology has developed in the segments of intelligence maintenance, supply chain, and customer service. Machine learning and deep learning are helpful for these applications. Further development in the inspection of fuel efficiency

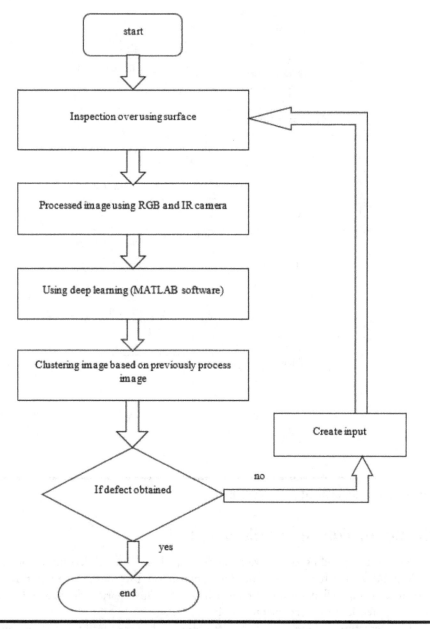

Figure 9.12   Algorithm Based on Deep Learning.

with the help of an AI model can analyze how much fuel is consumed in the climb phase for different aircraft to develop climb phase profiles for fuel conservation.

AI-based assistants can suggest alternate routes to pilots based on weather data from sensors and flight data using air traffic management. AI-enabled smart cameras can use facial recognition to identify the passenger and suspicious people at airports. Upcoming developments in the International Space Station is AI-based to assist astronauts are equipped with cameras, sensors, and microphones to see, hear, process, and display important in speaking and flying. AI-based computer vision and machine learning technologies enable self-piloted commercial aircraft to take off and land and to navigate and detect ground obstacles autonomously [8].

Conclusion

As the aircraft industry is constantly making progress with technological advancements, we look to improve one important aspect of this industry, which is inspection. With the help of artificial intelligence, the data can be acquired more accurately and quickly. UAV technology has a very good scope because of the increasing trend of UAVs in almost every field. With the modern world rapidly growing and trying to discover more efficient ways of working in every field, UAVs and Edge AI have a very important part to play in that.

In this chapter, we have discussed the various modes of wing failure and some of the NDT inspection methods including ultrasonic testing, infrared thermography, acoustic emission, eddy current testing, and laser stereography. The integration of UAV with Edge AI, deep learning, autopilot, infrared thermography, and image processing systems can play a major role in the inspection and maintenance of an aircraft, as well as in other fields.

References

[1] V. Tzitzilonis, K. Malandrakis, L. Fragonara, J. Gonzalez Domingo, N. Avdelidis, A. Tsourdos, and K. Forster. "Inspection of Aircraft Wing Panels Using Unmanned Aerial Vehicles." RECEIVED: 22 February 2019; Accepted: 11 April 2019; Published: 17 April 2019.

[2] A. Ramesh Kumar, S. Balakrishnan, and S. Balaji. "Design of an Aircraft Wing Structure for Static Analysis and Fatigue LifePrediction." *International Journal of Engineering Research & Technology (IJERT)* 2, no. 5 (2013). Department of Aeronautical Engineering, Nehru Institute of Engineering and Technology.

[3] S. Peruru and S. Abbisetti. "Design and FInite Element Analysis of Aircraft WIng Using Ribs and Spars." *International Research Journal of Engineering and Technology (IRJET) e-ISSN: 2395 -0056* Volumemac_mac 04, 06 (2017).

[4] H. Chao, Y. Cao, and Y. Chen. "Autopilots for Small Unmanned Aerial Vehicles: A Survey." *International Journal of Control, Automation, and Systems* 8, no. 1 (2010): 36–44. 10.1007/s12555-010-0105-z.

[5] H. Morton, B. Bishop and G. Clark. "NDT of AIrcraft Structures during Full-Scale Fatigue Testing." Airframes & Engines division, DSTO Aeronautical Research Laboratory, Melbourne.

[6] A. Khan and Y. Al-Mulla. "Unmanned Aerial Vehicle in the Machine Learning Environment." In The 10th International Conference on Emerging Ubiquitous Systems and Pervasive Networks (EUSPN 2019), Coimbra, Portugal, November 4-7, 2019.

[7] F. Pereira and C. Pereira. "Embedded Image Processing Systems for Automatic Recognition of Cracks using UAVs." Federal University of Rio Grande do Sul.

[8] Z. Zhou, X. Chen, E. Li, L. Zeng, K. Luo, and A. Zhang. Fellow IEEE. "Edge Intelligence: Paving the Last Mile of Artificial Intelligence with Edge Computing." Published data: 8, August 2019.

[9] S. Findlay and N. Harrison. "Why Aircraft Fail."

[10] S. Deane, N. Avdelidis, C. Ibarra-Castanedo, X. Maldague, A. Tsourdos, A. Williamson, H. Yazdani-Nezhad, and H. Zhang. "Autonomous Systems Imaging of Aerospace Structures." School of Aerospace, Transport and Manufacturing, Cranfield University, United Kingdom.

[11] H. Towsyfyan, A. Biguri, R. Boardman, and T. Blumensath. "Successes and challenges in non-destructive testing of aircraft composite structures", Institute of Sound and Vibration Research (ISVR), University of Southampton, Southampton SO17 1BJ, UK, received 19 November 2018; revised 17 December 2018; accepted 16 July 2019, Available online 9 October 2019.

[12] J. Saura, A. Reyes-Menendez, and P. Palos-Sanchez. "Mapping Multispectral Digital Images using a Cloud Computing Software: Applications from UAV Images".

[13] S. Moustakidis, A. Anagnostis, P. Karlsson, and K. Hrissagis. "Non-destructive inspection of Aircraft Composite Materials using Triple IR Imaging."

[14] https://debuggercafe.com/convolutional-neural-network-architectures-and-variants/

[15] S. Deane, N. Avdelidis, C. Ibarra-Castanedo, H. Zhang, H. Nezhad, A. Williamson, T. Mackley, X. Maldague, A. Tsourdos, and P. Nooralishahi. "Comparison of Cooled and Uncooled IR Sensors by Means of Signal-to-Noise Ratio for NDT Diagnostics of Aerospace Grade Composites." Received: 8 April 2020; Accepted: 28 May 2020; Published: 15 June 2020.

[16] J. Chen, S. Chen, S. Luo, Q. Wang, B. Cao, and X. Li. "An Intelligent Task Offloading Algorithm (iTOA) for UAV Edge Computing Network."

[17] S. Sharanya and S. Karthikeyan. "Classifying Malicious node in VANETs using Support Vector Machines with Modified Fading Memory." *ARPN Journal of Engineering and Applied Sciences* 12, no. 1 January (2017).

[18] S. Sharanya. "Revathi Venkataraman, an Intelligent Context Based Multi-layered Bayesian Inferential Predictive Analytic Framework for Classifying Machine States." *Journal of Ambient Intelligence and Humanized Computing* (2020). 10. 1007/s12652-020-02411-2.

[19] R. Minu and G. Nagarajan. "Bridging the IoT Gap Through Edge Computing." In *Edge Computing and Computational Intelligence Paradigms for the IoT*, pp. 1–9. IGI Global, 2019.

[20] G. Nagarajan, R. Minu, and A. Jayanthiladevi. "Cognitive Internet of Things (C-IOT)." In *Sensing Techniques for Next Generation Cognitive Radio Networks*, pp. 299–311. IGI Global, 2019.

[21] S. Simpson and G. Nagarajan. "An Edge based Trustworthy Environment Establishment for Internet of Things: An Approach for Smart Cities." *Wireless Networks* (2021): 1–17.

Chapter 10

Edge AI–Based Aerial Monitoring

S. Karthikeyan, G. Bharath Ajay, N. Raakin Ahamed, and A. Sharun

Department of Aerospace Engineering, B. S Abdur Rahman Crescent Institute of Science and Technology, Chennai, India

Contents

DOI: 10.1201/9781003145158-10

Introduction

Being born in a world rife with lots of advanced technologies and rapidly growing industrial inventions, aerial monitoring using drone technology along with advanced imaging sensors created a life and time-saving revolution. Technologies like deep learning (DL), machine learning (ML), and artificial intelligence (AI) technology made drone technology more advanced and autonomously enabled. In the era of Industry 4.0, unmanned aerial vehicles (UAV) have rapidly grown and made themselves useful in almost every industry. In past years, drones have been used in structural defect detection, disaster management, security surveillance, educational purposes, photography, parcel delivery, and agriculture. As drone use is increasing day by day, drones are becoming more useful in monitoring the photovoltaic (PV) field. Solar industries started to adapt drone technologies for their PV structural defect monitoring due to their advanced surveillance capability, efficient data logging capability, long-range inspection, and instant defect analysis capabilities. The massive increase in population across the globe led to an exponential increase in energy demands. Electricity utilized nowadays is from fossil fuels, which are responsible for the increase of greenhouse gas emissions. The availability of fossil fuels is decreasing rapidly. This creates a gap between energy produced by the environment and the demand for energy resources. Hereafter, alternative energy sources mainly cover all the areas with a viable and nature-friendly manner. When the idea of better energy emerges, it should be selected according to site, availability, transportation, viability, etc. [1,2].

The better energy source would be solar energy from the sun, which has a rising demand in the global market due to its large availability, easy operation, market development, and eco-friendliness. When we have a large power plant available above us, then what is necessary is to mainly focus on developing power from oil and coal. Sun gives energy with clean, non-stop energy. The major content in the sun is accumulated atomic power that has more energy on board to operate our system associate other for an extra for one more 5 billion year and solar panels will turn this energy into a never-ending, convenient source of electricity. The photovoltaic panels generate electricity by absorbing solar radiation, which does not require an external energy source to operate. The fast growth of photovoltaic power generation has produced electricity on a higher scale and plays an important role in protection from global warming issues by reducing the fossil fuel usage and greenhouse gas emissions. Rigorous research development and technological advancements have made an increase in photovoltaic cell efficiency, reducing the photovoltaic structure panel cost, and getting as much power as possible from the photovoltaic panel. Despite all, the photovoltaic systems are sensitive and affect the efficiency, reliability, and safety of the solar system. Major drawbacks are limits of factors affecting the loss not measured which leads to energy loss and it is not detected. The problems we need to focus on in the solar power system are to identify the causes. Continuous monitoring of a photovoltaic plant could enable solutions for identifying defects. Continuous monitoring cannot be achieved by human inspection as it takes a lot of time and improper identification. Aerial monitoring using drones could be a time-saver and, with proper imaging, AI systems can be easy to identify major and minor defects in photovoltaic panels. Drones can be especially useful when monitoring a large PV field, because it also decreases the human workforce involved. The defect identification can be achieved by using electroluminescence imaging and IR-thermal imaging and infrared imaging [3,4].

The content based on implementing engineering technologies for automated intelligent drones to monitor the solar plants is the major objective of this chapter.

We also discuss the photovoltaic systems and defects caused in the PV systems and identification of those faults and defects using aerial inspection. Later, we discuss the hardware and software involved in the drone system for effective monitoring and scope of drones in remote monitoring and photovoltaic industries [2].

Solar Cell

A solar power cell, conjointly called a photovoltaic cell, is a tool that converts the energy of the sunlight from the sun into power through the electrical phenomenon result. Photovoltaic cells are dimensions of an adult's palm and colored bluish black. They are usually bundled along to form larger units known as solar modules. Solar modules' area unit is even coupled along to make solar panels. Like battery cells, solar panels' area unit is manufactured to get electricity. The battery cells build electricity from chemical components; photovoltaic cells generate electricity by arresting daylight. That is why they are called photovoltaic (PV) cells, because the name photovoltaic cell comes from the Greek word known as *light* and the word *voltaic* became relevant due to an Italian electricity pioneer named Alessandro Volta. The bulk of solar cells' area unit fictitious from the element with increasing potential energy and decreasing value, the fabric ranges from non-crystalline to crystalline single crystal element formation. The solar battery does not have any moving elements. In solar cells, silicon material is a semiconductor and other materials, such as metal, allow electricity to flow down them. A solar cell system is a sandwich structure of two layers up and down of silicon doped together to allow the electricity flow. The solar cell consists of n-type (negative-type) silicon and p-type (positive-type) silicon layers together [5].

Once the light particles reach the cell, they bombard the upper surface. The energy of the photon is carried through the solar cell. These photons give their maximum energy to the electrons in the p-type silicon layer. In the future, this energy are used by the electrons to hop across the sandwich wall to the n-type silicon layer and move into the route and then the circuit distributes the electricity. The solar cell follows the basic physics rule of law of conservation of energy. The efficiency of solar cells has drastically increased by more than 50% compared to its first-generation solar cells. A single-junction solar cell has an efficiency of more than 30%, called a SQEfficiency limit. Historically, solar cells are utilized in things wherever electric power from the grid structure is unprocurable, like in distinct space power systems, Earth-orbiting satellites systems, client systems; for example, application of hand-held calculators or radiocarpal watches, remote radio, and water pumping. Solar cells' area unit is terribly helpful in powering area vehicles like satellites and telescopes (e.g., Hubble). They supply an economical and reliable method of powering objects that might otherwise be pricey and cumbersome fuel sources [4,5].

The types of solar cells are first-generation (mono-Si, single, the simple junction point between p-type and n-type silicon layers), second-generation (thin wafers about 200 micrometers, also known as thin-film solar cells), and third generation (latest technology with maximum efficiency, made of materials other than silicon). Today's solar cells produce more than 2–6 kWh per day; multiplying it gives 700–2500 kWh per year. To make a large amount of solar power, solar farms are created to produce a huge amount of solar electricity during the daytime [6] (Figure 10.1).

Drones and Their Specifications

The drone, also known as an unmanned aerial vehicle (UAV), is an aircraft without a pilot or passenger on board. They are controlled by the transmitter by radio waves received by the receiver inside the drone body. As they are autonomous vehicles, they have a pre-programmed ruleset that enables them to make the choices on their own. Automatic systems incapable of enabling this "choice of

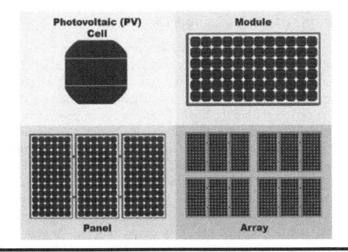

Figure 10.1 Difference between Solar Cell, Module, Panel, and Array.

freedom". Due to the absence of pilots, these drones usually have a definite level of autonomy. Drones are preferred due to their compact and small size, they reduce the human workforce, better inspection and task completion, autonomous and adapt to the situation, long-range travel, better high-altitude imaging, less noise, maneuverability, and obstacle detection. There are also categories in drones such as large drones and small drones, fixed-wing drones, and multirotor drones. Drones are also classified according to the number of motors, the position of the motors placed, speed of the drone, battery capacity, electronic speed controller specifications, flight controllers, propellers, angle of the propellers, etc. [4]. As drones are becoming more commercialized, many industries have adopted drone technologies for their industries. With no exception, the solar industry has adopted technologies for its solar panel defect or fault inspection in their large-scale solar farms. As they reduce costs for maintenance, inspections, and repairs, and man-hours, using drones in the solar industry gives new opportunities and replaces existing work. Without drones, the inspections are completed manually and would take more time. Moreover, the drone can give more accurate data on faults in the solar panel, the location of the panel, and whether it is a major defect or minor defect. Drones are easy to control and use many software and apps that have been developed to control drones according to their needs. There are three ways to receive data from drones: PDF inspection report, online web maps, and field repair application. The tracking system in the drones is becoming better day by day. Drones can be used for site development planning and construction; commissioning and asset transfers; maintenance inspections; roof measurements and inspections; and substation, pole, and line inspections in solar industries. The most common drone used for solar field inspection is a four propeller or six propeller-multirotor, as they provide more stability in the air [3,7].

Specifications of an Inspection Drone

The inspection drone should be licensed for commercial purposes and must be a multirotor all-purpose drone. The drone should offer a minimum of 30 minutes of flight time and a maximum of 55 minutes and above in a single flight. The drone must be compatible with advanced AI capabilities for autonomous flights and to make its own choices during the flight. Drones must be good for tackling situational awareness for emergency responses. Four to six directional sensing and positioning will be suitable for imaging and detection. An IP45 rating is preferred for emergency inspection during rain. A 15 km max transmission signal must be enabled for long-distance flight inspections. Features such as large-scale mapping can make the tracking issues easier. UAV health management software can frequently check the health of the drone during the flight and keep the drone pilot updated. The operating temperature of the drone must be −20 degrees Celsius to +50 degrees Celsius. Additional features like live mission recording: record mission actions like craft gesture, gimbal orientation, image shooting, and zooming level to form sample mission data files for forthcoming automatic inspections and AI Spot-Check: automate day-to-day inspections and capture compatible results when aboard AI acknowledges the topic of interest and identifies it in resulting machine-controlled missions to confirm accordant framing. A drone camera must be equipped with a 640 x 512 px radiometric camera with a frame rate of 30 fps. According to IEC standards, a minimum of a 640 x 480 thermal resolution is needed to perform an efficient thermal electrical device review. The IEC additionally says that a 9 MP camera is ample if you need RGB pictures to show thermal images [5,8,9] (Figures 10.2 and 10.3).

Figure 10.2 Drone Scanning Solar Panels for Fault Detection.

Figure 10.3   Thermal Image of Solar Array.

Ways Drones Deliver Value to Solar Industry

The drones can add value to the solar industry for inspections and mapping due to their comprehensive coverage. They mainly allow the inspection of the solar energy cell system using drone technology and it is comparatively better than a manual field-testing operation. This will be measured based on I-V curve tracing. Doing regular inspections of a solar system takes time, requires skilled labor, and has a possibility of uninspected areas. Even though the quantity of time it takes to carry out these checks can even cause a difference within the test outcomes, capturing aerial footage of a complete solar field takes a noticeably short period of time to remove inconsistencies and inevitable errors in the scrutiny information. O&M groups that have enforced drones in use have reduced the time by 90% [2].

Enhanced Visibility – Use of drones to carry out aerial diagnostic technique inspects all problems at intervals a solar site all the way downcast to the cell side. Using the capturing elaborated imagery data of the whole PV system than made groups area connection than unit made ready to establish, classify, and localize every anomaly and perceive the performance influence. Technicians are then ready to speedily range irregularities by the extent of severity, visit every anomaly, and build acceptable maintenances. Site safety manually confirms a solar cell location and if it is working the most effective way using technicians. They should sporadically open combiners and inverters for checking. Direct interaction with open equipment is very unsafe and puts a technician's life at risk. Wherever an unsafe location is present, we need to use drones to check that location to avoid any danger. Scalability across solar sites - Since C&I sites area unit usually is set in extremely inhabited regions, and drone technicians area unit wide on the market for rent. Drones permit little groups to additionally examine massive utility-scale solar places in the same day, rather than causing a crew of technicians to seek out a needle in very risk work. Mostly single technicians will show up to a website and accomplish an IR and high-resolution imaging review at intervals of some hours. Drones' area unit sanctioning plus executives to extend the number of websites their groups will manage while not adding additional accomplished technicians.

Improved operational excellence made with PV systems encircling many thousands of panels arranged. Aerial high-resolution and thermal inspections have taken the lead economically thanks to sight anomalies like failures, spots, soiling, shading, and string. The O&M and quality organization at intervals the solar cell trade accepting drone technology thus on enhance their flow of labor, productivity, growth, reduction of labor charges, and improve protection [5,8].

Edge AI

As we are living in an era that is rapidly developing in autonomous technologies, artificial intelligence (AI) is leading the way. We came to the realization that AI requires large-scale information support and cloud storage that relies on a massive quantity of coaching and learning of an enormous variety of sample information and tests [10].

As current information within the network shows a high increase in growth rate, it might produce challenges to current information design, so it needs to cut back pressure on the network because of the volatile growth of information.

Edge computing knowledge arose into existing technologies. AI and edge computing are becoming two popular technologies. The industrial applications of edge computing are cloud service–based edge computing "cloud service drainage", site facility edge alliance/site provider "site + computing service", fixed operator-oriented edge computing "fixed connection + computing services", and mobile operator-centric edge computing (MEC) "mobile connectivity + computing services". The five technologies essential to perform edge AI is: 1. AI application on Edge – AI should provide intelligent services and edge computing for systematically organizing the technical frameworks; 2. AI inference in Edge – AI concerning edge computing must fulfill various requirements, such as latency and accuracy; 3. Edge computing for AI – AI computation is supported by edge computing in terms of network architecture, hardware, and software; 4. AI training at Edge – under resources and privacy constraints AI models are trained for edge intelligence; 5. AI for optimizing Edge – maintaining and managing various functions of edge computing as applied by AI [11] (Figure 10.4).

Edge AI reduces the consumption of power and improves battery life. It also reduces costs for data communication because less data is transmitted. Edge AI allows real-time operations within milliseconds; real-time operations are foremost

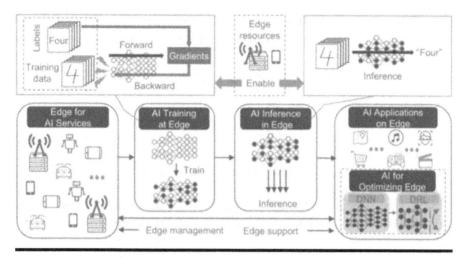

Figure 10.4   Landscape of Edge AI.

for self-driving cars, robots, and drones. Edge AI can be used in image analytics for recognizing various types of objects; image analytics with AI will help in people identification, obstacle avoidance recognition, and multi-object detection and also in other cases such as surveillance and monitoring, autonomous vehicles, and for analysis in online shopping. In audio analytics, Edge AI is useful for audio scene classification and audio event detection such as a baby crying, glass breaking, gunshot, etc. And at the same time for human voice recognition and keyword recognition can be analyzed. For factories, Edge AI plays a major role in predictive maintenance in factories for measuring noise level, temperature, and vibrations for early detection of failures. Edge AI is also used for body monitoring; the information can be correlated with stress level, health, diet, and alerts. Not only these, with multi-model analysis by receiving a huge amount of data from a variety of data sources and applying with specific neural network and with deep learning, but Edge AI can also perform more than the given uses [4,10,11].

Analysis of Various Modes of Solar Cell Failure (FMEA)

Safety and reliability are main issues in a semiconductor plant, mainly when it comes to flammable and toxic substances. However, the green industry is rising rapidly these days and new materials and technologies are immerging, producing higher photovoltaic efficiencies. Still, these technological advancements can accelerate the complex nature and risk of solar cell safety management. Failure mode and effect analysis (FMEA) is a safety analysis method that can identify the effects and modes of failure in components. It has two categories: Design FMEA

(DFMEA) and Process FMEA (PFMEA). The Design FMEA predicts the possibility of product malfunction and product safety from factors such as material geometry and properties, material tolerance, and engineering noises. The Process FMEA predicts the impact of a decrease in reliability of the process, quality of the product, customer feedback and dissatisfaction and safety from materials used, environmental factors, and human factors [12].

So, why we need to do failure mode and effects analysis (FMEA), the earlier the defect or failure is discovered, the less it will cost, and vice versa. The benefits of FMEA are that it provides a lower cost solution, verification of changes, standard work, a design collaboration between product and process. The FMEA needs to be performed when designing a new process or product, improving the goal for a process, understanding and improving the failures of a process, while performing the existing production process differently. There are seven steps to perform FMEA: 1. Assemble of the FMEA team and pre-work, 2. Path-1 Development, which is required by way of severity ranking, 3. Path-2 Development, which requires prevention cause through occurrence ranking, 4. Path-3 Development, which requires testing and detection through detection ranking, 5. action assignments and priority, 6. actions take and design review. 7. re-ranking closure. This paper states the FMEA of the solar plant [4,13].

Solar Cell Failure

Encapsulant Tarnish Failure

The solar cell module gets tarnished or discolored when exposed a long time to the sun's ultraviolet radiation, air, and dust. This tarnishing happens due to high-temperature exposure, which causes the degradation of the encapsule and metal parts get corroded. These happen by catalyzing carboxylic and aldehyde acid. This reduces the efficiency of photovoltaic cells and affects their performance over time and degrades the encapsule material. As it is not a major failure, it needs to be treated as it affects the performance of the solar cell. Traditionally, visual inspection was made to determine the discoloration, but the use of drones can determine the effects for a larger area in less time and it also gives clear, visual images and enables us to analyze whether it is needed to be treated as soon as possible and it is a minute effect [14].

Voltage Failure

Voltage current plays a major role in photovoltaic performance. The resistance is series resistance and shunt resistance. The series resistance affects the performance of the photovoltaic module higher when comparing it to shunt resistance. The current-voltage curve of the solar module is similar at night with the group of diodes in the module. But during the daytime, when exposed to direct light, and while generating power, the curve turns toward negative voltage. This can damage the performance of the solar cell. The series resistance can increase by five times higher and it can cause serious problems. The side effect can cause a loss in the cell, degradation of the encapsule, shunting of cell joints, shorting of bypass diode, and even corrosion of metals and connections [15].

Corrosion Failure

Due to the climate changes and ingression of wetness during rainy and foggy climates the sodium can accumulate close to the solar module. The aerobic degradation effect of the compound material tends to increase the amount of ingression of wetness. The construction of encapsule laminate and glass lamination can act as a sort of protective layer. Most of the solar module failures that happened today happened due to corrosion. So, corrosion becomes a major driven factor in solar cell failure, and it needs to be treated immediately [16].

Failure in Junction Bay Box

These boxes give the connection between the solar cell module and the solar cell system. These modules are prone to ingression of moisture and formation of corrosion. The junction bay boxes are highly vulnerable to degradation due to more adjacent potentials when compared to the single solar cell. The risk of dangerous faults is more likely to happen in the junction bay box. These boxes should be examined often for any moisture present or corrosion formation. A slight improper check-up can damage the whole solar module and can be costly [17,18].

Failure Due to Delamination

One of the most common failures or defects in the photovoltaic module is delamination. It happens due to more time in the solar field. The delamination can cut down the transmission and the performance of the cell. The delamination can cause the moisture to be ingress inside it and results in corrosion. It plays a main role in thin or additive photovoltaic cell materials. Visual and drone inspections can identify this failure and inspect it [16].

Bubble Formation Failure

Due to continuous heating on the layer of the solar cell, some gases' area unit free from the EVA backside for the formation of bubbles. The greenhouse gases and ethyl hexanol are the reason for the formation of bubbles. The bubble formation failure is less effective compared to delamination. The bubbles can be treated by the lamination process. Relatively frequent check-ups are needed to avoid the formation of bubbles [16].

Failure Due to Cracks

The density of the solar cell has decreased. It decreases the standard of cloth used, which decreases the grade of the PV module. However, the prospect of solar cell crack damage rises. Eight percent of photovoltaic cell cracks happen throughout creating a solar module. Damage in an exceedingly photovoltaic module may well be a handicap; however, usually it does not sight by a vacant eye. EL imaging technique is the best way to get the cracks within the electrical device. Cracks occur in PV modules because of vibration, applied a whole bunch, and radiation heat effect. The damage can happen where the bars are fused onto the element and generate because of fatigue in the cyclic bending. Excluding these modes of failures, there are aspects wherever the failure of solar power cells will happen like ground faults, line-line faults, arc faults, shade faults, and faults in block diodes. So, star cell scrutiny is turning into a serious issue for property [16,18,19] (Figure 10.5).

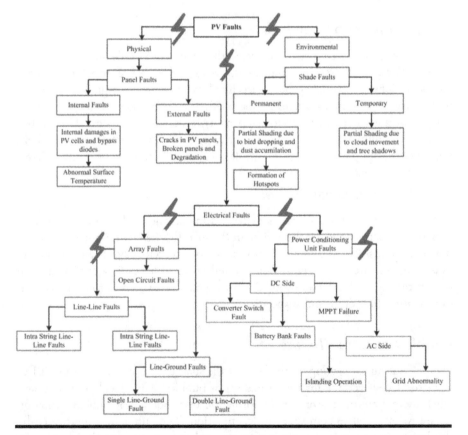

Figure 10.5   Various Modes of Failure in PV Module.

Existing Inspection and Rectification Methods

As the PV industry is growing rapidly day by day, the need for high-volume inspection of PV modules is more important. The increase in size of large-scale PV plants, tracking the source of failures, financial support, and increasing awareness of module failures among investors are the major factors for rigorous inspections [4].

Manual Ground-Level Inspection

Manual ground-level inspections contain the scanning of PV modules by means of mounted EL cameras on transportable constructions that are manually moved by field engineers. The investigated ground-level review includes two totally different systems. As these are traditional methods, and it requires a high number of human forces. The failures cannot be fully detected [19].

One-Camera Tripod System

A one-camera tripod system option has high flexibility. It will be used as a high-tripod, a "small" camera-tripod combined with a cherry picker or simply as a standard tripod. The system is simple to move during a plane with the ordinary bags. Therefore, this method does not want a long preparation. The operation will be assured by one or two engineers, which may alter the setup configuration easily. This enables elaborated pictures of unclear or unknown defects. The most important disadvantage of the system is the place of the measuring and its perhaps unsuitable ground. Only some of the modules match one image promptly, making the system very slow (max zero 0.2 MW/night) and hence is merely restrictedly applicable for giant scale analysis [19].

Multi-Camera Tripod System

Multi-camera systems are tailor-made for specific power plant layouts. So, an interval to regulate the construction is important. Contrary to the tripod system, the transport is large and a minimum of four persons is needed. The number of modules per image is additionally higher; even the standard of the images is adequate and last, however not least, the position of the modules at intervals the images are usually similar. The last characteristic especially helps throughout the process steps, where cropping and equalizing are conducted. As an associate in nursing example, a fast and standardized capturing of EL-images is conferred here, for a project a particular setup was developed with two high-resolution EL-cameras operating in parallel. The higher camera captured a pair of three modules and the lower camera captured a pair of two modules. With the conferred two-camera system, which was moved on a rail system victimization the construction, up to

Figure 10.6   One-Camera Tripod System.

0.8 MW can be recorded per night. This method will also be adjusted for different power plants to suit every need of each plant [9] (Figures 10.6 and 10.7).

AI-Based Methods in Solar Cell Failure Analysis

Drones are proven to show that they provide a large variety of assistance in many kinds of zones as well as in the photovoltaic power sector. Still, there are few

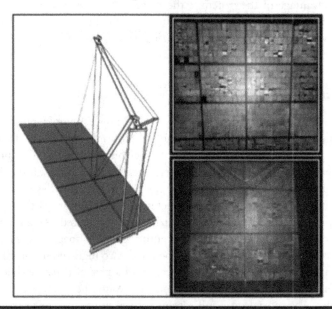

Figure 10.7   Multi-Camera Tripod System.

challenges are faced in processing and analyzing the data, automatic flight planning, wireless connectivity, and other autonomous protocol. To overcome these challenges, AI, ML, DL, RT, and other technologies can empower the drone's potential of being to act showing intelligence with an automatic action arrange with instant processing [4].

Artificial Intelligence (AI)

The performance of artificial intelligence would be the same as the human brain. In distinction to the abilities owned by the human brain, the artificial intelligence put together the ability of doing testing models, image assisting, data identification, and adapting and learning new skills. The principal motivation behind the applications is the extraordinary ability of finding the problems. Distinguishing and common artificial intelligence applications incorporate information analyzing, data processing, etc. Artificial intelligence would possibly modify the surveillance inside the drones used for alternative energy field observance. Drones capable of an artificial intelligence analytics platform would possibly brace in distinctive the liability within the solar cell plant. Drones with artificial intelligence can increase the standard of review. This allows quick functioning and prolongation. It eases communication between the drone and control center with operation and maintenance. Artificial intelligence collaboratively can facilitate the drones to accommodate the operation and maintenance team for workable fault incidence and restorative supported the monitored data. During this manner, collaboration would possibly build the drone more intellect [1].

Recognition Technology

In PV energy fields, the succeeding recognition technologies (RT) have more scope: for image recognition authorized drones for validation for approved record. Image recognition authorized drones to observe the solar cell system parts and elucidate them. From the image, authorized persons can analyze the information data and operation of the solar cell systems. This could modify all to assemble considerable interpretations of the tracked footage and images (EL and IR thermal images) by the maintenance specialists. With RT capability, the drones are authorized to become further intelligent in imaging technology. Recognition technology in solar cell review cameras will modify the drones to spot even the smaller cracks and alternative faults effectively [4].

Machine Learning

Machine learning (ML) is observed as an intense, deep learning and neural technique. It is chiefly painted as an exploitation of the mathematical algorithms that

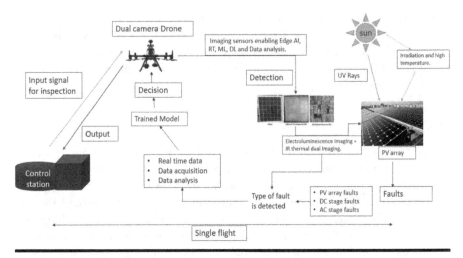

Figure 10.8   Flow Chart of Edge AI-Based Aerial Monitoring.

facilitate the tutorial methodology with an outsized kind of practical occurrences. Machine learning (ML) is of three types: Unattended learning that suggests having the capability to hunt out a variety of patterns (capacity to sight testing patterns). The opposite is supervised learning at intervals that preparation and categorization square measure the previous algorithms, and last is reinforcement learning where the use of loots and chastisements were stick to the strategic observance of solar cell fields. Exploitation of machine learning (ML) the drones square measure typically created intelligence and independent decision making by pre-programming the drones with the formula and arithmetic tools [3,20] (Figure 10.8).

Architectural Design of Edge AI-Based Solar Cell Inspection System

AI requires large-scale data to assist and cloud storage, which is based on an enormous amount of priming and learning of a huge number of trail data and tests. So, edge computing with AI technology can give the solution. Using electroluminescence and IR thermal imaging can even detect minor cracks and extreme faults. Real-time data acquisition can scan hundreds of images and detect failures. AI and ML in a drone can enable its autonomous intelligence and allow it to make its own decisions. Aerial mapping and location of the PV module can be sent by drone for inspection [7].

The control station enables the drone for inspection and gives it commands to perform. The drone is equipped with IR and EL imaging cameras with recognition technology and artificial intelligence; it starts to scan the PV arrays. Once it detects the faults, it processes the image to find which type of failure occurred, whether it is minor or major, PV array faults or DC stage faults, or AC stage faults; it compares the data with predefined models, now the data is analyzed, and the type of fault is determined with the trained models. Now the images are stored and scanned in cloud storage with the help of Edge AI and the drones are allowed to decide on their own to provide the importance of the failure and whether it should be treated earlier or it is a very minor crack, which can be replaced later. The location of the PV array is sent to the control center using GPS and aerial imaging. Finally, all the output data is given to the control station. The whole process takes place in a single flight [21].

Motivation: Need of Edge AI–Based System

The combination of artificial intelligence and edge computing is innate since there is a clear convergence in the middle of them. Precisely, edge computing focus and synchronize an oversized variety of cooperative edge computing devices and distribute the technique to generate information in accessibility, and artificial intelligence attempts to simulate intelligence of human behavior in devices or machines by learning from data information. Apart from liking the general advantages of edge computing, driving artificial intelligence to the additional benefits each other within the following aspects. Because of the application of the skyrocketing variety and sorts of mobile phones and IoT devices, giant volumes of multimodal data of substantial surrounding units are endlessly detected at the device facet. Throughout these circumstances, artificial intelligence is practical, thanks to its capability to quickly analyze those large data volumes and extract data from them for high-quality decision making. Joined with the foremost widespread AI techniques, deep learning brings the flexibleness to automatically establish patterns and observe anomalies inside the data detected by the sting device, as epitomized by population distribution, traffic flow rate, humidity, temperature variant, pressure variant, and air quality. The data extracted from the detected data unit is then sustained to the amount of your pattern prophetic decision making (e.g., public transportation coming up with, stability, and driving rate alerts) in reaction to the fast-changing environments, enlarging the operational coherence. Because the world is moving towards renewable energy, several investors and countries began to invest in PV industries and different renewable energy industries. Once the demand increases, the failure and defects review rate additionally will increase. Manual and stand inspections cannot do inspections for large areas during a short time, likewise as they do not notice minor faults. So, there is a desire for brand-new technology with effective results. The standard course of action for providing associate artificial intelligence service embraces coaching a ML model from info, and arts thinking with the testing model. The performance of a ML model is measured by its model accuracy, which could in all probability be improved by grouping additional employment information. However, employment of a ML model from giant information is pattern intense to teach a model with efficiency, administer architectures unit usually take on, that can initiate further communication costs for interchanging info beyond nodes. The estimation and communication value grow extremely high for high-dimensional models like deep neural networks. To boot, low latency is vital for thinking in applications like smart vehicles, good drones, etc. We tend to therefore sum up the key execution measurements of edge AI in regards of facsimile precision and comprehensive inactivity [10,11,22].

Implementation of Algorithm

Suggested Algorithm-Design Framework

The algorithm (Figure 10.9) is used to acquire real-time data for PV array inspection and process it to compare with the trained model. If the trained model and the PV faults match, it allows the drone to take the decision through Edge AI, whether it is a major or minor failure and sends the data to the control center with the location of the PV module using GPS and aerial imaging [4,9,23–26].

Software Requirement

Managing the program of drone operations is a complex process. It can be eased by using drone software, but finding the right and best software is a challenge for the developer to complete their operations. Using a software resolution for several functions like potential work orders, resource management, flight designing, and pursuit, program coverage, compliance, and information management can assist you to contour your operations and manage your program with efficiency. You will even have the program oversight that a lot of giant companies ought to guarantee systematically safe and compliant execution of all aspects of their drone program [7].

Flight Application Software

A flight application is employed to manage the drone throughout the flight. A flight application designed specifically for business use is usually the higher alternative. A poster flight application ought to supply a simplified interface with solely the functions needed, and it ought to be orientated toward safety and security with options like pre- and post-flight checklists, integrated airspace advisories and authorization, and native information mode. Having a flight application that is integrated with your program management code offers further edges, like automatic

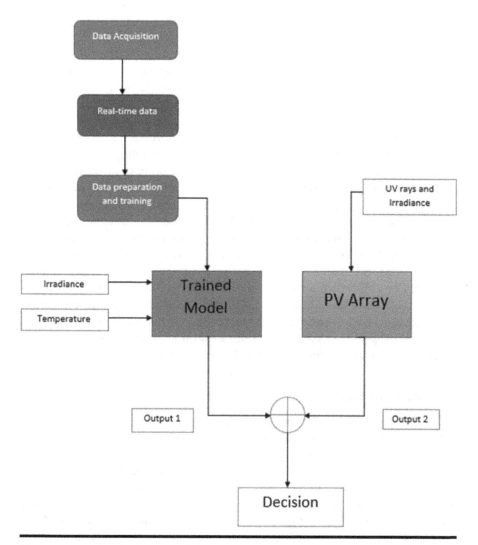

Figure 10.9 Monitoring Algorithm.

uploading of all flight information. Flights in conjunction with completed checklists and screenshots will be simply and systematically captured, tracked, and reported on, in conjunction with notifications of any flight activities that do not adhere to safety best practices. A live communication system that integrates a program management platform with a flight application, conjointly includes options like flight playback, wherever the flight is re-created on-screen; moreover, the power to translate flight logs into a drone and battery usage information that informs maintenance selections [3].

Data Software (Drone)

Drone knowledge is usually uploaded into varied package platforms for process, analysis, and visual image. Completely different package platforms are best suited to differing kinds of applications and knowledge desires. Some tools are designed to be used just for the raw data set process, whereas others are solely helpful for analysis or visual images of processed knowledge. Analytical tools specifically are typically targeted to a particular industrial application. ArcGIS is most ordinarily utilized by life for analyzing and viewing knowledge for utility-scale PV inspections, whereas ArcGISis is also used for connected inspections of electrical transmission lines and poles, vegetation assessments, etc. What knowledge package you would like can rely upon whether you will be processing and analyzing drone knowledge internally, or whether you will be outsourcing this operation. If you do not attempt to do internal processing and analysis, you merely have to worry about the best way to integrate the ultimate drone knowledge product into your operations. Some organizations can wish to integrate ArcGIS knowledge, as an example, whereas others can use online drone knowledge platforms on an individual basis. Victimization the associate in nursing source model, access to those platforms can generally be provided by your seller. Certify that the process, analyzing, and visual image of your drone knowledge ends up in an information deliverable which will drive higher choices for your business operations [3,4,7].

Hardware Requirement

The hardware provides the function of the inspections; lack of even a single hardware and the inspection cannot be done effectively. The required hardware is a multirotor drone and transmitter to transmit the signal to the drone, ground control station for transmitting commands and collecting data from the drone, IR thermal imaging camera for defect identification, electroluminescence camera for identifying the minor cracks, camera mount to hold both the IR thermal imaging camera and electroluminescence camera, RGB (Red, Green, Blue) sensor for mapping, GPS, autopilot system, obstacle detection sensors for a safe flight, LED lights for signaling, PV module tracking sensor, ImageRecognition sensors for detecting the PV module in a large solar field and to get the clear image for identifying the cracks depth, Li-poly battery with more storage capacity for long duration flights, IP45 rated drone body for emergency inspections during rain, and backup data storing hard disk [4,9].

Challenges in Edge AI–Based Solar Cell Inspection System

The main challenges can be selecting the proper drone for the inspection, proper coding and algorithm for edge computing and artificial intelligence, and collection of proper data using data analytics used to be done by an experienced data scientist. These data should be professionally trained for allowing the drones to make their own decision. If the model is not trained properly, the results can be errors and it would be a failure. The selection of cameras with a good configuration from a universally recognized brand is recommended; using low-quality IR and EL cameras cannot give proper image and the trained models will not be able to predict the faults. Use of recognition technology is recommended but the technology must be implemented properly in the imaging system and should be monitored frequently. Edge computing should be able to send data and store these data properly and be segmented. If the AI is not enabled properly, the drone cannot execute the commands and the tasks effectively. The biggest challenge is training the model with lots of solar cell failure and defect models and images for recognition [10,12,27,28].

Scope for Future Deployment

When the demand for renewable energy such as solar energy increases, the inspection for these PV modules also increases. It reduces the workforce, time, and maintains the constancy of electricity flow. So, the scope of drone technology rapidly increases and provides jobs for drone pilots, data scientists, and AI developers. Artificial technology and edge computing with machine learning are becoming more in demand. Tech companies predicted that it would create more employment and increase the intelligence of the machine [2].

The costs of PV power have steadily reduced, whereas additionally rising potency, however, it still needs giant extensions of land to supply electricity. This can be wherever the AI software package developed makes its biggest contribution. The buildup of mud and dirt on the surface of the PV panels is one of the culprits in deteriorating potency over time. The drones are not only used for detecting faults and failures; in the future they can be deployed for cleansing. The case is worsened in arid and regions, wherever the presence of sand hampers operations, and people are the favored regions to put in PV farms. Thus, cleansing tasks will account for up to hours of operational prices of those plants. Here, however, drones have additionally returned to the rescue by providing autonomous cleansing devices. Brush-equipped drones for the arid cleansing of PV panels, one of the key benefits of their computer science system, is the ability to perform those tasks without the help of human operators [11].

Conclusion

A review analysis on the observation of solar cell field exploitation workforce and remote observation is depicted, highlighting their pros and cons relating to the limited and large-scale PV plants. The role of drones in observation of small-scale and large-scale solar cell systems was mentioned, varieties of drones and their configuration were deliberated and from that one can choose the appropriate drone for their demand. The technologies that may authorize the intelligence and automation abilities of the drone observation system are mentioned and illustrate the future roles of them in solar cell plants [2,4].

References

[1] N. Kerle, F. Nex, M. Gerke, D. Duarte, and A. Vetrivel. "UAV-Based Structural Damage Mapping: A Review." *22 November 2019; Accepted: 23 December 2019; Published: 26 December 2019.*

[2] A. Dhoke, R. Sharma, T. K. Saha, A. Dhoke, R. Sharma, and T. K. Saha. www.elsevier.com/locate/solener

[3] S. Koch, T. Weber, C. Sobottka, A. Fladung, P. Clemens, and J. Berghold. "Outdoor Electroluminescence Imaging of Crystalline Photovoltaic Modules: Comparative Study Between Manual Ground-Level Inspections and Drone-Based Aerial Surveys." In 32nd European Photovoltaic Solar Energy Conference and Exhibition. https://www.researchgate.net/publication/308166800

[4] D. S. Pillai, and N. Rajasekar. "A comprehensive review on protection challenges and fault diagnosis in PV systems, Solar Energy Research Cell, School of Electrical Engineering, VIT University, Vellore, India." Received 29 July 2017; Received in revised form 19 March 2018; Accepted 26 March 2018.

[5] N. M. Kumar, K. Sudhakar, M. Samykano, and V. Jayaseelan. "On the Technologies Empowering Drones for Intelligent Monitoring of Solar Photovoltaic Power Plants." *Procedia Computer Science* 133 (2018): 585–593.

[6] M. Diethelm, L. Penninck, M. Regnat, T. Offermans, B. Zimmermann, C. Kirsch, R. Hiestand, S. Altazin, and B. Ruhstaller. "Finite Element Modeling for Analysis of Electroluminescence and Infrared Images of Thin-film Solar Cells." ISSN: 0038-092X.

[7] J. M. Malof, K. Bradbury, L. M. Collins, and R. G. Newell. "Automatic Detection of Solar Photovoltaic Arrays in High Resolution Aerial Imagery." Department of Electrical & Computer Engineering, Duke University, Durham, NC 27708 2 Energy Initiative, Duke University, Durham, NC 27708 3Nicholas School of the Environment, Duke University, Durham, NC 27708.

[8] J. Teubner, I. Kruse, H. Scheuerpfluga, C. Buerhop-Lutza, J. Haucha, C. Camusa, and C. J. Brabec. "Comparison of Drone-based IR-imaging with Module Resolved Monitoring Power Data." In *7th International Conference on Silicon Photovoltaics, SiliconPV 2017.*

[9] P. Bauer, R. Venkataraman, B. Vanek, P. J. Seiler, and J. Bokor. "Fault Detection and Basic In-Flight Reconfiguration of a Small UAV Equipped with Elevons." *IFAC PapersOnLine* 51, no. 24 (2018): 600–607.

[10] Y. Shi, K. Yang, T. Jiang, J. Zhang, and K. B. Letaief. "Communication-Efficient Edge AI: Algorithms and Systems." arXiv:2002.09668v1 [cs.IT] 22 Feb 2020.

[11] Z. Zhou, X. Chen, E. Li, L. Zeng, K. Luo, and J. Zhang. "Edge Intelligence: Paving the Last Mile of Artificial Intelligence with Edge Computing." 107, no. 8 (August 2019).

[12] O. Menéndez, R. Guamán, M. Pérez, and F. A. Cheein. "Photovoltaic Modules Diagnosis Using Artificial Vision Techniques for Artifact Minimization." Received: 6 May 2018; Accepted: 19 June 2018; Published: 28 June 2018.

[13] C. Liu, S. Hwang, and I. Lin. "Safety Analysis of Combined FMEA and FTA with Computer Software Assistance ± Take Photovoltaic Plant for Example." In 7th IFAC Conference on Manufacturing Modelling, Management, and Control International Federation of Automatic Control June 19-21, 2013. Saint Petersburg, Russia.

[14] E. Wang, H. E. Yang, J. Yen, S. Chi, and C. Wang. "Failure Modes Evaluation of PV Module via Materials Degradation Approach." *Energy Procedia* 33 (2013): 256–264.

[15] B. Nehme, N. K. Msirdi, A. Namaane, and T. Akiki. "Analysis and characterization of faults in PV panels, 8th International Conference on Sustainability in Energy and Buildings, SEB-16, 11–13 September 2016, Turin, ITALY." *Energy Procedia* 111 (2017): 1020–1029.

[16] P. Rajput, M. Malvoni, N. M. Kumar, O. Sastry, and G. N. Tiwari. "Risk priority number for Understanding the Severity of Photovoltaic Failure Modes and their Impacts on Performance Degradation." (2019): 100563. *ISSN 2214-157X.* 10.1016/j.csite.2019.100563.

[17] L. Hocine, K. M. Samira, M. Tarek, N. Salah, and K. Samia. "Automatic Detection of Faults in a Photovoltaic Power Plant based on the Observation of Degradation Indicators." www.elsevier.com/locate/renene

[18] S. Wiegholda, A. E. Morishigea, L. Meyera, T. Buonassisia, and E. M. Sachsa. "Crack Detection in Crystalline Silicon Solar Cells using Dark-field Imaging." *7th International Conference on Silicon Photovoltaics, SiliconPV 2017, Sarah Wieghold et al. / Energy Procedia* 124 (2017): 526–531.

[19] M. Dhimish and V. Holmes. "Solar Cells Micro Crack Detection Technique Using State-of-the-art Electroluminescence Imaging." ISSN: 2468-2179.

[20] F. Bayrak and H. F. Oztop. "Effects of Static and Dynamic Shading on *Thermodynamic and Electrical Performance for Photovoltaic Panels.*" www.elsevier.com/locate/apthermeng

[21] M. H. Ali, A. Rabhi, A. E. hajjaji, and G. M. Tina. "Real Time Fault Detection in Photovoltaic Systems." *Energy Procedia* 111 (2017): 914–923. 8th International Conference on Sustainability in Energy and Buildings, SEB-16, 11–13 September 2016, Turin, ITALY.

[22] S. Sharanya and S. Karthikeyan. "Classifying Malicious node in VANETs using Support Vector Machines with Modified Fading Memory." *ARPN Journal of Engineering and Applied Sciences* 12, no. 1 (January 2017).

[23] S. Sharanya and R. Venkataraman. An Intelligent Context Based Multi-layered Bayesian Inferential Predictive Analytic Framework for Classifying Machine States. *Journal of Ambient Intelligence and Humanized Computing* (2020): 1–9.

[24] R. I. Minu and G. Nagarajan. "Bridging the IoT Gap Through Edge Computing." In *Edge Computing and Computational Intelligence Paradigms for the IoT*, pp. 1–9. IGI Global, 2019, USA.

[25] G. Nagarajan, R. I. Minu, and A. Jayanthiladevi. "Cognitive Internet of Things (C-IOT)." In *Sensing Techniques for Next Generation Cognitive Radio Networks*, pp. 299–311. IGI Global, 2019, USA.

[26] S. V. Simpson and G. Nagarajan. "An Edge based Trustworthy Environment Establishment for Internet of Things: An Approach for Smart Cities." *Wireless Networks* (2021): 1–17.

[27] M. Falvo and S. Capparella. "Safety issues in PV systems: Design choices for a secure fault detection and for preventing fire risk." DIAEE – Electrical Engineering, University of Rome Sapienza, Via Eudossiana 18, 00184 Rome, Italy, Received 6 July 2014 Received in revised form 25 November 2014 Accepted 30 November 2014 Available online 18 December 2014.

[28] A. Mellit, G. Tina, and S. A. Kalogirou. "Fault Detection and Diagnosis Methods for Photovoltaicsystems: A Review." ISSN: 1364-0321, Received 10 February 2017; Received in revised form 14 February 2018; Accepted 17 March 2018.

Chapter 11

Object Detection in Edge Environment: A Comparative Study of Algorithms and Use Cases

D. Aishwarya and S. Sony Priya
Research Scholar, Department of CSE, SRM IST, Chennai, India

Dr. R. Minu
Associate Professor, Department of CSE, SRM IST, Chennai, India

Contents

DOI: 10.1201/9781003145158-11

Introduction to Object Detection

With the emergence of applications such as self-driving cars, augmented reality and automated surveillance, the need to process, perceive, and exploit the important features of the images and videos has considerably increased. These applications are primarily based on the visual recognition problems like classification of objects in the image, localization of objects after classification [1], and semantic and instance segmentation. Image classification identifies the different types of objects present in the image and assigns categorical class labels. Image classification is one application of computer vision used to classify images or objects based on their visual information. Image classification is used in a wide range of applications like self-driving automobiles, visual search engines, cancer diagnosis, etc [2]. Image categorization is used in conjunction with localization to obtain more information about the item. Object detection categorizes the objects and shows the location of each object using a bounding box (see Figure 11.2(b)). Computer vision also has applications for object identification like tracking, content-based picture retrieval, facial recognition, and other applications. Semantic segmentation processes each pixel and categorizes it according to its categorical class, but does not differentiate object instances of each class. Instance segmentation differentiates each object and each categorical class (Figure 11.1).

    Object detection, similar to other visual recognition problems, helps in understanding and analyzing images and videos. The unique features of object

(a)

(b)

(c)

(d)

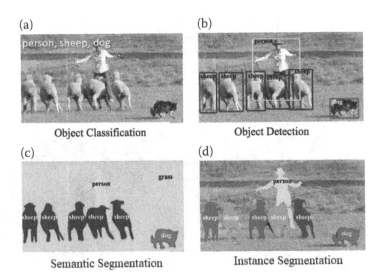

Object Classification

Object Detection

Semantic Segmentation

Instance Segmentation

Figure 11.1 Visual Recognition Problems.

detection that differentiate it from other recognition processes include the ability to locate the objects in the image, multiclass classification (Figure 11.2), counting the number of instances in each object class and tracking these objects irrespective of the shape, size, and effect of occlusion and illumination, view obtained with respect to the camera, and pose associated with the view. Object detection also allows identification of a particular class of objects from the given image. Some of the key applications of object recognition include self-driving cars (see Figure 11.3), video surveillance, and object tracking.

Figure 11.3 shows how a road view is processed by an object detection algorithm. It is understood that these detection algorithms employed in a self-driving car try to perceive the environment the same way a human eye and brain processes the road view while driving. Hence, detection of objects plays a key role in computer and machine vision. Object detection can even be considered the first

Figure 11.2 Object Detection.

Figure 11.3 Object Detection Using Self Driving Car.

step for the vision of robots. Because the objects are first detected and localized using object detection, then the resultant data is processed by a separate set of algorithms that determine the action to be performed. For example, after identifying the location of a traffic signal [3], the sign is processed and then the action to be performed by the autonomous car is determined (Figure 11.4).

Object detection uses various algorithms to perform categorization and localization. They are described in Section 2. The different environments where object

Figure 11.4 Traffic Signal Processing.

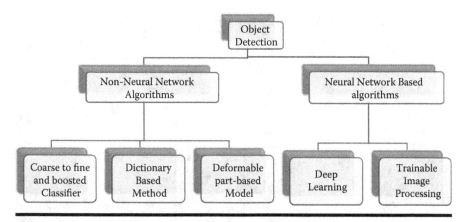

Figure 11.5   Classification of Object Detection.

detection is deployed is discussed in Section 3. Applications of object detection are elaborated in the next section. Section 5 discusses the three important metrics of object detection. Sections 6 and 7 discuss the challenges and research directions of object detection, respectively, followed by conclusion and references.

Object Detection Algorithms

Object detection algorithms fall under two major categories. These two categories and their sub-categories are shown in Figure 11.5.

The object detection performed using the traditional/non-neural method is categorized as image processing. Object detection using neural networks is categorized as computer vision. There are differences between both of the methods (see Figure 11.6).

From Figure 11.6, it can be understood that image processing performs the processes of an eye, but computer vision performs processing similar to that of a brain. Computer vision is a fast-developing field and has gathered a lot of attention from various industries. The algorithms that belong to both of these classes are shown in Figure 11.7.

Traditional/Non-Neural Methods

Traditional object detection algorithms basically work on the handcrafted features, i.e., the feature engineers work on images to identify the set of features based on which the object detection process has to take place. Due to the lack of structured image representations and computational resources, complicated image feature representations. Object detection using traditional methods involves many feature detection and algorithms associated with it (Figure 11.8).

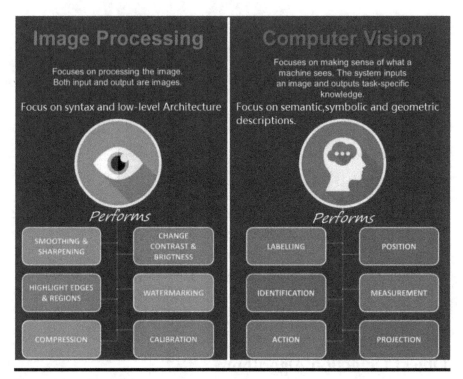

Figure 11.6 IP vs CV.

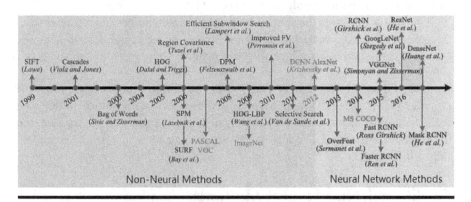

Figure 11.7 Major Milestones in Object Detection Algorithms.

To perform object detection using the non-neural methods, the part feature detectors specified previously are used. Apart from the ones specified previously, HAAR features classifier play a key role in object detection. HAAR cascade classifier used along with the Viola Jones detector for face recognition invariant to skin color, is an important milestone in the classical object detection algorithms age.

Feature detection

Edge detection	Ridge detection

Edge detection

Canny · Deriche · Differential · Sobel · Prewitt · Roberts cross

Corner detection

Harris operator · Shi and Tomasi · Level curve curvature · Hessian feature strength measures · SUSAN · FAST

Blob detection

Laplacian of Gaussian (LoG) · Difference of Gaussians (DoG) · Determinant of Hessian (DoH) · Maximally stable extremal regions · PCBR

Ridge detection
Hough transform

Hough transform · Generalized Hough transform

Structure tensor

Structure tensor · Generalized structure tensor

Affine invariant feature detection

Affine shape adaptation · Harris affine · Hessian affine

Feature description

SIFT · SURF · GLOH · HOG

Scale space

Scale-space axioms · Implementation details Pyramids

Figure 11.8   Feature Detection Techniques.

The first step in object detection is extracting features like edges, corners, blobs, etc. using filters. These extracted features are associated with a predefined set of definitions (Bag of Words). These features are handcrafted. From these features, the objects are detected. The span of 1999 to 2011 comes under this category where a majority of tradition algorithms were created. All of these algorithms share a common flow of processing the images (Figure 11.9).

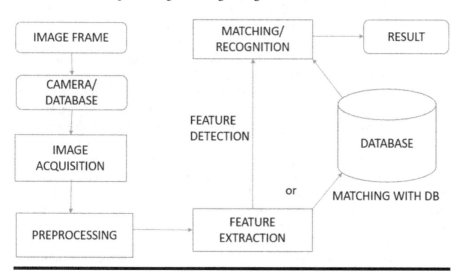

Figure 11.9   General Architecture of Tradition Image Processing.

Some of the important milestones in traditional object detection algorithms include:

■ SIFT (Scale Invariant Feature Transform) generates image features by converting the image into a large number of local vectors representing the features. These vectors are invariant to the scaling, translation, and rotation.
■ HOG (Histogram of Oriented Gradients) is an improved version of SIFT [4], that is invariant to illumination effects as well. It is computed from the dense grid of uniformly spaced cells [5].
■ Deformable Part-based Model (DPM) is an extended version of the HOG detector. It basically consists of a main filter and many part filters.
■ Coarse to fine cascades and boosted classifier method [6], is one in which cascades of filters obtain the features from a coarse to a fine manner and then the obtained images are sent as input to the classifier that performs the detection part [7].
■ Bag of Words or dictionary method is one in which a single object is detected at a time and, after removing it [8], the next object is detected.

Neural Network–Based Algorithms

By combining computer vision and AI, we can make the computers think and do various operations like humans based on the input image or video. Neural network–based image processing is performed in two ways: by combining the feature detection algorithms from a previous section with an artificial neural network classifier, which is primarily a machine learning (ML) network. This require an explicit feature engineering process, which is a time-consuming and tedious task.

The machine learning part from Figure 11.10 shows the role of ML. The neural network in the ML is relatively shallow. The set of algorithms being created beginning from AlexNet (2012) [9], are all based on a deep neural network structure called the convolutional neural network (CNN), shown in Figure 11.10. The CNN is a class of deep learning, created especially to process the images and videos. Traditional techniques that depend on manual efforts are burdensome and time-consuming. However, deep learning, a subset of machine learning, overcomes these challenges. Deep learning involves training a model with a massive number of samples to automatically learn to do tasks such as image classification with the help of various deep learning algorithms [10]. Deep learning employs a specialized algorithm neural network to extract patterns from input data samples. The working of the neural network algorithm is based on the workings of the human brain.

Computer vision empowers computers to observe and comprehend, and AI helps computers to think. Computer vision trains computers with massive quantities of

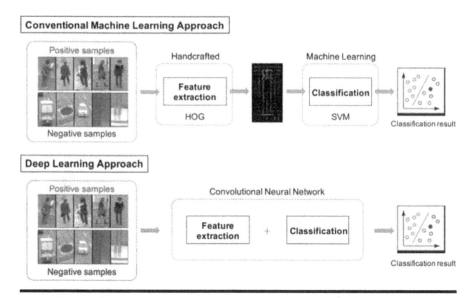

Figure 11.10 Machine Learning vs Deep Learning Approach for Processing Images.

data again and again to enable them a high-level comprehension of digital images or videos. For example, to make a computer recognize dogs [12], we must train it with a wide variety of different dog photos. Several real-world applications are being developed in the field of computer vision, which is crucial for security, agriculture, product manufacturing, and so on. The untrained neural networks are trained with the data set of objects and the trained network is tested using samples of different object types (see Figure 11.11(a)). With the emergence of CNN, working with images has become easier than ever but a larger computational resource is required for the CNN as it is a deep-layered architecture [12]. One main advantage of CNN is that the features are learned by the neurons themselves [12], and no explicit handcrafting of the features is required. The general architecture of CNN is shown in Figure 11.11(b).

It can be seen from Figure 11.11 that CNN contains a repetitive pair of convolution and pooling layer and a fully connected layer that performs classification. The repetition of convolution and pooling layer can be for any number of times and it corresponds to deep neural network architecture [13]. The architecture in Figure 11.11 only does classification, to perform object detection, i.e., classification with localization, an additional bounding box architecture has to added at the end of this architecture. One important thing [14] to be noted from Figures 11.10 and 11.11 is that the deep learning method shows no pre-processing of input image. Most of the time CNNs do not require pre-processing and feature engineering. The feature extraction and learning process is automatically taken care by the convolutional layer (Figure 11.12).

(a)

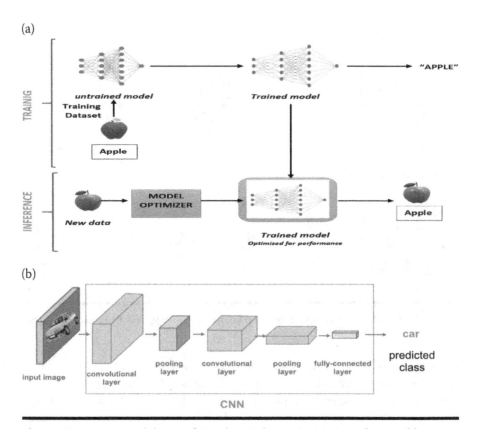

(b)

Figure 11.11 (a) Training and Testing Using a Deep Learning Architecture; (b) CNN Architecture.

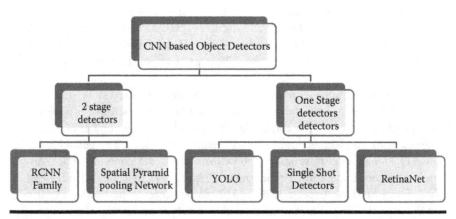

Figure 11.12 Types of CNN-Based Object Detection Algorithms.

Object detection using CNN [15,16] is done in two ways: two-stage detectors and single-stage detectors. The former method is similar to coarse to fine cascades of filter followed by a detector structure. The two-stage detectors use a separate region proposal network that identifies all the suspectable bounding boxes with images; these proposed regions are then passed to a convolution neural network–based classifier. The Single-stage detectors form a grid of anchor boxes in the image; the filters in the convolution layer check each bounding box for any chance of object, and if any is found, it is directly classified in a single-stage network.

Two-Stage Detectors

Region-based convolutional neural network and its improved versions, namely Fast RCNN and Faster RCNN, fall under two-stage detectors (Figure 11.13).

- The region proposals for the RCNN [17] algorithm are generated using selective search. The selective search algorithm generates regions in the image but doesn't classify them. The generated region proposals are then classified using a previously trained CNN architecture.
- The spatial pyramid pooling (SPP) [18,19] network was created to reduce the computational complexity by sharing the computing process of RCNN. The SPP net computes the convolutional feature map for the entire image and then detects each object [20].
- Fast RCNN contains region proposals and images as input. The region proposals are pooled by region of interest pooling that converts the features

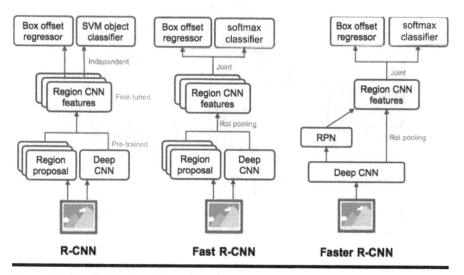

Figure 11.13 RCNN Family Architectures.

of the same size. The second CNN architecture matches the feature map and the region proposal maps and generate the final output.

■ Faster RCNN works faster than the other two RCNN architectures. It has a separate region proposal network (RPN) that concurrently predicts the object bounds and the probability scores.

Single-Stage Detectors

■ YOLO (You Look Only Once) [21] justifies its name by using the input image only once for the computation of objects localizing bounding boxes and their respective class probabilities. This is done using a single convolutional neural network. YOLO splits the input into "s" grids and uses the anchor boxes to look for objects (Figure 11.14).

■ Single shot detectors (SSD) use a multiscale feature map instead of fully connected CNN layers. The input image [22] frame is split into grids and every single grid is made accountable for detecting objects with in it. It is faster than Faster RCNN and YOLO.

■ RetinaNet is better in terms of accuracy and speed when comparing its performance with architectures like YOLO and SSD. It uses feature pyramid networks and focal loss as important [23,24] improvements and it uses the previously trained Resnet architecture Figure 11.15.

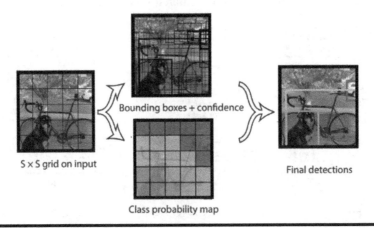

Figure 11.14   YOLO.

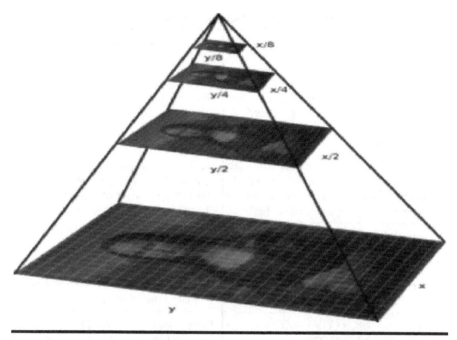

Figure 11.15   Image Pyramid Helps in Identifying Objects Irrespective of the Scale.

Comparison between Traditional Algorithms and Neural Networks

See Table 11.1.

Object Detection Environments

Object detection environments include the environment where the image sources are captured and whether the object detection process is done instantaneously or in offline mode.

Image Source Environment

Image source environment denotes the place where the images and videos are extracted. Some of the common environments are as follows:

- Buildings, pathways – Video surveillance [26]
- Road – Traffic lights detection, speed violation, self-driving cars
- Hospitals – Medical image processing [27]

Table 11.1   Non-Neural vs Neural Network Algorithms for Architecture

Traditional Object Detection Algorithm	*Neural Network–Based Algorithm*
Handcrafting of features is an important task, but selecting an ideal set of features to be extracted is erroneous and is fine-tuned only through repeated trial-and-error method [28].	CNN-based algorithms perform feature engineering automatically.
With increase in number of different object classes, the feature selection and extraction is more tedious [29].	The number of parameters increase with the number of object classes but the process is also automated.
Fine-tuned to improve accuracy.	Provide better accuracy.
It is domain specific.	Flexible to be used for any use case.
Extracts part features [30].	Each network learns the complete set of features of an object.
They are not object class specific, i.e., the features extracted are general features [31].	Features extracted are learned and associated with the object class; hence, object class specific.
It does not require higher computational capability [32]. Can be implemented on low-cost microprocessor chip.	Higher and better processors like graphical processing unit (GPU) are required for smooth operation.
It requires pre-processing of input image during test	It most often does not require pre-processing techniques to be implemented over the input during testing.
Does not require training of the model.	Requires training of neural network, especially over a large amount of data, for which data augmentation (a pre-processing technique, is used).
Potential applications include robotic vision, virtual reality, motion capture, etc.	Applications include self-driving cars, surveillance monitoring, tracking, etc.
Applications mostly belong to offline processing.	Most applications are based on real-time processing.

The environmental factors that affect the image quality and the object detection accuracy include the following:

- Shadows of other objects
- Reflections caused by lighting
- Contrasting lights
- Objects occluding each other
- Night light images
- Heavy activity scenes

Object Detection Extraction Environment

Once the image sources are extracted, the object detection process can be done either in offline mode (with time gap) or in real-time mode (instantaneous processing); see Table 11.2.

Edge Computing

Real-time processing requires microprocessor devices to be embedded to the camera. Processing the data near its source is referred to processing at the edge and is termed edge computing. Also, it is important to note that these microprocessor chips have limited computational capability [33]. There are edge computing devices like robots, smaller devices like raspberry pi, and field programmable gate arrays

Table 11.2 Object Detection Environments

Real-Time Processing	Offline Processing
Requires higher computational ability to process the images	Offline processing does not require computational ability
Time delay has to be reduced	Time complexity does not play a major role
Accuracy is compromised while trading off with time delay	Higher accuracy is strived for
Applications: automated video surveillance, traffic light, vehicles monitoring	Applications: medical images processing

(a)

(b)

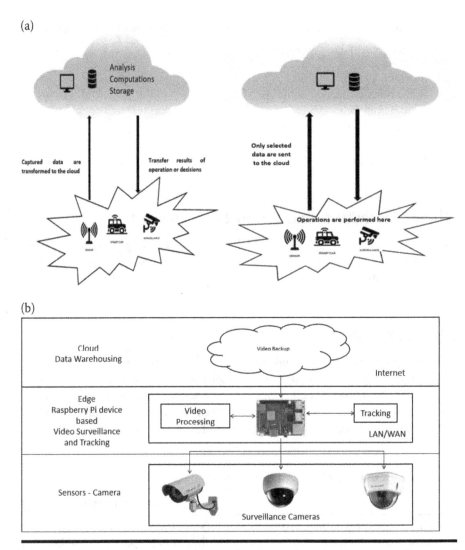

Figure 11.16 **(a) Cloud Computing vs Edge Computing; (b) Edge Computing–Based Surveillance.**

(FPGAs), etc. An example architecture of edge computing is shown in Figure 11.16. It is an example [34] of edge computing–based video surveillance. An edge device (raspberry pi) is attached to a surveillance camera, which detects the object detection process near the source itself. The surveillance feed is then uploaded onto the cloud storage. The algorithms discussed in the section 1.2, all these algorithms require higher computational complexity, especially the neural network-based algorithms. Hence, for real-time processing of images and videos, the lighter version of these algorithms and hybrid versions [35], including part filters of tradition object detection methods and the CNN layers, would be better. A few of these are discussed in this section.

Object Detection Algorithms for Edge Computing Environment

SqueezeNet

This compression architecture was developed in 2016. It works on the principle "reducing the parameters and improving accuracy". It has replaced filters of size 3 × 3 to 1 × 1 and input channel size to 3 × 3 to [36] reduce the number of parameters. Down sampling is done only at the latter stages of the network. Its core building block is called the fire block that contains squeeze and expand architecture, and here the strategies specified previously are implemented (Figure 11.17). This improves accuracy. These make the CNN efficient and lighter enough to work in an edge device. But SqueezeNet is basically a classification problem solver. Hence, this can be used along with region proposal networks for better accuracy.

MobileNet

MobileNet architecture uses two additional hyper-parameters: width multiplier "α" and resolution multiplier "ρ". The width multiplier controls the depth or number of channels in an input image and the resolution multiplier controls the resolution of the input image. These hyper parameters help in making [37] the architecture more compact and efficient. MobileNet is primarily built using the depthwise separable convolution (Figure 11.18) rather than the normal convolution layer. The primary goal of MobileNet is not just to have a smaller architecture but improve the execution

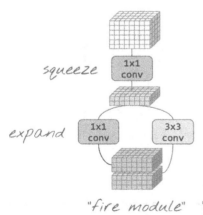

Figure 11.17   Fire Module.

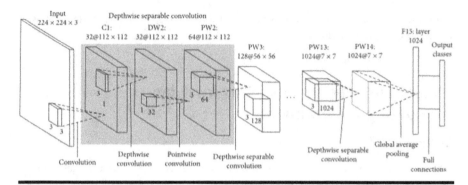

Figure 11.18 MobileNet.

speed of the architecture as well. Using the depthwise separable convolutions, the computation process is minimized by eight to nine times when compared to the standard convolution operation.

ShuffleNet

ShuffleNet focuses on devices with limited computational capability like smart-phones, drones, and robots. The ShuffleNet architecture tries to provide the best accuracy while limiting computational requirements to 10 or 150 of MFLOPS (Million FLoating Operations Per Second) [38]. The ShuffleNet utilizes channel shuffle and point-wise group convolutions. Channel shuffle (Figure 11.19) refers to shuffling feature maps of input channels and then passing it to the other com-putational layers. This feature helps in building efficient architecture.

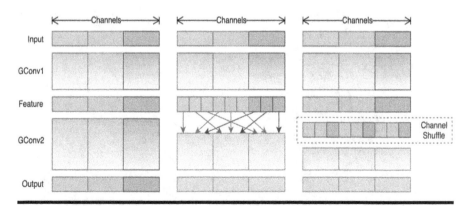

Figure 11.19 Channel Shuffle in ShuffleNet; GConv Refers to Group Convolutions.

NASNet

Neural architecture search (NAS) network was developed by Google Brain. This architecture is basically for classification of a problem and, similar to SqueezeNet, it is used along with a region proposal network algorithm like the ones in Faster R-CNN. NASNet with Faster R-CNN [39] outperforms MobileNet and ShuffleNet. NASNet algorithm, creates a NASNet search space, in which it deploys series of convolutional layers over a CIFAR-10 data set. The algorithm identifies which convolution layer or cell of the network has the best feature map and uses the same set of parameters and implements the repeated copy over the ImageNet data set. This method has created a new regularization method named "Scheduled Drop Path" (Figure 11.20).

EdgeAI

The deep learning model needs substantial storage space, but it is overcome by combining it with cloud computing. Deep learning is intrinsically a time-consuming task, but with cloud computing technology, we can design, develop, and train deep learning applications faster. There are various disadvantages to using cloud computing technologies [40]. The most significant drawback is network latency due to Internet traffic. For example, with video surveillance, when monitoring anomalies in a public venue, we should make decisions in a fraction of a second to keep people safe. In the cloud, the data needs to travel back and forth, so it takes more time to deliver good results. A significant number of users store their data on the cloud, reducing data privacy. Furthermore, data transfer from/to the server from remote places is quite challenging. Figure 11.16(a) shows the difference between cloud and edge computing. These problems are avoided by EdgeAI. EdgeAI is the process of combining a trained model with an accelerator like Jetson Nano (NVIDIA), TB-96AI (Rockchip) [41], CoralDevboard (Google), AIAM5729 (Beagle Bone), OpenVINO etc., which will process the incoming new data to

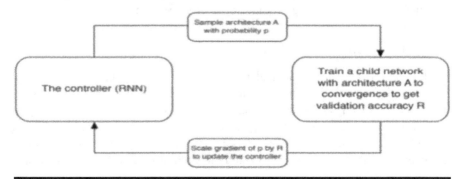

Figure 11.20   NASNet Architecture.

detect if it correctly predicted or not. EdgeAI is a system that uses deep learning algorithms to process data generated by a hardware device at the local level, i.e., the device itself or a nearby device. Here, the network connection is not necessary. Also, the decisions are made in real time [42], within milliseconds. It reduces the communication cost for transferring the data between the cloud and the device. The response time also decreased. EdgeAI is used in many applications like self-driving cars, robots, Siri, surveillance systems, and many other areas. However, edge technology will not replace the cloud technology; the only difference is the data generated by the users will be operated and processed on the edge. There are several advantages by using EdgeAI, including:

- Increase privacy because of local processing
- Reduces data communication costs
- Real-time processing
- Cost and network latency are reduced

Applications of Object Detection

Object detection plays a key role in understanding and analyzing a scene. Traditionally, deep learning models depend on cloud data centers to perform various operations, but it doesn't provide real-time services due to network latency. To overcome this issue, EdgeAI (a combination of edge computing and artificial intelligence) is used. With the emergence of edge computing, real-time applications based on images and videos have increased and [43] the accuracy of the processing has also been increased considerably. The advantages of using edge computing, in spite of its computational limitedness, proves to be advantageous in terms of lower latency, fewer network issue, faster processing, security issues of transferring important data to remote location is reduced, and excessive use of data centers could be reduced. EdgeAI is used in various fields like video surveillance, health care, industries, transportation, security, robotics etc. Various applications of object detection using edge computing are discussed in this section.

Object Tracking

With increased need for scene analysis, object tracking has become a key application of object detection. Almost applied in every use case, object tracking is the process of identifying and locating objects on the image/video and then tracking its movements across the image. Tracking can also be used [44] to access the trajectory of the object. Using part filters and features like blobs, edges could be used for object detection. Using simple blob (color) feature identification, to recognize objects and

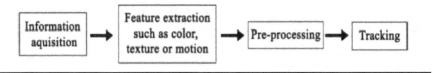

Figure 11.21   Object Detection Using Part Filter.

tracking process is shown using bounding boxes. The architecture of this model is shown in Figure 11.21.

Since the previous algorithms are very light, they could be effectively implemented in an edge device. Since tracking is done with moving objects, the frame differencing method is efficient with the object detection process. In frame differencing, consecutive frames are extracted and the presence and the position of the object are identified at a regular interval (Figure 11.22).

The deep learning, Siamese architecture could be used to identify if the two objects detected at consecutive frames are the same are not using the feature vectors obtained for both detected objects. Object tracking using bounding boxes is shown in Figure 11.23. Apart from Siamese, object tracking is done through three different class of algorithms (Figure 11.24). The generalized object detection flow is shown in Figure 11.25.

Robotic Vision

Visual servoing denotes the ability to control the movements and activities of the robot based on the visual feedbacks. This phenomenon is fundamental for controlling robots with visual system. It means to capture the image and perceive it effectively so that activities can be performed better and navigation of the robots can be done effectively without clashing into other objects. Robots could also be considered as edge devices, but with higher computational [45] ability than the system on chip devices. Since robots are automated devices, deep learning–based object detection techniques that are fully automated are generally preferred. An example of a robotic eye is shown in Figure 11.26. Object detection is the primary task for

Figure 11.22   Object at Different Frame Interval.

Figure 11.23   Tracking Specific Objects.

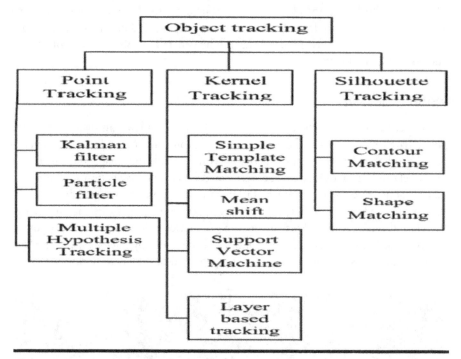

Figure 11.24   Tracking Algorithms.

visual servoing. It can be seen from Figure 11.27 that object detection forms the base for interactions like handing over objects (Figure 11.28) or getting objects, movement across the area, etc. Figure 11.29 shows how the hand-part is detected during the interaction and how it is segmented from the vision of the robot.

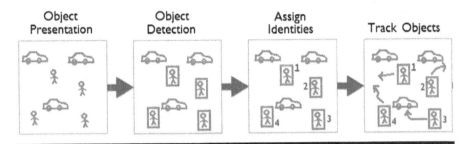

Figure 11.25   Object Tracking General Process Flow.

Figure 11.26   Robotic Eye.

Self-Driving Cars

A self-driving car, also known as an autonomous car, uses a variety of sensors and cameras to perceive the environment and drive the car. The structure of the autonomous driving system is very complex due to the integration of many technologies for sensing, localization, observation, decision making, and interaction with other cloud servers. Its working principle is: "sense-plan-act", like robotic systems. It is the combination of AI, edge, and cloud technologies. An autonomous vehicle operates in the following manner: first, it collects data via sensors and sends

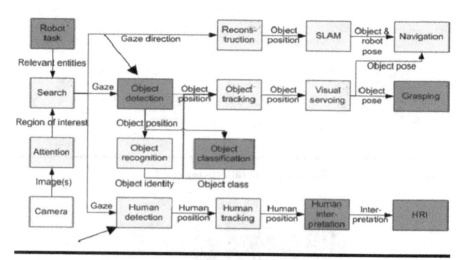

Figure 11.27 Robotic Vision Architecture.

Figure 11.28 Hand-in Interaction with Robot.

it to edge devices, and then AI calculates the appropriate action to take and provides orders to the autonomous vehicle. It transmits all data to the cloud at each step, but it does not wait for a response. There are several difficulties like high accuracy and robustness in various weather conditions, localizing the vehicle to obtain location information and path, decision making based on pedestrian

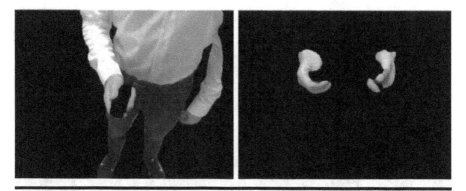

Figure 11.29   Robotic Perception for Hand-in Interaction.

movement and communication between them, and making plans to drive the car in traffic. The perception system consists of multiple sub-systems that localize the car, does obstacles (objects) detection and tracking, path planning, traffic signal detection and monitoring, etc., and generates data, based on which movement decision is made by the decision-making system. Deep learning algorithms such as YOLO and Faster RCNNs are used for the object detection process. The camera setup over the self-driving for environment perception is shown in Figure 11.30. The map in which the destination is selected, shows the path for the self-driving car and the movement of the car in that direction is shown in a display screen (Figure 11.31).

Self-driving cars capture input from cameras, sensors, lidar, radar, GPS, etc. From Figure 11.32, it can be understood how vital is an object detection algorithm for self-driving cars in the perception of the environment.

Figure 11.30   Camera in Self-Driving Car.

Figure 11.31 Display Screen Showing Map and Direction.

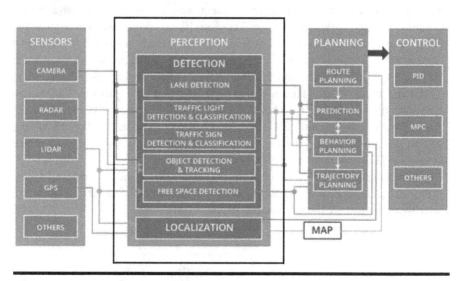

Figure 11.32 Self-Driving Car Architecture.

Surveillance

EdgeAI intelligent security measures uses current camera infrastructure to enable autonomous monitoring and alerts across the venture. Organizations can now install, manage, and receive security alerts and warnings in real time, thanks to the EdgeAI platform. To offer efficient video surveillance, the distributed intelligent video surveillance system, which allows for parallel processing with multiple models like CNN and LSTM by enabling each edge node to do a distinct job, was created. Ruiminet a.l., introduced a smart parking surveillance system that uses an SSD-MobileNet detector created using Tensorflow Lite and Raspberry Pi to automatically recognize parking spaces. Zhao,

Y et al., suggested a lightweight DL-based intelligent edge surveillance (INES) technique to minimize network resource consumption and system responsiveness.

Smart City

The construction of a smart city is very difficult due to the large amount of data. To address this problem, EdgeAI is used. In EdgeAI, all the operations and decisions are made in edge devices, thus reducing the network latency, communication delay, and cost. Simulation models can be used to achieve better resource allocation without degrading network performance. For navigation and street object detection using EdgeAI, a Secure Smart Cities framework to secure IOT communications by black network and AI techniques are developed.

Health Care

EdgeAI is also widely used in medical field. Some of the applications in the medical field are monitoring the patients and their rooms to find abnormalities like fall detection and to record the patient details like temperature and heart rate; if there is any abnormality in this, it automatically gives an alert. It is also used in radiology to detect fractures, cancers, and cardiovascular abnormalities.

Object Detection Metrics

- **Precision:** The measure of accurate predictions.
- **Recall:** It is the count of number of correct predictions out of all predictions.
- **Intersection Over Union:** It is the ratio of the area in the image identified as a particular object by the bounding box to the area of intersection between the original area and detected area. (Figure 11.33).
- **Mean Average Precision (mAP):** It is the measure of precision of the entire model.

Challenges of Object Detection in an Edge Computing Environment

- **Computational Capacity:** Limited computational capacity is the major challenge in object detection in edge computing environment. Coping with the limited computational complexity and being mindful of not exhausting the resource is important while developing the algorithm or architecture.
- **Images with Interlace Background and Foreground Object:** In images like Figure 11.30, it can be seen that the foreground objects like pedestrians and cars are interlaced with the background. This is caused by lighting and crowding. These images acquire very low accuracy upon object detection (Figure 11.34).

Figure 11.33   IoU = Area Covered by Red/Area Covered by Pink.

- **Multi-class Objects:** In real-time processing, classifying multi-class objects is a very tedious task. Using edge computing and deep learning, the task has better accuracy than with traditional methods, but each has its own disadvantages and challenges. With a traditional method, deciding and choosing the best set of parameters to be detected from the image is a tedious task, whereas with neural networks, training the network for multiclass classification requires a larger number of data samples for every class, which is burdensome. Collecting and augmenting the data for training is very important since it directly affects the accuracy of the object detection process.
- **Intra-Class Variation:** Within the objects of the same class itself, each object instance could differ from the other through certain features like, color, shape, size (see Figure 11.31), etc. It is important to consider these while developing the algorithm. For example, face detection, in which faces of

Figure 11.34   Image with Interlaced Foreground and Background.

Figure 11.35   Intra-Class Variations.

different skin tone, hairstyles, changes in size of face, distance from camera that affects the size, are all factors to be considered (Figure 11.35).

■ **Change in Pose, View Angle of Camera, and Resolution:** Different object differently at different pose and from the angle of view of camera. These two issues are very challenging for object detection algorithms to overcome as they cannot be altered. Only the algorithm has to be made flexible and efficient enough. Resolutions of the image can be corrected by using proper lighting at the source or by using pre-processing techniques prior to the object detection process.

■ **Partial and Full Occlusions:** Occlusion denotes one object blocks the other either partially or fully, such that the object at the back is not clearly visible. The solution to this challenge is still in the development state.

■ **Requisite of Temporal Information:** To clearly identify some objects at a time, one image may not be enough. The requirement of data from the consecutive image frames is also required. This information from a series of frames is called temporal data.

Research Directions

■ Increasing the computational capability of the edge computing devices.
■ Instead of trying to identify objects of different scale using sliding window or feature pyramid method, pixel-level detection of the same could be done.
■ Similar to foreground extraction, identifying interesting objects at the background like the buildings or the sceneries could help in the process of navigation of robots and drones using object detection methods.
■ Using multiple views and their fusion data could help overcome occlusion problems. But multi-view fusion of image sources is still in the development state.
■ An incremental learning technique could be used for training the neural network, which would avoid training each application separately.

Conclusion

Object detection is an important task in the visual recognition–based applications. Both sets of algorithms, i.e., traditional non-neural and neural network–based method, serve some unique purposes of object detection and both have their own advantages and disadvantages. Looking on to the environment where object detection is deployed, it can be seen that an edge computing–based real-time environment has more scope and applications than the non-real-time environment. On exploring the various tasks to be performed for the applications at the edge computing environment, it can be understood that the combination of both the non-neural and neural network–based method algorithms best fit the lower computational capability of the edge computing devices and offer faster and accurate solutions. The applications of object detection in edge computing were then discussed. The metrics for object detection, challenges, and research scope were then discussed.

References

[1] K. He, X. Zhang, S. Ren, and J. Sun. "Deep Residual Learning for Image Recognition." In Proceedings of the CVPR, 2016.

[2] S. Rajalingappaa. *Deep Learning for Computer Vision: Expert Techniques to Train Advanced Neural Networks Using TensorFlow and Keras*. Packt Publishing, 23 Jan 2018.

[3] R. Kulkarni, S. Dhavalikar, and S. Bangar. *Traffic Light Detection and Recognition for Self-Driving Cars using Deep Learning*. IEEE, 2018.

[4] R. Verschae and J. Ruiz-del-Solar. *Object Detection: Current and Future Directions*. Frontiers in Robotics and AI, 2015.

[5] Z. Zou, Z. Shi, Y. Guo, and J. Ye. "Object Detection in 20 Years: A Survey." arXiv:1905.05055v2 [cs.CV] (2019).

[6] D. G. Lowe. "Object Recognition from Local Scale-Invariant Features." In *Proc. of the International Conference on Computer Vision*, 1999.

[7] J. Redmon, S. Divvala, R. Girshick, and A. Farhadi. "You Only Look Once: Unified, Real-Time Object Detection." arXiv:1506.02640v5 [cs.CV] (2016).

[8] N. O' Mahony, S. Campbell, A. Carvalho, S. Harapanahalli, G. V. Hernandez, L. Krpalkova, D. Riordan, and J. Walsh. "Deep Learning vs. Traditional Computer Vision. arXiv:1910.13796v1 [cs.CV] (2019).

[9] R. Girshick. "Fast R-CNN." In *IEEE International Conference on Computer Vision*, 2015.

[10] W. Liu, D. Anguelov, D. Erhan, C. Szegedy, S. Reed, C. Fu, and A. C. Berg. "SSD: Single Shot MultiBox Detector." arXiv:1512.02325v5 [cs.CV] (2016).

[11] T. Lin, P. Goyal, R. Girshick, K. He, and P. Dollar. "Focal Loss for Dense Object Detection." arXiv:1708.02002v2 [cs.CV] (2017).

[12] IBM. Environmental Factors for Object Detection. https://www.ibm.com/docs/en/iva/2.0.0?topic=analytics-environmental-factors-object-detection.

[13] Natasa, Smart Imaging Blog, 2019. https://www.smartimagingblog.com/2019/04/07/what-is-real-time-processing-online-vs-offline/.

[14] V. Tsakanikas and T. Dagiuklas. "Video Surveillance System-Current Status and Future Trends." *Computers and Electrical Engineering* 70 (2018): 736–753.

[15] F. N. Iandola, S. Han, M. W. Moskewicz, K. Ashraf, W. J. Dally, and K. Keutzer. "SqueezeNet: alexnet-level accuracy with 50x fewer parameters and <0.5 mb model size." arXiv:1602.07360v4 [cs.CV] (2016).

[16] A. G. Howard, M. Zhu, B. Chen, D. Kalenichenko, W. Wang, T. Weyand, M. Andreetto, and H. Adam. "MobileNets: Efficient Convolution Neural Networks for Mobile Vision Application." arXiv:1704.04861.v1 (2017).

[17] X. Zhang, X. Zhou, M. Lin, and J. Sun. "ShuffleNet: An Extremely Efficient Convolutional Neural Network for Mobile Devices." arXiv: 1707.01083.v2 (2017).

[18] B. Zoph, V. Vasudevan, J. Shlens, and Q. V. Le. "Learning Transferable Architectures for scalable Image Recognition." arXiv:1707.07012v4 [cs.CV] (2018).

[19] P. Singh, B. Deepak, T. Seth, and M. D. P. Murthy. *Real-Time Object Detection and Tracking Using Color Feature and Motion.* IEEE ICCSP, 2015.

[20] G. Chandan, A. Jain, and H. Jain. *Mohana, Real Time Object Detection and Tracking Using Deep Learning and OpenCV.* IEEE ICIRCA, 2018.

[21] L. Bertinetto, J. Valmadre, J. F. Henriques, A. Vedaldi, and P. H. S. Torr. "Fully-Convolutional Siamese Networks for Object Tracking." *Computer Vision – ECCV Workshops* (2016).

[22] D. Kragic and M. Vincze. "Vision for Robotics." *Foundations and Trends in Robotics* (2009).

[23] P. Rosenberger, A. Cosgun, R. Newbury, J. Kwan, V. Ortenzi, P. Corke, and M. Grafinger. "Object-Independent Human-to-Robot Handovers Using Real Time Robotic Vision." *IEEE Robotics and Automation Letters* (2021).

[24] C. Badue, R. Guidolini, R. V. Carneiro, P. Azevedo, V. B. Cardoso, A. Forechi, L. Jesus, R. Berriel, T. M. Paixão, F. Mutz, L. D. P. Veronese, T. Oliveira-Santos, and A. F. De Souza. "Self-Driving Cars: A Survey, Expert Systems with Applications." (2021).

[25] https://en.wikipedia.org/

[26] Jetson Nano Developer Kit, https://developer.nvidia.com/embedded/jetson-nano-developer-kit, last accessed 2019/11/15.

[27] https://www.rock-chips.com/a/en/products/RK33_Scrics/2018/0130/874.html

[28] https://coral.ai/products/dev-board/

[29] https://beagleboard.org/ai

[30] https://docs.openvinotoolkit.org/latest/

[31] J. Chen, K. Li, Q. Deng, K. Li, and S. Y. Philip. "Distributed Deep Learning Model for Intelligent Video Surveillance Systems with Edge Computing." *IEEE Transactions on Industrial Informatics* (2019).

[32] R. Ke, Y. Zhuang, Z. Pu, and Y. Wang. "A Smart, Efficient, and Reliable Parking Surveillance System with Edge Artificial Intelligence on IoT Devices." *IEEE Transactions on Intelligent Transportation Systems* (2020).

[33] Y. Zhao, Y. Yin, and G. Gui. "Lightweight Deep Learning Based Intelligent Edge Surveillance Techniques." *EEE Transactions on Cognitive Communications and Networking* 6, no. 4 Dec. (2020): 1146–1154. 10.1109/TCCN.2020.2999479.

[34] https://www.aitrends.com/ai-insider/edge-computing-ai-self-driving-cars/

[35] J. Janai, F. Güney, A. Behl, and A. Geiger. "Computer Vision for Autonomous Vehicles." *Foundations and Trends®inComputerGraphics and Vision* 12, no. 1–3 (2020): 1–308. 10.1561/060000007.

[36] M. Al-Gaashani, M. S. Ali Muthanna, K. Abdukodir, A. Muthanna, and R. Kirichek. "Intelligent System Architecture for Smart City and its Applications Based Edge Computing." In 12th International Congress on Ultra-ModernTelecommunications and Control Systems and Workshops (ICUMT), pp. 269–274, 2020. 10.1109/ICUMT51630.2020.9222460.

[37] S. Nagaraj, B. Muthiyan, S. Ravi, V. Menezes, K. Kapoor, and H. Jeon. "Edge-based Street Object Detection, 2017 IEEE SmartWorld, Ubiquitous Intelligence & Computing, Advanced & Trusted Computed, Scalable Computing & Communications, Cloud & Big Data Computing." In *Internet of People and Smart City Innovation (SmartWorld/SCALCOM/UIC/ATC/CBDCom/IOP/SCI)*, pp. 1–4, 2017. 10.1109/UIC-ATC.2017.8397675.

[38] S. Chakrabarty and D. W. Engels. "Secure Smart Cities Framework Using IoT and AI, 2020 IEEE Global Conference on Artificial Intelligence and Internet of Things (GCAIoT)." pp. 1–6, 2020. 10.1109/GCAIoT51063.2020.9345912.

[39] L. U. Khan, I. Yaqoob, N. H. Tran, S. M. A. Kazmi, T. N. Dang, and C. S. Hong. "Edge-Computing-Enabled Smart Cities: A Comprehensive Survey." *IEEE Internet of Things Journal* 7, no. 10 Oct. (2020): 10200–10232. 10.1109/JIOT.2020.2987070.

[40] A. Kaur and A. Jasuja. "Health Monitoring based on IoT using Raspberry PI." International Conference on Computing, Communication and Automation (ICCCA), pp. 1335–1340, 2017. 10.1109/CCAA.2017.8230004.

[41] P. Magaña-Espinoza, R. Aquino-Santos, N. Cárdenas-Benítez, J. Aguilar-Velasco, C. Buenrostro-Segura, A. Edwards-Block, and A. Medina-Cass. "WiSPH: A Wireless Sensor Network-based Home Care Monitoring System." *Sensors* 14, no. 4 (2014): 7096–7119.

[42] L. Greco, G. Percannella, P. Ritrovato, F. Tortorella, and M. Vento. "Trends in IoT based Solutions for Health Care: Moving AI to the Edge." *Pattern Recognition Letters* 135 (2020): 346–353.

[43] R. I. Minu and G. Nagarajan. "Bridging the IoT Gap Through Edge Computing." In *Edge Computing and Computational Intelligence Paradigms for the IoT*, pp. 1–9. IGI Global, 2019, USA.

[44] G. Nagarajan, R. I. Minu, and A. Jayanthiladevi. "Cognitive Internet of Things (C-IOT)." In *Sensing Techniques for Next Generation Cognitive Radio Networks*, pp. 299–311. IGI Global, 2019, USA.

[45] S. V. Simpson and G. Nagarajan. "An Edge based Trustworthy Environment Establishment for Internet of Things: An Approach for Smart Cities." *Wireless Networks* (2021): 1–17.

Chapter 12

Ambient Intelligence: An Emerging Innovation of Sensing and Service Systems

V.J.K. Kishor Sonti

Associate Professor, Department of ECE, Sathyabama Institute of Science and Technology, Chennai, India

G. Sundari

Professor, Department of ECE, Sathyabama Institute of Science and Technology, Chennai, India

Contents

DOI: 10.1201/9781003145158-12

Introduction

History has proven that technology is making human lives comfortable. The controllability, observability, and adaptability of any technology make it a frontrunner for divergent applications. The shady side of the technology reveals the limitations in application. Ambient intelligence (AmI) is a promising technology just like artificial intelligence (AI), disruptive in nature and creating an impact on day-to-day lifestyles. Edge AI and associated applications are further extended and strengthened by the emergence of ambient intelligence. This chapter of the book emphasize AmI and its potential in offering innovative solutions for developing service systems through intelligent sensing and computing.

Ambient intelligence (AmI) implies "Smart Surrounding". Research in this field necessitates the convergence of pervasive computing, sensors, and artificial intelligence (Lee [1]). One of the predicted outcomes of this innovation is human well-being, which is the driving force for any technology.

Ambient intelligence was invented and developed by Eli Zelkha and team in 1998 [2,3] in a report quoted that AmI should be handled in the next decade by ordinary people. In a survey paper, Sadri [4] highlighted about the attitudes of humans towards intelligent technologies. A. Nijholt et al. [5] discussed the social aspects of AmI. These include social belief, interaction, and judgment.

The most interesting element of applying this knowledge is the social impact. Confidence, trust, and choice of the end user are the most important parameters of this study. Various approaches have been proposed earlier about the application of ambient intelligence in diverse fields.

This chapter of the book exactly suits the theme of edge AI for different industry cases. An attempt has been made in Section 3 of this chapter to analyze primarily the health service systems and consumer electronics sector through intelligent sensing and an eagle-eye view in other sectors. Unobtrusive hardware, adaptive software, and distributed networks are the components of AmI. There is a

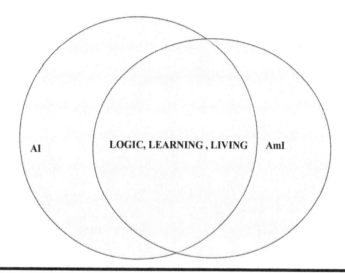

Figure 12.1   Logic, Learning, and Living in Comfort – AmI and AI.

natural linkage of AmI and AI in enriching the lifestyle of the humans. AmI shall also be considered as the extension of AI; hence, the AI circle is shown extended to AmI in Figure 12.1.

The fascinating truth of AI and AmI can be expressed in terms of logic, learning, and living. These are the focal points of evolution and application of these technologies. In general, logic is behind the intelligence, learning is the process by which error control takes place, and comfortable living is the outcome of AI and AmI. Therefore, both of these intelligent systems' development revolve around developing realizable logic and adaptive systems with the ability to learn and to be efficient in ensuring a smart living environment.

Intelligence has logic; every logic is based on a rule or set of rules, every rule is conditioned, every condition emerges from the capacity to perform, every capacity is a sign of ability; therefore, if the logic possesses the fragrance that may lead to innovation, an indirect process of developing creative ability systems. Both in AI and AmI the logic is exciting, and the systems are adaptive and consistently updating information based on instant data by a sensing environment [6]. Incidentally, smart living is the objective and outcome of these technologies.

Ambient intelligence emphasize upon how the machines interact with surroundings, whereas artificial intelligence is the emulation of human cognitive functions. Application of AI algorithms makes AmI more productive. There was general opinion that AmI can't be achieved without AI, but in recent attempts, efforts have been made to develop AmI without using AI (Matjaz [7]).

AmI is sensitive to the presence of the people. Personalized, adaptive, non-invasive, and unobtrusive are the most common features of AmI [8]. An interdisciplinary approach often leads to innovative solutions; AmI is one of the best

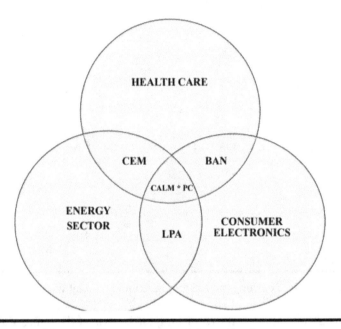

Figure 12.2   Ambient Intelligence – Potential Applications.

examples for interdisciplinary model. This is prominently known as "calm technology".

Figure 12.2 depicts the expansion of ambient intelligence otherwise known as "calm technology" to other sectors. Developments in the energy sector result in the design of low power and economically viable healthcare and consumer electronics systems with a common intersection point in the context of this chapter of the book as "calm technology" powered by pervasive computing. Edge AI requires such an approach for the effective realization of AI algorithms to suitable hardware, leading to innovative solutions.

BAN refers to body area networks, CEM refers to clean energy driven medical systems, and LPA refers to low-power applications of electronic systems' design and development. CALM*PC refers to ambient intelligence supported by pervasive computing. Calm technology extended its services not only in a human presence but also in absence.

Mark Weiser [9–12], in an article titled "The Computer for the 21st Century", quoted that "*the most profound technologies are those that disappear. They weave themselves into the fabric of everyday life until they are indistinguishable from it*". He also quoted that this disappearance is not merely due to the elegance of the technology, but because of the psychology of humans. This is true in word and spirit, when it comes to Internet revolution. The history of human civilization is going to observe the same in the case of artificial intelligence (early results are indicative) and ambient intelligence. The psychological perspective of this intelligence systems development is resonantly interesting, which is elaborated on in Section 3.

Optimization algorithms, regression methods and data analytic techniques are in literature, which are used for prediction. There is a good amount of research that was carried out in the past two decades related to optimization (M. [13]) and adaptive nature of intelligent systems. A. Liu Cheng and H. H. Bier in 2016 mentioned the advantages of integrating AmI with available adaptive architectures (A. [14]). Vladimir Villarreal et al. [15], in a review, described the influence of AmI in day-to-day activities. The challenges of AmI in the context of smart urban cities were presented by Norbert Streitz et al. [16].

AmI technologies are in general sensitive, responsive, adaptive, transparent, and ubiquitous. The base for AmI is the pervasive computing and its applicative model was presented by Guruduth Banavar et al. [17]. Stan Kurkovsky, in 2008, presented the past, present, and future of pervasive computing.

Section 2 focuses upon the rudimentary aspects of pervasive computing and its potentiality in finding applications pertinent to various fields. The influence of pervasive computing and its applications in various fields are comprehensively presented; the components of the pervasive computing are discussed.

Pervasive Computing – Backbone of Ambient Intelligence

As quoted by Mark D Weiser [9] – "Technology recedes into the background of our lives", Pervasive refers to ubiquitous presence or "existing everywhere". Pervasive computing is known as the backbone of AmI, because of the simple fact that it spreads the intelligence. This is invisible, socialized, and convergent in nature. It informs us, but doesn't demand our attention.

Pervasive computing indicates to the user the availability of the resources and suggests the possibility of effective usage. The core principles of pervasive computing are decentralization and connectivity (Aleksander [18]). Relative and well-associated terms in the context of pervasive computing are artificial intelligence, sensor networks, and human-machine interaction.

The elements of pervasive computing are presented in Figure 12.3. The prime issue of pervasive computing is context awareness. This term was first coined in 1994 by Schilit. Context awareness brings the awareness about the situation to the systems [19]). It also helps in personalizing applications. One of the challenges exists in terms of minimum data availability to infer the context. Mike Addlesee et al. [20] discussed another context-aware application called a sentient computing system and its implementation. This computing system is also observed to be prospective.

Sensors are available for different types of data acquisition. These sensors play a crucial role in sensing the human presence or the changes in the surroundings and

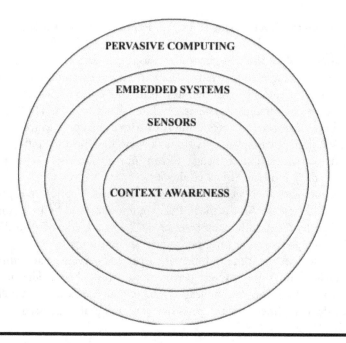

Figure 12.3 Elements of Pervasive Computing.

generate data accordingly. Position, pressure, temperature, moisture, light, and acoustic sensors are often used for data acquisition in AmI.

Embedded systems are the next level of integration, generally imbibed by the powerful processors. A real-time operating system (RTOS) empowers embedded units for acting instantly to the updated inputs; process them as per the requirement and deliver the required output.

From business class to domestic life, everything has been influenced by the evolution of the Internet of Things (IoT). A high degree of automation is supported by the pervasive computing methods. Pervasive computing is a blend of context awareness, mobile computing, and embedded systems (Diane J. [21]). All the existing technologies such as Wifi, Wimax, Bluetooth, and Zigbee serve in pervasive computing.

"Impromptu inter-operability" is another exciting feature of pervasive systems. Privacy and security need major attention in exploring a further scope of the pervasive computing applications.

Pervasiveness

Research and development have taken a new leap with the advent of novel technologies and computing methods. Pervasive computing facilitates interdisciplinary research. This has become a powerful instrument for researchers and techno-thirsty innovators.

"Emergence of convergence amidst divergence" is the order of pervasive computing. This truly changed the dimension and direction of 21st-century smart living. Intelligence algorithms such as particle swarm optimization, ant colony optimization driven systems, and integrated development environments, leading to smart enabled environments, which have lifted human standards of living from one-computer-one user days to pervasive computing or ubiquitous computing.

The consumer electronics market has received unprecedented growth; healthcare service systems have become more precise and fast; and mobile networking, remote communications, industrial IoT, and robotics have seen a dynamic growth pattern with pervasive computing making quiet contributions. Stan Kurkovsky [22] pointed out that smartphones are recognized as the best modes to interface with a pervasive environment, until or unless natural and other pragmatic solutions for interfacing are explored.

Smart spaces, mobile networks, and security systems are some of the areas where pervasive ambience has been prevalent in the past two decades [3]. Managing smart spaces has become more feasible with pervasive computing. Pervasive applications make the user operate at a sub-conscious level. This is, in other words, understood as a silent operative environment (SOE).

The increased demand for smart spaces also leaves challenges for developing effective interfaces. The human-machine interaction level deepens with the randomness associated (psychological aspects of humans). In the future, scalability becomes a major issue in pervasive computing (M. [23]).

Technological advancements have made significant contributions to imbue humans towards a sophisticated lifestyle. Pervasive computing is one such advancement, which encourages invisible intelligence to prevail in the surroundings. This facilitates the emergence of intelligent sensing and service systems development, otherwise known as ambient intelligence.

Pervasive Computing in AmI

Intelligent algorithms, fuzzy-based expert systems, machine learning, genetic algorithms, pattern search, image processing and fusion techniques, system-on-chip, wireless sensor networks, wearable electronics, nano-materials, nano electronic mechanical systems (NEMS), and micro electronic mechanical systems (MEMS) have brought a noticeable shift in computer science–driven development and its applications. Machine learning is the heart of artificial intelligence (Maximilian [24]), similar to the role of pervasive computing in AmI.

Qualitative and quantitative progress was observed across the globe in pervasiveness-based applications. This pervasive computing has redrafted the generic rules of computation. Naturally, this progression succeeded in the design and development of intelligent systems well supported by the intelligence infused ambience. This context awareness has made pervasive computing the suitable contender for ambient intelligence.

Ambient Intelligence in Health Care and Consumer Electronics

Ambient intelligence is a sensing, decision making, and applicative approach that uses pervasive computing and intelligent user interfaces [25]). Contextual awareness, ubiquitous wireless access, and hands-free interaction are the fundamental components of ambient intelligence. This applies to domestic as well as work spaces.

AmI takes the inputs/changes from/in the environment using sensors. This process is known as data acquisition. This data is processed using general or specific purpose processing units (usually embedded processors). Appropriate inferences are made out of the processed data and the timely decisions are to be taken. Figure 12.4 is a block diagram of a typical AmI environment.

Data is important for prediction. Real-time data, statistical data, and other experimental observations generate a huge amount of data. Classifying, analyzing, and interpreting data is a herculean task. Information from sensors, interfacing modules, and monitoring systems has to be critically examined for arriving at logical and timely inferences.

Prediction models, decision-making approaches, and optimization algorithms are available to assist in making timely and apt decisions. Data-driven design modules are updated or implemented based on these decisions by the previous sub-module of this AmI system. But the key module is data acquisition as the data generated by human actions (cognitive or behavioral) most of the times is random. Every module of this ambient intelligent environment shall undergo modification, when behaviorism is taken into consideration (which requires huge attention by researchers to make AmI a best choice for smart living).

Behavior desire relations with human and environment is exciting to explore. These behavior desires are challenging to emulate or simulate. An understanding or

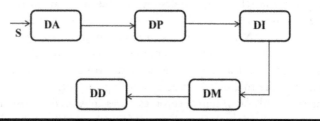

Figure 12.4   A Typical Ambient Intelligent Environment.

knowledge about the human emotions, beliefs, and the randomness involved is essential to design and develop ambient intelligent service systems.

Human Psychology – Behaviorism – Futuristic Ambient Intelligent Systems

Cognitivists and Piagetians have contributed for the development of behaviorism. Psychology can assist people in making behavioral changes in social and personal life (Albert [26]).

Scientific psychology emphasizes describe, predict, and adapt. Human behavior is random in most of the situations. The cognitive information is often challenging to translate/decipher and to process.

Various theories on cognitive psychology have an underlying string of addressable uncertainty. Human interaction with surroundings was studied by Piaget in his famous theory on cognitive development. Vygostky also suggested that such development shall be understood through social perspective. The individual and his/her culture determine the nature of interaction with the surroundings is the key point of observation for ambient intelligence future research and development.

One can also understand that "classical conditioning" proposed by Ivan Pavlov, a Russian psychologist, has an analogy in the implementation of AmI. In AmI also we are conditioning the environment to be vigilant and to perceive the changes and adapt accordingly. The true excitement in using this technology exists in the prediction of the surrounding's (ambience) response to the human cognitive randomness [27]).

Sternberg's [28] theory of intelligence suggested that adaptive sense prevails in humans, similar to the ability of AmI systems. Cattell [29] concluded that fluid and crystallized intelligence are major components of human intelligence. Fluid is based on reasoning with the available information at that instant, whereas crystalline is the "experience bank". Crystalline intelligence is accumulated knowledge due to experiences. In the future AmI, the services offered by the systems shall be designed to possess both types of intelligence. Therefore, the feedback should be very precise and fast for timely updating of inputs.

Biological aspects of behaviorism are also interesting. Neurons and their activity based on activation function are topics worth reading to understand the biological background. The exciting point in AmI is the ability of electrical and electronic sensors to tap the signals from the natural sensors of the human body or the changes in the optical energy in a smart space.

Social psychology also suggests that influence of ecological variables is on people's unpredictable behavior. Cultural context cannot be ruled out in social behavior (especially using AmI systems in a work space). In terms of social psychology, the attempt to develop an efficient AmI system is not less than infusing altruistic behavior of humans in machines.

Aggression and depression are the emotions that alter the behavior of an individual instantly and over a period of time. The intelligent environment assisting such individuals shall be equipped with updates of mental health status of those individuals. This will enable futuristic AmI systems to deliver services in a better manner, but it is a great challenge for this technology to surpass.

Behaviorism

Bandura's theory (1974) on behaviorism and Watson's [30] behavioral model on prediction of one's behavior and controlling it certainly need to be studied or shall be taken into consideration by AmI experts. This knowledge to a certain extent will help them to make forthcoming AmI systems more user-friendly in smart environments.

Behavioral psychology is the branch of psychology that deals with the study of observable behavior. This observational element is crucial in advanced ambient intelligence (AAmI). The change in the behavior that would reflect a gesture or some sort of identifiable action shall be perceived by the smart environment that is empowered by the sensors. The typical scenario of this psychological perspective positioning is depicted in the flow diagram (Figure 12.5).

Any expected or unexpected change in human behavior shall be recognized and the data acquisition has to be repeated for offering the best AmI services. Smart spaces require smart actions. These smart actions are possible only when behaviorism-infused AmI systems are developed.

Generalization is another bigger challenge in AmI systems. These AmI systems shall be customized. If it has to happen, the human psychology perspective becomes crucial in this process. Therefore, the success of AmI systems or enabled

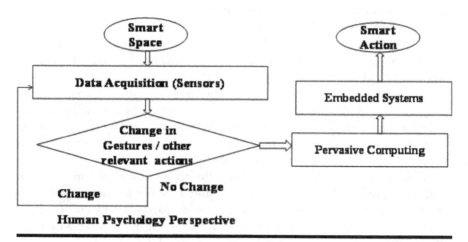

Figure 12.5 Human Psychology Perspective in Ambient Intelligence.

services greatly depends upon the customization rather than generalization, for which knowledge pertinent to psychology is essential.

Neglecting psychological perspective; AmI systems may offer services at the cohort level, but may not be efficient in serving individual requirements for long time. For example, the needs and choices of an individual change over a period of time. The automated systems should have the track of the information and upgrade accordingly the quality of service.

The gray shade of using AmI in a future domestic purpose has another dimension. For example, children become habituated to this technology-driven living, and it may hamper their creative intelligence. The natural common sense that comes with the balanced use of fluid and crystalline intelligence may become obsolete at times. Imagine a child was grown in an AmI-enabled domestic environment; this child may face challenges in leading a normal life outside this environment.

Even though the present advantages are attractive, other side of the coin should be concentrated before putting this technology to the best use of common people. The critical query is the effectiveness of the intelligent environment that would predict or quickly recognize the behavioral change of all ages, genders, cultures, and cohorts (especially at work space). A balanced approach model shall make the intelligent systems have sufficient potential to address the psychological aspects of behaviorism in order to interlace the technology.

Balanced Approach Model

A two-dimensional balanced approach model is suggested here for the effective implementation of AmI, fundamentally at the domestic level and shall be extended with necessary modifications to the work environment. AmI systems and services are predominantly developed to make the smart living a reality. Technological aspects are well taken care of, but in AmI implementation, the behavior of humans remains crucial. In this balanced approach model, it is suggested that both technological and psychological dimensions shall be considered while developing AmI-enabled services and systems for effective long-term usage. Vigorous analysis of both dimensions shall take place before the installation of these AmI systems. Necessary modifications shall be suggested to mitigate the challenges of instant changes in the human behavior using fluid intelligence of statistical data in the form of crystalline intelligence. But this information is generated only by the human behavior in a given situation. A balanced approach method exactly points out and gives appropriate importance to behaviorism while developing AmI systems.

AmI – Technology Dimension

Technology makes lives simpler and easier. AmI invites and demands technological advancements in sensors, interfacing units, and fast communication systems.

Research on smart devices, material physics studies, microelectronic mechanical systems (MEMS), nanoelectronic mechanical systems (NEMS), algorithms, and architecture contribute to the development of fast computing and communicating systems and user-interface units are necessary and happening now.

AmI needs technology that shall create components and systems that can be scaled down, flexible, and have fast learning. Intellectual circles, industry, and academia shall coordinate and contribute to meet these requirements.

AmI – Psychology Dimension

AmI systems work effectively in a limited sense of individual behavior. Psychological studies on human behavior in individual and group behavior are instrumental in the design and development of efficient AmI service systems.

According to techno-ethics, wisdom that originates from balanced mind is the best path to decision making. Moral attitude and ethical decision making are much needed when deploying AmI systems in sensitive service sectors such as healthcare systems. AmI systems make timely and intelligent decisions imbibed with an emulated segment of behavioral intelligence. This conducive AmI environment–based progress makes "business intelligence" more productive. In simple terms, equation 1 summarizes this balanced approach model.

Computational Intelligence + Behavioral Intelligence = Efficient Ambient Intelligence (1)

This lessens the ill effects that occur due to the use of AmI like smart yet sensitive technologies in usage. In this section, two cases were taken for analyzing the AmI impact on service systems and sensing. The healthcare industry and consumer electronics are discussed in the following sub-sections from this balanced approach model point of view.

Ambient Intelligence – Healthcare Industry Transition

The human body has random variants. The healthcare industry faces a variety of issues in handling the randomness associated with the health data of an individual or a cohort.

Technology Dimension

Ambient intelligent system–enabled health environments are the boon to the healthcare industry, as timely sensing and inferring the crucial health-related data is of utmost importance.

Most of the times, the patient's health is monitored at home (not in the case of emergency or abnormal situations). Wearable devices, robots, and medical help assistance using advanced communication systems have become more prominent.

The Internet of Medical Things (IoMT) is a collection of entities that collect, analyze, and transmit health data.

Ambient intelligence in the future shall present a scenario where the doctor will be in a position to access all the basic vital information and other relevant data of the medical history before the patient enters into the cabin. Early treatment methods are strengthened with the use of these technological advancements. The healthcare industry is closely monitoring the impact of these disruptive technologies; AmI is one such advancement under intense observation [31]).

The digital revolution has changed the face of front-office operations in hospitals. Patient registration, self-care helping tools, and various health apps add more value to the healthcare services (Hammad [32]). Newly evolved technologies such as IoT, AI, and wearable devices are helping in saving time for the doctors, patients, and clinic staff.

The use of AI and AmI improves the speed and accuracy in healthcare services. AI-enabled interactive message systems are useful in addressing the patient's general queries. Diagnostic treatment procedures received a big push in the quality of service with the advent of these technologies. The use of robots offer minimum invasive operations.

Another remark is human involvement in monitoring the vitals has been greatly reduced. Accurate identification of veins for blood extraction is possible. The use of robots in health care is increasing, and most of the healthcare operations are taken up with IoMT. Health update information is communicated to patients and it helps in maintaining good health.

Pervasive computing helps in analyzing the statistical data and prediction models become crucial with decent accuracy in readings. Electronic health records (EHRs) will be helpful in identifying the parallels at symptom level or patient response in analyzing or predicting the future course of treatment. But a huge amount of data associated with EHR poses a challenge to decipher, infer, or interpret manually all the time. Smart computing methods are very useful at this juncture. There will be a scenario where the information is auto processed with the available EHR repository and the crucial information shall be shared to physicians and other authorized supporting staff by this "calm technology".

Psychology Dimension

AmI services in health care are promising. But as aforementioned in this section, the generalization may be more than a challenging task. Monitoring and assisting patients suffering from mental health disorders such as schizophrenia and ADHD, and mood disorders such as hypomania and depression, may be tough customers for this technological experience. Early childhood response, adolescent behavior, and late-adulthood gestures may not be predictive and sometimes misleading. AmI systems are not suggestible to people living in these environments without considering all of these age- or hormonal change–induced behavioral responses.

A customized approach of implementing a patient's behavioral pattern will be essential as in the case of mental health issues. A behavioral psychology study of a patient is useful when deploying AmI systems. A data log or crystalline intelligence is handy for the AmI to make the learning or training easy and accurate. Medical assistance errors shall be greatly reduced with this knowledge, even though the patient is under AmI assistance and supervision.

There are various ethical considerations and legal aspects to be considered while using AmI in the healthcare industry (Leena V [33]). All of these obligations should be addressed in the process of making AmI a potential destiny for providing smart healthcare systems.

AmI – Consumer Electronics

Consumer electronics has grown over the years from tiny electronic gadgets to professional audio and video systems [34]). The market of consumer electronics is driven by the changing needs of customers. Advancements in electronic components/devices support the consumer electronics market to meet the customer requirements. This saga is successful and also mitigated various challenges in terms of speed, accuracy, and size. AmI has significantly contributed to consumer electronics industry growth with the need created for sensors and embedded units.

The evolution of very large scale integrated circuits (VLSI) technology and the emergence of artificial intelligence boosted consumer electronics like never before. These developments in electronics and computer science paved the way for fusion thinking. Technocrats, scientists, and researchers took this innovation forward to the form of Internet of Things (IoT), the most sought-out technology today.

Technology Dimension

The Internet of Things brought the concept of machine-machine interaction (M2M). IoT systems make use of devices, data, analytics, and connectivity. The industrial Internet of Things (IIoT) is the extension of IoT. The Internet of Medical Things (IoMT) has its applications in the health sector. Such categories of IoT are motivating to produce the necessary suitable devices and systems, which are flooding the commercial market. Similarly, the ambient intelligence impact on consumer electronics has been vivid and intense.

Ambient intelligence supports a spectrum of human activities including smart living, security, health care, work, and personal communications [35].

Psychology Dimension

The psychology dimension of consumer electronics is an amazing topic for research. The study of behaviorism or behavior psychology of a particular cohort adds value to business intelligence–based data analytics. Knowledge of behaviorism helps AmI experts to develop more sensible smart spaces that suit an individual or to an office.

Prime objectives of AmI services and systems are in offering a secure, safe, and smart living. But overreaching out to these objectives remains challenging over these years. Even though technology excellence is empowering the AmI-driven consumer electronics market, the silver lining feature of adaptability to changes in human behavior is missing and needs improvement. For example, the presence of a man near a door is detected by means of an optical sensor and opens it without his complete willingness, may push him into an unforeseen threat or troubled situations.

Security and safety of the people living in this environment may be compromised. Long usage of AmI-enabled electronics products may force us in losing natural human instinct based responses.

Other Possible Applications of AmI

The capacity of AmI allows exploring applications across the domains. A few of the possible areas are listed below:

- Public transport systems
- Banking sector
- Mass production industries (where human monitoring and data analysis is a challenge)
- Aviation industry
- Hospitality and tourism industry

The application of AmI in various fields driven by behavioral psychology is a thought-provoking research prospect. The future may also witness another interesting development in the form of business intelligence driven by behavioral intelligence.

Social Issues and Research Prospects of AmI

Social issues associated with ambient intelligence are the critical issues to be handled. Sensing is the core element in ambient intelligence. Awareness about the human presence, recognition of any activity by an individual or a cohort, and adapting the needs of them are the key points in the delivery mechanism of AmI.

Group behavior is different from the individual. Choices made in a cohort are different from an individual response at times. Social living enforces a change in regular habits, which AmI systems might have tuned and requires special attention and training to change accordingly.

User adoption or addiction to this calm technology may not be comfortable, and rather confusing for non-techno-friendly individuals. A multi-user AmI-enabled environment poses a variety of problems to be solved. For example, a guest for a few days to this AmI-enabled domestic environment must be accommodated with no disturbance to normal living. Watching entertainment is a specific user choice and an AmI system tuning to multiple users is an interesting development to wait and watch. General assistance may be offered in the healthcare industry using AmI, where optimal adaptation may be the case. But the real issue is when customization is required and implemented.

Technology versus Ethics

Ethics technology nexus is a time-tested phenomenon. Technology brings comfort to living, but limitations in the usage of it unfold ethical aspects. The technology implementation is a guided process; technology ethics governs this process. Ethical dilemmas coexist with the merits and demerits of technology at every juncture of technology-driven development.

Revolutionary technology such as ambient intelligence also has ethical hiccups in the early implementation stage. Privacy and confidentiality of the personal information is at stake with the undue intrusion of technology into lives. Social vulnerability has been an issue to be addressed. The implementation strategy of technology should carefully interweave the development aspects with ethical and moral issues that may emerge.

Technophilia and technophobia are the different elements of relationship between technology and society. An AmI-enabled environment may not be the early choice of technophobic individuals. But time has proven that humans are natural habitants of technology. The evolution of a technology also gives scope for the emergence of techno-ethics (Jürgen [36]). Techno-ethics helps in the ethical assessment of technological implications.

Research Prospects

Ambient intelligence is interestingly promising. There are multiple research areas that would contribute to the fast developments in AmI implementation. Most prominent among those areas are naturally sensors, embedded systems, and intelligent mathematical techniques; studies on behavioral psychology; microelectronics; and advancements in the energy sector. Research in these following areas has a direct or indirect impact on the design and development of AmI sensing and service systems.

■ Design and Development of Sensors

Accurate, fast sensing, and economic sensor development are the focal points of research in this domain. Designs of compact structures, enhanced compatibility with other interfacing hardware, and micromachining are the most promising topics of interest. Characteristic modeling of sensors has scope forever. Bio-compatible invasive sensors development has a huge potential and is an interdisciplinary study. Research on sensors is mostly customer-driven. Trends in the sensor development crafts platform for more intelligent systems in future [37].

Reliability, adaptability, robustness, less maintenance, low energy-consumption, and self-calibration are guiding the progress of research. Exponentially increasing the commercial market in order to meet the requirements of the future is an inviting major scope for researchers. Miniaturization and multi-sensor integration are other demands from the IoT industry. In the context of AmI applications in health care and consumer electronics, any breakthrough in the research on sensors is highly anticipated.

■ Embedded Systems

The technology of the future highly depends upon embedded systems. Real-time responses require real-time data processing. DSP processors and high-end embedded processing units are the new market demands. This potentiality of embedded systems is due to the adaptability with other hardware modules or peripheral systems. Embedded systems use micro-controllers and are used in controlling various devices in numerous real-time applications. Resolving co-design issues, developing advanced interfacing units, and industry-specific protocol development are widely researched across the globe.

Some of the applications of embedded systems are industrial control systems, medical electronics, consumer electronics, automotive, aerospace, and communication industries (Oluwole O. [38]). Due to this wide range of applications, any step towards progress in embedded research is much appreciated.

In the AmI perspective, embedded systems research will reduce the latency in communication among hardware modules. Multi-user scenarios demand an efficient integrated development environment, which is a far reality without a good amount of research in embedded systems and their programming.

■ Intelligent Algorithms/Computing Techniques

Pervasive computing holds the major computational portion of AmI. Context awareness is the central principle. To be more context aware, the data processing requires better approaches. Research on the application of various intelligent algorithms is rapidly growing. Ant colony optimization, particle swarm optimization, artificial bee colony algorithm, glowworm swarm optimization, and artificial fish swarm algorithm are the most explored applications ranging from smart grid management to predicting financial markets [39].

Any intense focused work on cuckoo search algorithm, differential evolution, bat algorithm, firefly algorithm, shuffled frog leaping algorithm, fruit fly optimization algorithm, bacterial foraging optimization, chicken swarm optimization algorithm, wolf pack algorithm, and artificial plan optimization algorithm takes the process of optimization to new boundaries. Swarm based algorithms unfold new dimensions of social interaction [40]. This kind of work is much needed for exploring new avenues of applications based on computational intelligence.

Apart from the above optimization algorithms, intelligent systems development depends upon fuzzy, neuro-fuzzy modeling; genetic algorithms based modeling; molecular computing; and other artificial intelligence algorithms.

In the context of AmI, such research on computing techniques has a great scope. This is an exciting opportunity to researchers in mathematics, computer science, electronics, and bioscience disciplines.

■ Psychology Studies

Behavioral problems in preschool children, orphans, and anti-social behavior youngsters are most studied in the recent past. Behavioral intentions, evaluative conditioning, social intelligence, and emotional intelligence are giving scope for research problems. Mood disorders and genetic disorders causing impulsive behavior patterns in individuals will be a breakthrough research for the holistic and realistic implementation of ambient intelligence systems.

■ Microelectronics

Microelectronics in the past six decades was guided by Gordon Moore's law. Increased package density, on-chip testing, fault-tolerant systems development, and nano-electronics are increasing the research demands in this field.

Increased ternary compounds usage in the development of high-speed devices and monolithic microwave integrated circuits is a potential research gap. Any amount of progress in low-k dielectrics, carbon nanotubes for interconnect and sensor applications, circuit and system design, integrated circuits for NEMS/MEMS, photovoltaic, low-power consumption integrated circuits, and solar cells have direct influence on the development of AmI systems.

■ Energy Sector

Research in the energy sector is p rogressive. The availability of renewable energy sources made the smart grid technology more productive (Mohamed [41]). Smart grid management, renewable energy resources optimum utilization, and in predicting or forecasting the renewable energy resources availability, reduction of loss incurred in energy transmission and distribution are the major trends in research of the modern energy sector.

In the context of AmI, research in the energy sector helps in reducing the load on the energy sector, which also encourages the manufacturing of clean energy compatible devices. This will have a long-term and indirect effect on the progression of AmI-enabled smart enviornments.

AmI-compatible hardware development, communication infrastructure advancements, experimental studies on nano-materials, novel display and energy management systems, and fast computing and processing units design and development are some of the most promising areas for research.

Conclusion

Ambient intelligence is going to be the new normal. The post-pandemic scenario will push for more research in such intelligent systems, where human intervention becomes minimal. Ambient intelligent systems evolution, fundamentals, and future research is elaborated in this chapter of the book.

The inception stage to fading of technology into a natural process of living is a gradual transition; the transformation may not be smooth and accepted readily in all cultures and social clusters. AmI is not an exception to this transition, and it is expected that these social and ethical hurdles are successfully handled by the expertise propelling this technology. This chapter of the book addressed the behavioral psychology viewpoint, which will be a valuable addition in this transformation.

A reasonable amount of control over situations is necessary. We can make use of this AmI to the extent of prediction and assisting in most needed service sectors like health care and also in consumer electronic systems.

In the future, ambient intelligence shall have strong footprints in public transportation, education sector, and in developing business intelligence models. Undergraduate curriculum in medicine shall include techno-driven medical diagnosis methods and pre-diagnosis data acquisition methods using an AmI-enabled smart space (as special or open electives).

In spite of the positive outcomes, AmI-enabled domestic life is exciting and equally alarming to the self-thinking abilities of humans. Creativity of the children is a threat when the human-machine interaction occurs through ambient intelligence.

Technological and psychological dimensions shall be given appropriate significance in the design and implementation of AmI services and systems. Technology shall be embraced to make lives easy, but not complex and perplexing.

Acknowledgments

We express our deep sense of gratitude to Mrs. Sumathi Srinivasan, special educator and counseling psychologist for adding value to the psychological viewpoint in this chapter.

References

[1] L. Spector. *Evolution of Artificial Intelligence. Artificial Intelligence*, pp. 1251–1253, Elsevier, 2006. 10.1016/j.artint.2006.10.009.

[2] E. H. L. Aarts and J. L. Encarnação. *True Visions: The Emergence of Ambient Intelligence*. Springer, 2006. ISBN 9783540289746 – via Google Books.

[3] K. Ducatel, M. Bogdanowicz, F. Scapolo et al. *J.-C. Scenarios for ambient intelligence in 2010*. IST Advisory Group Final Report, European Commission, EC. Brussels, 2001.

[4] F. Sadri. "Ambient Intelligence: A Survey." *ACM Computing Surveys* 43, no. 4 (2011): Article 36. 10.1145/1978802.1978815.

[5] A. Nijholt, O. Stock, and T. Nishida. *Social Intelligence Design in Ambient Intelligence*. Springer, 2009. 10.1007/s00146-009-0192-7.

[6] A. Sharma, A. Kumar, and A. Bhardawaj. "A Review of Ambient Intelligence System: Bringing Intelligence to Environments." *International Journal of Information & Computation Technology*. ISSN 0974-2239 4, no. 9 (2014): 879–884, International Research Publications House.

[7] M. Gams, I. Y. Gu, A. Härmä, et al. "Artificial Intelligence and Ambient Intelligence."*Journal of Ambient Intelligence and Smart Environments* 11 (2019): 71–86. 10.3233/AIS-180508 IOS Press.

[8] J. C. Augusto. "Ambient Intelligence: Basic Concepts and Applications." In J. Filipe, B. Shishkov, and M. Helfert (eds), *Software and Data Technologies. ICSOFT 2006. Communications in Computer and Information Science*, vol. 10. Springer, Berlin, Heidelberg, 2008. 10.1007/978-3-540-70621-2_2.

[9] M. Weiser. "The Computer for the Twenty-first Century." *Scientific American* September (1991): 94–110.

[10] R. I. Minu and G. Nagarajan. "Bridging the IoT Gap Through Edge Computing." In *Edge Computing and Computational Intelligence Paradigms for the IoT*, pp. 1–9. IGI Global, USA. 2019.

[11] G. Nagarajan, R. I. Minu, and A. Jayanthiladevi. "Cognitive Internet of Things (C-IOT)." In *Sensing Techniques for Next Generation Cognitive Radio Networks*, pp. 299–311. IGI Global, USA. 2019.

[12] S. V. Simpson and G. Nagarajan. "An Edge based Trustworthy Environment Establishment for Internet of Things: An Approach for Smart Cities." *Wireless Networks* (2021): 1–17.

[13] M. Javad Akhlaghinia, A. Lotfi, and C. Langensiepen. "Soft Computing Prediction Techniques in Ambient Intelligence Environments." (2007) 1-4244-1210-2/07. IEEE.

[14] A. Liu Chenga and H. H. Biera. "An Extended Ambient Intelligence Implementation for Enhanced Human-Space Interaction." 33rd International Symposium on Automation and Robotics in Construction (ISARC). (2016).

[15] V. Villarreal, J. Fontecha, R. Hervás, et al. "Ambient Intelligence: Technological Solutions for Wellness and Supporting to Daily Activities." Tenth LACCEI Latin American and Caribbean Conference (LACCEI'2012), Megaprojects: Building Infrastructure by fostering engineering collaboration, efficient and effective integration and innovative planning, July 23-27. Panama City, Panama. (2012).

[16] N. Streitz, D. Charitos, M. Kaptein, et al. "Grand Challenges for Ambient Intelligence and Implications for Design Contexts and Smart Societies." *Journal of*

Ambient Intelligence and Smart Environments 11, no. 2019 (2019): 87–107. 10.3233/AIS-180507. IOS Press.

[17] G. Banavar, J. Beck, E. Gluzberg, et al. "Challenges: An Application Model for Pervasive Computing." Proceedings of the Sixth Annual ACM/IEEE International Conference on Mobile Computing and Networking (Mobicom). (2000).

[18] A. Bai, H. C. Mork, and T. Halbach. "Norwegian Computing Center, Oslo, Norway, A Review of Universal Design in Ambient Intelligence Environments." SMART ACCESSIBILITY 2016: The First International Conference on Universal Accessibility in the Internet of Things and Smart Environments, 2016. ISBN: 978-1-61208-525-8.

[19] V. Kostakos and E. O'Neill. *Introducing Pervasive Computing to Society.* 1st UK-UbiNet Workshop, 25-26th September 2003. London, UK: Imperial College, 2003.

[20] M. Addlesee, R. Curwen, S. Hodges, et al. "Implementing a Sentient Computing System" *IEEE Computer* (2001).

[21] D. J. Cook, J. C. Augusto, and V. R. Jakkula. "Ambient intelligence: Technologies, applications, and opportunities." *Pervasive and Mobile Computing* 5, no. 2009 (2009): 277–298. 10.1016/j.pmcj.2009.04.001.

[22] S. Kurkovsky. "Pervasive Computing: Past, Present and Future." 2008. 10.1109/ITICT.2007.4475619, IEEE Explorer.

[23] M. Satyanarayanan. "School of Computer Science, Carnegie Mellon University, Pervasive Computing: Vision and Challenges." *IEEE Personal Communications* (2001).

[24] M. Hüttenrauc, A. Šošić, and G. Neumann. "Deep Reinforcement Learning for Swarm Systems." *Journal of Machine Learning Research* 20 (2019): 1–31.

[25] J. H. Søraker and P. Brey. "Ambient Intelligence and Problems with Inferring Desires from Behaviour." *International Review of Information Ethics* 8, no. 12/2007 (2017) ISSN 1614-1687.

[26] A. Bandura. "Behavior Theory and the Models of Man." *American Psychologist* (1974): 859–869.

[27] A. de Ribaupierre and T. Lecerf. "Intelligence and Cognitive Development: Three Sides of the Same Coin." *Journal of Intelligence* 2017, no. 5 (2017): 14. 10.3390/jintelligence5020014.

[28] R. J. Sternberg. "Toward a triarchic theory of human intelligence." *Behavioral and Brain Sciences* 7 (1984): 269–287.

[29] R. Cattell. "Theory of Fluid and Crystallized Intelligence: A Critical Experiment." *Journal of Educational Psychology* 54 (1963): 1–22. 10.1037/h0046743.

[30] J. B. Watson. "Psychology as the Behaviorist Views It." *Psychological Review* 20 (1913a): 158–177.

[31] N. Dey and A. S. Ashour. "Ambient Intelligence in Healthcare: A State-of-the-Art." *Global Journal of Computer Science and Technology* XVII, no. III Version 1 (2007).

[32] H. Durrani. "Healthcare and healthcare systems: inspiring progress and future prospects." *mHealth*2 (2016): 3. 10.3978/j.issn.2306-9740.2016.01.03.

[33] L. V. Gangolli, R. Duggal, and A. Shukla. "Review of Healthcare in India, Centre for Enquiry into Health and Allied Themes." 2005 ISBN: 81-89042-40-8.

[34] J. Hart. "Consumer Electronics." 1993 1993/08/01.

[35] E. Aarts and R. Roovers. "Philips Research Laboratories. IC Design Challenges for Ambient Intelligence." Proceedings of the Design, Automation and Test in Europe Conference and Exhibition (DATE'03) 1530-1591/03. 2003.

[36] J. Bohn, V. Coroamă, M. Langheinrich, et al. "Institute for Pervasive Computing, ETH Zurich, Switzerland." *Social, Economic, and Ethical Implications of Ambient Intelligence and Ubiquitous Computing.* 2004 10.1007/3-540-27139-2_2.

[37] O. Kanoun and H. Tränkler. "Sensor Technology Advances and Future Trends." *IEEE Transactions on Instrumentation and Measurement* 53, no. 6 (2004): 1497–1501.

[38] O. O. Oyetoke. "Embedded Systems Engineering, the Future of Our Technology World; A Look Into the Design of Optimized Energy Metering Devices." *International Journal of Recent Engineering Science (IJRES)* 18 (2015): 17–25. ISSN: 2349-7157.

[39] L. Rosenberg, N. Pescetelli, and G. Willcox. "Artificial Swarm Intelligence amplifies accuracy when predicting financial markets. IEEE 8th Annual Ubiquitous Computing. "*Electronics and Mobile Communication Conference (UEMCON)* (2017): 58–62. 10.1109/UEMCON.2017.8248984.

[40] M. Oliveira, D. Pinheiro, M. C. Macedo, et al. "Uncovering the Social Interaction Network in Swarm Intelligence Algorithms." *Applied Network Science* 5 (2020): 24. 10.1007/s41109-020-00260-8.

[41] M. Zahran. "Smart Grid Technology, Vision Management and Control." *WSEAS Transactions on Systems* 12, no. 1 (2013).

Index